THE
SHINAR
DIRECTIVE

THE SHINAR DIRECTIVE

PREPARING THE WAY FOR THE SON OF PERDITION

DR. MICHAEL LAKE

DEFENDER

CRANE, MO

The Shinar Directive:
Preparing the Way for the Son of Perdition
Defender
Crane, MO 65633

ISBN: 978-0-9904974-3-1

A CIP catalog record of this book is available from the Library of Congress.

Cover illustration and design by Daniel Wright: www.createdwright.com.

Except in the passages noted, all Scripture quotations are from the Holy Bible, Authorized King James Version.

Dedication

I dedicate this book to all those who long for truth,
revival, and to walk in the kingdom of God.
May God empower His Remnant in this generation.

Contents

Foreword

By Thomas Horn

As far back as the beginning of time and within every major culture of the ancient world, an astonishingly consistent story is told of "gods" that descended from heaven and materialized in bodies of flesh. From Rome to Greece—and before that, to Egypt, Persia, Assyria, Babylonia, and Sumer—the earliest records of civilization tell of the era when powerful beings known to the Hebrews as *Watchers* and in the book of Genesis as the *Benei ha-Elohim* ("Sons of God") mingled with humans, giving birth to part-celestial, part-terrestrial hybrids known as *Nephilim*. The Bible says this happened when men began to increase on earth and daughters were born to them. When the Sons of God saw the women's beauty, they took wives from among them to sire their unusual offspring. This event is recorded in Genesis 6:4 this way:

> There were giants in the earth in those days; and also after that, when the sons of God came in unto the daughters of men, and they bare children to them, the same became mighty men which were of old, men of renown.

When this Scripture is compared with other ancient texts, including *Enoch, Jubilees, Baruch, Genesis Apocryphon, Philo, Josephus*, and others, it unfolds to some that the giants of the Old Testament, such as Goliath, were the part-human, part-animal, part-angelic offspring of a supernatural interruption into the divine order of the species. The apocryphal *Book of Enoch* gives a name to the angels involved in this cosmic conspiracy, calling them "Watchers." We read:

> And I Enoch was blessing the Lord of majesty and the King of the ages, and lo! the Watchers called me—Enoch the scribe—and said to me: "Enoch, thou scribe of righteousness, go, declare to the Watchers of the heaven who have left the high heaven, the holy eternal place, and have defiled themselves with women, and have done as the children of earth do, and have taken unto themselves wives: Ye have wrought great destruction on the earth: And ye shall have no peace nor forgiveness of sin: and inasmuch as they delight themselves in their children [the Nephilim], The murder of their beloved ones shall they see, and over the destruction of their children shall they lament, and shall make supplication unto eternity, but mercy and peace shall ye not attain." (1 Enoch 10:3–8).

According to Enoch, two hundred of these powerful angels departed "high heaven" and used women (among other things) to extend their progeny into mankind's plane of existence. Departing the proper habitation God had assigned them was grievous to the Lord and led to divine penalization. Jude described it this way:

> [The] angels which kept not their first estate, but left their own habitation, he hath reserved in everlasting chains under darkness unto the judgment of the great day. (Jude 6)

Yet beyond such historical accounts from apocryphal, pseudepigraphic, biblical, and Jewish traditions related to the advent of the Watchers and the "mighty men" born of their union with humans, mythologized accounts say these "gods" used humans to produce demigods (half-gods). In fact, when the ancient Greek version of the Hebrew Old Testament (the LXX or Septuagint) was made, the word "Nephilim"—referring to the part-human offspring of the Watchers—was translated *gegenes*, the same terminology used by the Greeks to describe the Titans and other legendary heroes of partly celestial and partly terrestrial origin, such as Hercules (born of Zeus and the mortal Alcmena) and Gilgamesh (the two-thirds god and one-third human child of Lugalbanda and Ninsun).

This is where things get quite interesting, as on the back cover of this book you will find an unsettling statement involving what some would call the greatest of all "demigods" on the ancient plains of Shinar—a geographical locale in ancient Mesopotamia that the Hebrew Bible refers to as Babylon—where an evil was born: the first world king, the prototype transhuman, the ultimate despot named Nimrod in the Bible, Osiris by the Egyptians, Gilgamesh by the Sumerians, and Apollo by the Greeks. This part-human hybrid was the original Son of Perdition who later devised the "Shinar Directive"—a plot to enslave humanity through a global false religion that would turn men against God and the order of His creation. Of course, we all know how God intervened at the Tower of Babel and dispersed Nimrod's original coup, but few understand that this story is not over yet—it's coming around and was prophesied to do so in a final end-times conflict during which the primeval powers of Mystery Babylon would gather to build a new Tower of Babel for Nimrod/Apollo's second coming.

Over the years, my good friend and biblical scholar Gary Stearman has written extensively about the connection this historical figure had with the original Babylonian mystery religion as well as his reanimation in the end-times as Antichrist. "But who is this Assyrian[?]" he asked a while back. "He is none other than the spiritual inheritor of the first great post-Flood religious apostasy. He is the keeper of the great heritage that began at the Assyrian capital, Nineveh. Its founder was Nimrod.... He is the Antichrist, the future despot who comes in the name of the ancient mystery religion."

Stearman continues:

He was a rebel who allowed himself to be worshipped as a god. After the Flood, his rebellion became the foundation of mankind's greatest religious apostasy. Down through the generations, this system of false worship became known simply as the "Babylonian Mystery Religion." Its basis is quite clear. *It attempts to channel the power of the ancient gods through the figure of one, powerful man. Nimrod became that god* [emphasis added].

Alexander Hislop, in his classic text, *The Two Babylons*, substantiates the thesis that the Babylonian mystery religion was based on the worship of this proto-Antichrist. "It was to glorify Nimrod that the whole Chaldean system of iniquity was formed," he wrote.[1] Yet the mystery religion continued since its beginning secretly through the ages, shrouded in hiding by adepts of the occult in anticipation of a final moment when the ancient spirit should be awakened:

Corrupt priesthoods have flourished, carrying with them the shadow of Nimrod and his ancient mysteries. Their inner secrets have been known by various names, including alchemy, magic, sorcery, conjuring, soothsaying and so forth.... waiting for the prophesied day when it would rise once again. [A movement that] will result in the reign of the Antichrist.

Enter Dr. Michael Lake, founder and chancellor of Biblical Life College and Seminary, whose shocking essay you now hold in your hands—a work that argues beyond doubt that we have entered the final time frame in which the spirit of Nimrod/Apollo is rising. Dare I say, with this book, that Lake emerges as one of the most judicious observers of the ages harkening back to those ancient occult-science endeavors—from megalithic building sites to the founders of Atlantian-like societies that to this day astonish scholars and laymen alike. Yet, argues Lake, there is more. In *The Shinar Directive*, he tackles the timeline between the first incursion of a mighty evil to its return and final encounter. Lake exceeds in making this near future chillingly ominous. Our eyes are opened to a biosphere and exosphere that have become a vast and stunningly dreadful battleground—a terrain as forgotten as prehistory, yet is as close to us now as our own tomorrow. This lethal and toxic reality was foreseen by Scriptures, both Old and New Testament, but soon will, by necessity, be traversed by gutsy end-time heroes, not highly trained black-ops teams or Elite commandos, *but a revived and triumphant Church!*

In the end, the greatest achievements of *The Shinar Directive* are apt, profound, and conveyed in riveting fashion: With this work, the past and future legacy of wisdom and revelation clearly shine forth in multifaceted grandeur—from the forgotten "knowledge" of so-called "gods" and their reconnection to the latest scientific advances to the terrifying underbelly of a boiling Armageddon and, finally, the brilliant and thrilling endgame that God has in store for His own.

A Journey Down the Rabbit Hole

The Matrix is the world that has been pulled over your
eyes to blind you from the truth.
—Morpheus, *The Matrix*

I t's amazing how God will take you on journeys of discovery, especially when you are in ministry and clueless as to where the Church is prophetically in the "war against the saints." I remember in 1999, as I was watching the new sci-fi thriller, *The Matrix*, I began identifying so intensely with Neo (the main character in the story) that I almost had a panic attack during the movie. Neo had a sense that something was off in his world, but the truth was beyond what his paradigm would allow. The scene in the movie had him asleep at his computer keyboard when Trinity (the main heroine in the movie) typed the now-famous words on his computer screen: "Knock, knock, Neo." From that moment on, Neo began a journey down the rabbit hole and discovered another reality existed.

I am not saying that the singularity² is already here or that AIs (artificial intelligence beings) have secretly taken over the world. Actually, what we are facing is something even more nefarious. We are living in a neo-pagan world that is completely controlled by the occult, and the Church is oblivious to this reality.

I was raised as a typical American Christian. I cannot remember a Sunday that I wasn't in church. In fact, I have vivid memories as a young child of taking naps under the pews (in contrast to the many adults taking naps while on them). I accepted Jesus as my Lord and Savior at a Missionary Baptist youth camp nestled deep in the woods of Missouri when I was just twelve. On my thirteenth birthday, I answered the call to the ministry and have been a student of the Word and a preacher/teacher ever since. I wish that I could tell you that everything was clear skies and rainbows after that, but it wouldn't be true. Like most Christians in America, I was only partially awake. To be truthful, the covert influence of the occult within society and the Church had left me nearly comatose spiritually. I would have moments of great spiritual lucidity while ministering in the pulpit, but would revert back to a type of spiritual slumber by the time I got home. (I have recently discovered that the luciferian community mocks the state of the Church today by referring to us as "zombies.")

Then something startling happened. In January of 1994, a sovereign act of God changed my life forever. My wife, Mary, had lived under the shadow of a dark depression most of her life. I must commend her. She was able to hide this depression from the public well, and was able to make herself get out of the bed in the mornings to take care of our children and home. I am sure she had to muster intestinal fortitude to make it through each day. Everyone thought she was a very cordial person with a bubbly personality. She always baked goodies for our children's activities at school and was involved in classroom parties and other extracurricular events, although she confessed to me later that these social atmospheres were exhausting for her. Mary tried to conceal her deep depression, because she did not want to burden the people around her. She would rather hurt on the inside than make everyone around her miserable, too. Yet, she continued each day under this huge burden that was blocking her spiritual growth and even keeping her from reading the Word of God.

Mary woke up one cold January morning, and the depression was gone. It took her several days to realize what had happened. Colors around her appeared brighter and more beautiful. The air seemed fresher that morning, and she felt a joy in her heart. Mary began reading (actually more like devouring) the Word of God, listening to teachings on Christian TV, and getting lost in prayer for hours with this wonderful God who had set her absolutely free. While the rest of the family was watching evening television, she would dress warmly and go sit outside in our van to pray. (I even believe that this step helped her hear from God, considering the wealth of knowledge that we now have concerning the use of television broadcasts for the purpose of interjecting attitudes and ideas at the subliminal level.) Most importantly (at least from my perspective), she began to pray for the husband whom she had just fallen in love with anew. She prayed that he would be set free from the spiritual slumber that he had lived in for 95 percent of his life.

To our dismay, after eight months of glorious freedom, the depression came back with a vengeance. This time, it was darker and even more oppressive than before. Finally, on a cold evening a few months later, she wrapped herself in a blanket and sat outside on a picnic bench behind our home to seek the face of God. She determined in her heart that she would remain there until she got an answer from God on how she could have regressed to such a state. About the time she felt chilled to the bone, God began speaking to her. He told her that she was under demonic oppression, and that she now had the knowledge and ability to fight. God told Mary to bind the power of these demons in the Name of Jesus, and that He would show her the path to freedom. As God continued the process of Mary's deliverance and healing, she had memories emerge of abuse by those in the occult. She was having a very difficult time believing that these memories could be true, and she would repeatedly ask me to pray that God would show us truth to ensure that she was not being led into error by a deceiving spirit. Much to my amazement, everything she told me was not only confirmed by people in her hometown right in front of my eyes, but many of the details that she was remembering were confirmed though my continual research (and many of the other aspects of her recollections are still being confirmed today). In our present time, the concept of chimeras (a hybrid that combines several types of animals into one new creature) is a common topic among those in the know; when she gave me details of these hybrid beings in 1995, I must confess that it was very difficult to believe. In 2000, we viewed a series of huge lights flashing in a particular sequence over her hometown. As our research has continued, it is more apparent than ever that these lights were impacting the citizens of that town (the people in that town are totally unaware that they are being affected). I am convinced that these lights are an integral element of the unfolding saga of mind control in our nation (especially considering that the first time we viewed the lights was on election night of November 2000—is it possible that technology is being used to sway elections?).

As Mary's healing progressed and we stepped into the preliminary stages of discovering the deep roots of witchcraft in the Ozarks, God began working on me. Step by step, I began to awaken from the occult haze that had enveloped my soul. I was just like Neo in *The Matrix*. I knew there was something wrong, yet I was asleep at the keyboard of life. Then, through several sovereign moves of the Triune God, like Neo, I received a wake-up call. This did not lead me down a rabbit hole to discover that the world I had always known was a fabrication by an advanced AI to control my life. No—this rabbit hole led to the reality of just how embedded the occult is in every aspect of our society, and to what extent we are under its control. The luciferian agenda is well under way. I discovered that the multidimensional schemes of the enemy are more complex than anyone could ever imagine. In fact, these plans have been in motion since Nimrod walked the streets of Babylon. My discoveries included:

- Involvement by those in the occult in politics, education, and law enforcement
- The reality of mind control, satanic ritual abuse, and multiple personalities
- Systematic poisoning of our food, air, and water
- Secret societies' web of entanglement in every level of our society—worldwide
- The occult's deep intrusion into our churches, denominations, seminaries, and theologies—as well as spiritual warfare and psychic warfare aimed at our pastors

- How the luciferian agenda includes both aspects of completely controlling every individual on the planet and a deep passion to see the population reduced to just five hundred million

As Mary and I proceeded to realize the depth and span of Lucifer's plan for mankind, the warfare began to accelerate. We began ministering to several multigenerational members of the occult who were diagnosed with Multiple Personality Disorder (MPD[3]), which led to more research on mind control. We actually believe that these individuals were sent in to infiltrate and destroy rather than to seek help. It became obvious that someone was very concerned about what my wife was remembering. That was when all hell broke loose. To our astonishment, some of the greatest adversaries we had were Christians we had known for years in the churches of our community. We would run into these people, and it was apparent that they hated us (their appearances would be disturbing, and they would sneer at us or make bizarre comments). We would see the same people in the grocery store or on the street at other times, and they would seem normal and even talk to us like nothing odd had ever happened. This was "blowing our minds" until we finally understood the level of occult control in the town and the multifaceted concept of multiple personalities with programming. (As we learned more about mind-control experiments and the effects on the body, we concluded that their bright red faces were a result of histamine levels.) Once we read Russ Dizdar's book, *The Black Awakening*, we were able to make sense of the black uniforms that these Dr. Jekyll/Mr. Hyde types were wearing on certain dates. While this information caused my wife and me to sit back at our desks in unbelief as we continued our research, it explained what we were witnessing within that small town, and it also shed light on what had happened to Mary. We were able to connect some dots, convincing us that this secluded town had been a logical choice for such testing decades ago (with a military base about twenty miles away). Our investigations concluded that the experimentation was a success on a monumental scale. Keep in mind that, to the casual observer, this town looked like Mayberry from the *Andy Griffith Show*.

I could tell you about all the times when members of local covens circled our home at night uttering curses against my family, or when they poisoned us, or when they sabotaged our vehicle, or when they killed one of our pets and left the animal's body part on the edge of our yard for my children to find. But most of these stories have already been written by my dear wife in her book, *What Witches Don't Want Christians to Know*. Mary walked a fine line in writing her book. She wanted to share what we went through and how God delivered us to bring hope to those still trapped in the place where she had been raised. At the same time, she did not want to reveal names or provide too many details that would jeopardize the lives of those she was trying to reach. Few can even imagine the nights she spent in prayer, writing, rewriting, and weighing the words of every story and every detail. Although some have criticized her for not including all the "juicy" details, I am sure no one has walked in her shoes or cared as much about those still trapped in darkness. At this time, Mary believes she has done everything possible to show that God will protect those who want out of the trap she was born into. She believes she has fulfilled her promise to God to stand in the gap and pray. With sadness in her heart for those still in shackles, Mary agrees with me that God is telling us to move forward.

I am thankful that God is moving our family and ministry into another phase. The Holy Spirit very clearly stated that the old door of ministry has been closed and a new one has opened. This was also confirmed by several men of God whom I have the greatest respect for and trust greatly. The new door is all about the Remnant, preparing for what is coming, and learning how to walk in victory.

With the preparation of the Remnant in mind, I want to share the facts I have discovered through the process and the trials. I am an academic researcher and Bible teacher. I am also ex-military. So, I have a deep desire to "know my enemy." During those troubling times, I kicked into research overdrive. I read stacks of books and gleaned information from myriad websites. There were even books I considered so vile that I burned them after reading. I wanted to examine the mindsets of those involved in the occult so I could attempt to comprehend their warfare doctrine.

Although I'm not an expert on the subjects I will discuss in this book, I do have a better understanding of how trained occultists work to pull us into subjection and put us to sleep. Along the way, I have also discovered how the ancient Hebraic wisdom encoded into God's Word can make us aware of the enemy's tactics, identify paganism and its influences, break the power the kingdom of darkness has over our lives, and enable us to walk fully awake and in the freedom Jesus came to give us!

Today, the Holy Trinity is knocking at your door. "Knock, knock, Remnant." Are you ready to look beyond the world that has been pulled over your eyes and discover the truth? Are you ready to be equipped for end-time spiritual warfare and be enabled by our Sovereign and Holy God to walk out of Babylon? Are you ready to be that Bride whose garments are without spot or wrinkle? If so, read on and discover a reality that will set you free!

chapter one

The Reality of Conspiratorial History

A Brief Introduction

Coincidence is merely the puppeteers' curtain,
hiding the hands that pull the world's strings.
—Kaleb Nation, *Harken*

I spent most of my life with a general disinterest in human history. I believe that a large number of Americans fit into this category as well. Our culture has conditioned us to approach historical review with apathy, while simultaneously discouraging us from planning too far into the future. Everything we see in the media, from political speeches to commercials, emphasizes the "now." In fact, the "need it now" and "only the present matters" mindsets have been thrust into our society from every quarter. These cultural blinders establish fuel for the economy to fund the Elite and cultivate intellectual bondage. The enemy of our soul is limited concerning what he can use in his warfare against mankind (1 Corinthians 10:13). Since he has a limited bag of tricks, he needs to keep us in the dark regarding our real history. Without these psycho-spiritual blinders, we would recognize what is going on, cry out to God for intervention,

9

and implement spiritual strategies to overcome his intrusion and control of our lives.

As I said, I cared little about history until a series of events changed my worldview forever. As I mentioned in the introduction, my wife was in the middle of a miraculous healing season when several groups from the occult launched an incredible attack on our family. We eventually concluded that the attack was directly related to my wife's surfacing memories. These memories were bits and pieces of events that sounded like they were out of a script from some unknown sci-fi thriller. I must admit, there were times when Mary's memories caused my biblically trained and techno-oriented mind to reel in bewilderment. Later on, her memories were confirmed through the research of individuals such as Steve Quayle, Russ Dizdar, Walter H. Bowart, and Dr. Nick Begich (to name just a few). Some of her recovered memories were validated right in front of my eyes. I began to wonder: If the kingdom of darkness was so worried about what my wife was remembering about her past, maybe the history of mankind is replete with additional land mines of truth that the enemy desperately doesn't want us to discover, as well. In fact, today, the history of the United States is being rewritten with an Orwellian fervor. History was taught quite differently in times past; lessons included the portrayal of the heart and soul of each character. Students were imparted with a rich wealth of information that allowed them to both learn from history and be inspired by it. Books such as *The Christian Life and Character of the Civil Institutions of the United States* by Benjamin F. Morris were used in the educational process of our youth. Then the Progressive Movement began to take hold of our nation, and the deconstruction of our history began. During the time when I attended school (in the late 1960s and '70s), history had been reduced to memorizing events and dates. History had been separated from the passion, beliefs, and mistakes of those who had lived it.

Today, as part of the new Common Core curriculum in our schools, America's Founding Fathers are being referred to as terrorists, and they and the Constitution are looked upon with disdain.[4] At West Point's Combating Terrorism Center (WPCTC), the best and brightest of our young Army officers are being taught that radical Islam is not a real problem in America. The true potential enemies, according to a recent WPCTC report, are conservatives and patriots inside the United States.[5] Every effort to obscure our true history is being exerted from behind the scenes, allowing our leaders to create so-called historical justifications for whatever political agenda they are espousing. One of the recent historical fabrications is that George Washington would have wanted Obamacare for all US citizens.[6] (Since the original intent of the Founding Fathers was limited government, only those completely ignorant of American history could buy into such a sound bite.) An old axiom credited to Winston Churchill is more relevant today than ever before: "Those who fail to learn from history are doomed to repeat it."

We need to realize that the enemy is working overtime to hide our past so that he can keep us in bondage for a future he is covertly building.

After years of study—both in the Word of God and human history—since my wake-up call, I have become a strong believer in conspiratorial history. We have all been preprogrammed by our progressive culture to have a knee-jerk response to anyone who believes in conspiracies—they are the ones who wear aluminum foil on their heads. From our evening news to our favorite sitcoms, conspiracy theorists are depicted as either simpletons or mentally unstable. Few have taken the time to research for themselves and discover that there can only be one of two types of history. Noted historian, university professor, and believer A. Ralph Epperson provides an eye-opening introduction to the subject of understanding history in his book, *The Unseen Hand: An Introduction to the Conspiratorial View of History*:

> Wars start when one nation moves into the territory of another; depressions occur when markets take unexpected downturns; inflations occur when prices are driven up by shortages; revolutions start when the people, always spontaneously, rise up to overthrow the existing government. These are the traditional explanations of historical events. Events happen by accident. There do not seem to be any causes.

But this explanation of history leaves gnawing questions in the minds of serious students. Is it possible that government leaders and others planned these events and then orchestrated them to their desired conclusions? Is it possible that even the great catastrophes of history were part of this plan?

There is an explanation of historical events that answers these questions in the affirmative. It is called the Conspiratorial View of History, and it is the alternative to the Accidental View, the view commonly held today. It is possible, therefore, to summarize the major events of history into two alternative schools of thought:

1. The Accidental View of History: Historical events occur by accident, for no apparent reason. Rulers are powerless to intervene.

2. The Conspiratorial View of History: Historical events occur by design for reasons not generally made known to the people.[7]

We need to realize that we have been conditioned to believe everything that happens in the world today is merely by accident. There is no real cause and effect. We are expected to believe that an accidental event happening somewhere in another country caused a cascading series of events that ends up affecting both that nation and the entire world. The message is continually being reinforced within our global consciousness: "There is no secret cabal governing the affairs of this world. There is nothing to see here, folks; just watch another sitcom that amuses you, while it programs you to abandon social norms established by previous generations in exchange for a new agenda. Just slide back in your easy chair, be dazzled by the special effects in the new action movie, and enter another techno-induced stupor by the Elite-controlled entertainment industry."

Which of the following statements is harder to believe?

1. There is no rhyme or reason to anything that goes on here on the earth. Everything is just an accident. Any connections are just unexplainable coincidences.

2. There are those who plan our future from behind closed doors who can sway economies, control our energy resources, have complete control of the world's wealth through a centralized banking system, and topple or

cripple nations to suit their hidden agendas that move us toward a New World Order.

Let's analyze this and examine our own government:

- Do elected officials ever meet behind closed doors (under the cover of national security) to create policies and laws that even contradict the very platforms they ran on to be elected to office?
- Do the policies of both the right and left wings continually move us toward the same destination? (As far as I can see, the only difference is that one side prefers to move more quickly than the other.)
- Have we had national leaders speak of an agenda contrary to that of our own country? Are they warning us about or proclaiming the need for a New World Order?

Today the path to total dictatorship in the U.S. can be laid by strictly legal means, unseen and unheard by Congress, the President, or the people. Outwardly we have a Constitutional government. We have operating within our government and political system, another body representing another form of government—a bureaucratic elite. We have a well-organized political-action group in this country, determined to destroy our Constitution and establish a one-party state....

The important point to remember about this group is not its ideology but its organization. It is a dynamic, aggressive, elite corps, forcing its way through every opening, to make a breach for a collectivist one-party state. It operates secretly, silently, continuously to transform our Government without suspecting that change is under way....

If I seem to be extremist, the reason is that this revolutionary clique cannot be understood, unless we accept the fact that they are extremist. It is difficult for people governed by reasonableness and morality to imagine the existence of a movement which ignores reasonableness and boasts of its determination to destroy; which ignores morality, and boasts of its cleverness in outwitting its opponents by abandoning all scruples. This ruthless power-seeking elite is a disease of our century....

This group...is answerable neither to the President, the Congress, nor the courts. It is practically irremovable.

—Senator William Jenner, 1954[8]

In 1962 then Governor Nelson Rockefeller delivered a series of lectures at Harvard University on the future of federalism. In his presentation the governor dwelt at length on the interdependence of nations in the modern world, concluding with this statement: "And so the nation-state, standing alone, threatens in many ways to seem as anachronistic as the Greek city-state eventually became in ancient times."

Everything the governor said was true. We are dependent on other nations for raw materials and for markets. It is necessary to make defense alliances with other nations in order to balance the military power of those who would destroy us. Where I differ from the governor is in the suggestion implicit throughout the lectures that to achieve this new federalism, the United States must submerge its national identity and surrender substantial matters of sovereignty to a new political order.

The implications in Governor Rockefeller's presentation have become concrete proposals advanced by David Rockefeller's newest international cabal, the Trilateral Commission. Whereas the Council on Foreign Relations is distinctly national in membership, the Trilateral Commission is international. Representation is allocated equally to Western Europe, Japan, and the United States. It is intended to be the vehicle for multinational consolidation of the commercial and banking interests by seizing control of the political government of the United States.

—US Senator Barry Goldwater[9]

The depression was the calculated "shearing" of the public by the World Money powers, triggered by the planned sudden shortage of supply of call money in the New York money market....

The One World Government leaders and their ever close bankers have now acquired full control of the money and credit machinery of the U.S. via the creation of the privately owned Federal Reserve Bank.

—Curtis Dall, son-in-law to Franklin Delano Roosevelt[10]

We will succeed in the Gulf. And when we do, the world community will have sent an enduring warning to any dictator or despot, present or future, who contemplates outlaw aggression. The world can, therefore, seize this opportunity to fulfill the long-held promise of a new world order, where brutality will go unrewarded and aggression will meet collective resistance.

—President George H. W. Bush,
State of the Union address, 1991[11]

Well, to be honest, George Washington warned us about this cabal at the very beginning of our nation:

It is not my intention to doubt that the doctrine of the Illuminati and the principles of Jacobinism had not spread in the United States. On the contrary, no one is more satisfied of this fact than I am.

—President George Washington[12]

A Quick Review of the Tactics of Intelligence Agencies

All warfare is based on deception.
—Sun Tzu, *The Art of War*

Let your plans be dark and impenetrable as night, and when you move, fall like a thunderbolt.
—Sun Tzu, *The Art of War*

Few realize that conspiracy and campaigns of disinformation have been business as usual in international affairs since the time of Babylon! *The Art of War* was written by Sun Tzu around 500 BC. Many of the concepts postulated in that book were not necessarily originated by Sun Tzu. He simply organized and codified many that were developed well before his time and then added his own convictions, philosophies, and life lessons. History remembers Sun Tzu as a brilliant tactician and soldier. His legacy is that *The Art of War* is required reading in every war college and intelligence agency on the planet today (as well as in international corporations).

Nations have intelligence agencies because other countries and groups conspire against them. These same intelligence agencies that continually comb through tons of data each day to detect possible conspiracies are tasked with the duty of enacting their own governments' secret plans against other nations, as well. There is a continual cat-and-mouse game played on an international level involving conspiracies and campaigns of disinformation to hide the true agenda of any move by an intelligence agency against a competing nation. **Conspiracy/misinformation is the game of kings and thrones since civilization began.**

Whenever there is an influx of information pointing to various possible or opposing conspiracies and their debunking by self-appointed experts, it is usually a distraction to allow the real conspiracy to be enacted without being noticed by the general public. Intelligence agencies conduct such activities worldwide continually. In fact, part of their job is to make the false conspiracies look more creditable to keep investigators running after red herrings and prevent them from discovering the truth until it is too late. While the Elite-controlled media uses such stories to paint pictures of conspiracy theorists who look and act like Dr. Emmett Brown in the movie *Back to the Future*, in reality, both the fake conspiracies and their ever-so-carefully placed trail of bread crumbs were created by real conspirators to keep us from discovering their true agendas.

Clues to the Ultimate Conspiracy

[19]Then I would know the truth of the fourth beast, *which was diverse from all the others*, exceeding dreadful, whose teeth were of iron, and his nails of brass; which devoured, brake in pieces, and stamped the residue with his feet;

[20]And of the ten horns that were in his head, and of the other which came up, and before whom three fell; even of that horn that had eyes, and a mouth that spake very great things, whose look was more stout than his fellows.

[21]I beheld, and the same horn made war with the saints, and prevailed against them;

[22] Until the Ancient of days came, and judgment was given to the saints of the most High; and the time came that the saints possessed the kingdom. (Daniel 7:19–22, emphasis added)

The seventh chapter of Daniel speaks of ten kings who are a part of the fourth beast. Although many prophetic topics can be examined in these passages, I want to focus on just one for the discussion at hand. In the interpretation given to Daniel, a unique designator is given to this beast: "which was diverse [or different] than all the others" (Daniel 7:19). Why was it different? We have had kings throughout human history who have had vassal nations under them that maintained their own kings. In the book of Ezra, Artaxerxes was referred to as "a king of kings" (Ezra 7:12). Was it that the "little horn" waged war against three of the other kings? This has occurred at various times throughout human history, too. I believe the answer lies in the nature of this final kingdom. You see, there is a kingdom today that transcends all national borders. This kingdom controls kings, presidents, prime ministers, and nations. When its council of kings convenes, it determines which nations will prosper, which will fail, who will be elected president, and who will become expendable to accomplish the tacit global agenda. You see, this game of kings and thrones continues in the clandestine meeting rooms of the world's Elite. They use their own intelligence agencies and those of vassal nations both to conspire and to disseminate disinformation to keep the uninitiated from discovering the truth. The final kingdom, the kingdom that is different from all the others, in which the Antichrist will rise, is a financial empire that has subjugated the entire world under the weight of its power. All democracies, dictatorships, regimes, or even political parties are nothing more than tentacles of the same, final beast.

> Give me control of a nation's money and I care not who makes the laws.
>
> —Mayer Amschel Rothschild

   To set the proper foundation for understanding conspiratorial history from a prophetic view, we must understand that, at its very core, it is spiritual in nature. Therefore, the Word of God is our foundational source for understanding its nature and purpose.

chapter two

Conspiratorial History within the Bible

Part 1: Genesis 1–3

Remember the former things of old: for I am God, and there is none else; I am God, and there is none like me,

Declaring the end from the beginning, and from ancient times the things that are not yet done, saying, My counsel shall stand, and I will do all my pleasure.

—Isaiah 46:9–10

The more I grow in the grace of God and see Him and His majesty in the Word, the more I become enthralled at the splendor and wisdom of the One True God we serve. There are times when I sense what Solomon was feeling at the dedication of the Temple in Jerusalem in the tenth century BCE. We find an account of this event in 2 Chronicles:

But will God in very deed dwell with men on the earth? behold, heaven and the heaven of heavens cannot contain thee; how much less this house which I have built! (2 Chronicles 6:18)

At the moment the glory cloud of God (kaw-bode') filled the Temple, Solomon's heart was filled with awe. I believe this is of paramount importance for us to keep in the forefront of our minds as we seek to understand the level of warfare we find ourselves engaged in just before the Messianic Age. Although things may seem so complex at times that we cannot even begin to grasp the strategies of the enemy, our God was fully aware of His plan from the very beginning. With a word, the God we serve created our reality and used the speed of light as a container (or set the boundaries) of time itself. Never lose sight of this truth: There is none like our God!

God makes a powerful statement in Isaiah 46 that is essential to our study: He told us the end from the beginning. The entire Bible was inspired by God; it is immutable, infallible, and perfect. Yet there is something unique about the Torah. Would you be surprised if I told you that Moses did not author Genesis through Numbers? Did he write them down? Yes. But he did not author them. He was not moved upon by the Holy Spirit to write as the other men who penned the remaining books of the canon. The first four books of the Bible were dictated by God to Moses as he met with the Almighty face to face as a man would speak to his friend (Exodus 33:11). After years of meeting with God and taking dictation for the first four books, the residual anointing on Moses allowed him to author Deuteronomy with the same supernatural uniqueness the first four possessed. Deuteronomy (or *Devarim* in Hebrew) simply means "words." Moses provided the new generation of Israelites with a *Reader's Digest* version to instruct them before they crossed over into the Promised Land. So, the Torah (or the "loving instruction of the Father God"[13]) is five books in length; this is another reason we call it the Pentateuch. Five is the biblical number for grace.[14] As we proceed in our study, you will begin to realize why the kingdom of darkness has created such jaundice in the body of Christ concerning the Torah. Such prejudice against the foundations of our faith did not exist in the hearts of the apostles. In fact, they used the Old Testament *(Tanakh)* and the revelation of Jesus to turn the world upside down!

The End Times and the Writings of the Apostle John

Many consider the book of Revelation to be the last book written in the New Testament. Although it is true that the apostle John did write the final books that closed out New Testament canon, his last books were his epistles.

- **The Gospel of John**: John wrote this Gospel between AD 90 and 95. His purpose for writing it was so that all might have faith in the completed work of Messiah on the Cross.
- **The Book of Revelation**: John wrote this book while he was exiled on Patmos. Most commentators date this book as being written between AD 95 and 97. This prophetic book was written to the bondservants of God to reveal Jesus to them as "Messiah ben David." (We will cover this term later in our discussion.)
- **First Epistle of John**: The Apostle of Love wrote this book around AD 98. He had already experienced the vision about which the book of Revelation was written. This epistle was written to prepare the Remnant for the challenges John had already witnessed in the Revelation.

John begins both his Gospel and his first epistle with the phrase, "In the beginning." What we do not see with our twenty-first century, Gentile eyes is that he was referring to the Torah and, more specifically, to the book of Genesis. This Jewish apostle knew both the Torah and the book of Isaiah well. So, he was cognizant of the prophetic overtones encoded in the story of Creation. Before we can understand what John saw, we must first learn to view the Scriptures through Hebraic eyes.

A Quick Primer in Hebraic Hermeneutics

1. Jesus and the Torah

> For Christ is the end of the law for righteousness to every one that
> believeth. (Romans 10:4)

There has been much debate in theological circles on exactly what the
apostle Paul meant by this statement. Did Paul mean that the Torah was
completely done away with for New Testament believers, or was there a
more laser-like application to the statement he was making here? A. T.
Robertson, in his classic work, *Word Pictures in the New Testament*, provides additional insight:

> **The end of the law** (τελος νομου [*telos nomou*]). Christ put a stop
> to the law as a means of salvation (6:14; 9:31; Eph. 2:15; Col.
> 2:14) as in Luke 16:16. Christ is the goal or aim of the law (Gal.
> 3:24). Christ is the fulfilment of the law (Matt. 5:17; Rom. 13:10;
> 1 Tim. 1:5). But here Paul's main idea is that Christ ended the law
> as a method of salvation for "every one that believeth" whether
> Jew or Gentile. Christ wrote *finis* on law as a means of grace.[15]

First, Paul makes it clear that the only way to salvation is through
the completed work of Christ. Both the apostle Paul and the Council of
Jerusalem in Acts 15 put a stop to the misuse of the Torah as a means of
salvation for Gentiles by the erroneous teaching of the Pharisees from the
School of Shammai[16] that Gentiles had to first become physically Jewish (through circumcision) before they could receive the Messiah (Acts
15:1). Since the enemy has so successfully disenfranchised us from our
Hebraic heritage, nearly all Protestant theologians miss the fact that God
never intended the Torah to save anyone. When we examine the Exodus
story, the Torah was not handed to the children of Israel as a means to
free them from the clutches of the pharaoh of Egypt. Moses, a biblical
type and shadow of Messiah, was sent by God to deliver them first. Only

after they were a free people gathered around God's feet at Sinai did the Almighty begin giving them the Torah. The Torah is how free people in God conduct themselves, and it provides clear definitions of what sin is so that it might be avoided. Also encoded within the Torah is the promise of a greater deliverance: a salvation that is more than just physical. This salvation would free them from the one whom Pharaoh embodied: Lucifer himself. The One to come would be both like Moses and God. We call this One the Messiah. So Jesus is the goal of the Torah. The Torah first establishes the legal precedent for salvation through the suffering of Messiah. Then the job of the Torah is to act as a teacher to bring us before Him to receive that salvation through faith (Galatians 3:24). Jesus is the epicenter of the entire Word of God. Therefore, we can expect to see Him in every story, teaching, precept, and sacrificial offering required in the Torah. It is all about Jesus, from Genesis 1 to Deuteronomy 34!

2. Hebraic Hermeneutics

The next principle I need to touch on is the Hebraic methods of interpreting Scripture. The rabbis teach that there are four levels of Torah interpretation. The acronym for this is: *PaRDeS,* which is Hebrew for "paradise" and refers to a garden of delight (in other words, when we interpret God's instructions correctly, our lives can produce a garden of the Almighty's blessings). Let's take a look at what this acronym means.

Level One—*Pashat:* This is the literal meaning of the Scripture. It is the plain, simple meaning of the text in grammatical and historical context. We must remember that no method of interpretation can negate the Pashat level of the meaning of the text.

Level Two—*Remez:* This is the implied meaning of the text. The text is hinting at a deeper truth than what is being revealed.

Level Three—*Drash:* This is the allegorical, typological, homiletical meaning of the text being studied.

Level Four—*Sod:* This is the deep, hidden meaning of the text.[17]

Even in the hermeneutical principles used by evangelicals today, we have adopted the first three methods illustrated here. But for us to see what the apostle John was referring to, we will need to look at the original Hebrew and utilize the fourth level of Hebraic interpretation: the **Sod** level.

3. The Meaning of the Hebrew Letters

The rabbis recognize that each word, letter, and placement have specific meanings placed there by Almighty God as He dictated the Torah to Moses. The chart depicting the meaning of each Hebrew letter is on the following page.

So here are the three hermeneutical legs to our Hebraic platform:

- Jesus is the goal of the Torah.
- Any level of interpretation must agree with the plain meaning of the text.
- Every Hebrew letter has a specific meaning and can provide great interpretative insights.

Let's take a look at the **beginning** through the eyes of the apostle John.

Jesus Discovered in the Beginning

In the beginning was the Word, and the Word was with God, and the Word was God. The same was in the beginning with God. (John 1:1–2)

That which was from the beginning, which we have heard, which we have seen with our eyes, which we have looked upon, and our hands have handled, of the Word of life. (1 John 1:1)

I am Alpha and Omega, the beginning and the ending, saith the Lord, which is, and which was, and which is to come, the Almighty. (Revelation 1:8)

Gematria and Meaning for Hebrew and English

Number	Hebrew	English	Meaning
1	aleph - א	A	Strength – ox
2	bet - ב	B	house
3	gimel – ג	G	pride – lift up – camel
4	dalet - ד	D	door
5	hey - ה	H	behold – reveal – window
6	vav - ו	V	nail
7	zayin - ז	Z	cut off – weapon
8	het - ח	CH	Separate – fence
9	tet – ט	T	surround – snake – winding
10	yod - י	Y	hand
20	kaf - כ	K	open hand – cover – bent hand
30	lamed – ל	L	Staff – goad
40	mem - מ	M	water – chaos
50	nun - נ	N	fish – life
60	samech - ס	S	Support – prop
70	ayin - ע	-	eye
80	pey - פ	P	speak - mouth
90	tzadik – צ	TS	fish hook – (desire)
100	quof – ק	Q	back (least) – needle eye
200	resh - ר	R	front – first – head – chief
300	shin – ש	SH	Tooth – consume – destroy
400	tav - ת	T	sign – covenant – seal – mark - cross

Luciferianism teaches that Lucifer is the god that created the earth and mankind. It also teaches that *Elohim* was jealous of this new creation, portrayed Lucifer as evil, and took credit for the Creation. (This same concept is presented in the Masonic book, *Morals and Dogma*, by 33rd-Degree Mason Albert Pike.) In the minds of the followers of this belief system, Lucifer is wonderful and wants to fulfill his promise of imparting knowledge (that was forbidden to be given to mankind by Elohim) to make them like God. They believe that Elohim are evil, and Lucifer is the one who came to bring them light. I share this with you because you need to understand the belief systems of the Elite. They are luciferian to the very core. Every move they make in manipulating mankind is for one express purpose: to discover how to become gods through the knowledge promised by Lucifer. Yet God's Word paints a different picture for us. Is Lucifer in the Creation story before Genesis 3? Would you be surprised if I said, "Yes"? The good news is that Jesus is there, too (as well as in Genesis 3)!

The apostle John had a revelation of something that the rabbis had debated for centuries before Jesus ever walked the shores of Galilee. But to understand this debate and revelation, you would have to see through Hebraic eyes and view the **beginning** the way John did.

Jesus in Genesis 1:1

In the beginning (or *Bereshith*), there was a Word that sat right next to *Elohim* and was an active part of Creation. The rabbis understood the divine nature of the Torah and believed, since it was dictated directly from the mouth of God, that every word and its placement within Scripture held significant meaning. In Hebrew, this word was the *Aleph-Tav*. In Greek, it would have been represented as the *Alpha-Omega*. Grammatically, the *Aleph-Tav* in Hebrew is pronounced "et," and it is a connecting word. There is no corresponding word in English, so it remains silent. Yet, its impact upon our understanding of Creation is profound.

The *Aleph-Tav* predates Creation. This Word was considered by the apostle John to be the "Word of Life" (1 John 1:1). Since *Elohim* is the plural form for "God" in Hebrew, why is the *Aleph-Tav* residing outside of *Elohim*, yet considered equal with *Elohim* (Philippians 2:6)? I am convinced that it was the promise of salvation. There would be a distinct work of the *Aleph-Tav* separate, if you will, from the general work of *Elohim* in the plan for Creation and redemption. The *Aleph-Tav* (or *Alpha-Omega* in Greek) is none other than the preincarnate Christ! Now let's examine the *Aleph-Tav* using our chart to see if we can find Jesus in its meaning.

- Aleph = strength
- Tav = sign, covenant, seal, mark, and cross

The *Aleph-Tav* is the strength of the covenant and of the cross. Only Jesus can make that claim!

The *Aleph-Tav* is found throughout the Old Testament. What is intriguing to me is the placement of the *Aleph-Tav* in key Old Testament Scriptures. Here are just a couple of examples:

And Enoch walked with God after he begat Methuselah three hundred years, and begat sons and daughters. (Genesis 5:22)

Now here is the same verse in an Interlinear Bible:

Gen 5:22														
בָּנִים	וַיּוֹלֶד	שָׁנָה	מֵאוֹת	שְׁלֹשׁ	מְתוּשֶׁלַח	אֶת־	הוֹלִידוֹ	אַחֲרֵי	הָאֱלֹהִים	אֶת־	חֲנוֹךְ	וַיִּתְהַלֵּךְ	²²
ncmpa	vhw3msXa Pc	ncfsa	ucfpa	ucfsc	np	Po	vhcX3ms	Pp	ncmpa Pa	Pp	np	vtw3ms Pc	
sons	and begat	years,	hundred	three	Methuselah		he begat	after	God	with	Enoch	And walked	
1121	3205	8141	3967	7969	4968	853	3205	310	430	854	2585	3212	
bānîm	wayyôleḏ	šānâ	mēʾôṯ	šᵉlōš	Mᵉṯûšelaḥ	ʾeṯ-	hôlîḏô	ʾaḥᵃrê	Hāʾᵉlōhîm	ʾeṯ-	Hᵃnôḵ	Wayyiṯhallēḵ	

Enoch walked with God. What was between Enoch and *Elohim* that enabled the walk? The answer is the *Aleph-Tav!* The placement of the *Aleph-Tav* reveals the truth that it is impossible to walk with God without the enabling work of Messiah.

Now let's look at a prophetic Scripture dealing with the return of Christ:

And I will pour upon the house of David, and upon the inhabitants of Jerusalem, the spirit of grace and of supplications: and they shall look upon me whom they have pierced, and they shall mourn for him, as one mourneth for his only son, and shall be in bitterness for him, as one that is in bitterness for his firstborn. (Zechariah 12:10)

When we view this verse in our Interlinear Bible, we again discover the *Aleph-Tav*.

Zech 12:10

וְתַחֲנוּנִים	חֵן	רוּחַ	יְרוּשָׁלַם	יוֹשֵׁב	וְעַל	דָּוִיד	בֵּית	עַל־	וְשָׁפַכְתִּי 10
ncmpa Pc	ncmsa	ncbsc	np	vqPmsc	Pp Pc	np	ncmsc	Pp	vqp[2]1cs Pc
and of supplications:	grace	the spirit of	Jerusalem,	the inhabitants of	and upon	David,	the house of	upon	And I will pour
8469	2580	7307	3389	3427	5921	1732	1004	5921	8210
wᵉtaḥᵃnûnîm	ḥēn	rûaḥ	Yᵉrûšālaim	yōšēb	wᵉˁal	Dāwîd	bêt	ˁal-	Wᵉšāpaktî

הַיָּחִיד	עַל־	כְּמַסְפֵּד	עָלָיו	וְסָפְדוּ	דָּקָרוּ	אֲשֶׁר־	אֵ֣ת	אֵלַי	וְהִבִּיטוּ
amsa Pa	Pp	ncmsa Pp	PpX3ms	vqp[2]3cp Pc	vqp3cp	Pr	Po	PpX1cs	vhp[2]3cp Pc
only	his	for	as one mourneth	for him,	and they shall mourn	they have pierced,	whom		upon me	and they shall look
3173	9999	5921	5594	5921	5594	1856	834	853	413	5027
hayyāḥîd	ˁal-	kᵉmispēd	ˁālāyw	wᵉsāpdû	dāqārû	ˀăšer-	ˀēt	ˀēlay	wᵉhibbîṭû

In Zechariah 12:10, the word "me" is added to "upon" to make sense of the Scripture by the translators. It could easily have been translated, "They shall look upon the *Aleph-Tav* they have pierced."

Finally, let's look at an example of the **token** of covenant with God:

And God said, This is the token of the covenant which I make between me and you and every living creature that is with you, for perpetual generations. (Genesis 9:12)

Now in the Interlinear Bible:

Gen 9:12

כָּל־	וּבֵין	וּבֵינֵיכֶם	בֵּינִי	נֹתֵן	אֲנִי	אֲשֶׁר־	הַבְּרִית	אוֹת־	אוֹת	זֹאת	אֱלֹהִים	וַיֹּאמֶר 12
ncmsc	Pp Pc	PpX2mp Pc	PpX1cs	vqPmsa	pi1cs	Pr	ncfsa Pa	ncbsc		afs	ncmpa	vqw3ms Pc
every	and	and you	between me	make	I	which	the covenant	the token of	is	This	God	And said,
3605	996	996	996	5414	589	834	1285	226	9999	2063	430	559
kāl-	ûbên	ûbênēkem	bênî	nōtēn	ˀănî	ˀăšer-	habrît	ˀōt-		Zōˀt	ˀĔlōhîm	Wayyōˀmer

:עוֹלָם	לְדֹרֹת	אִתְּכֶם	אֲשֶׁר	חַיָּה	נֶפֶשׁ
ncmsa	ncmpc Pp	PpX2mp	Pr	afsa	ncfsa
perpetual	for generations:	with you,	is	that	living	creature
5769	1755	854	9999	834	2416	5315
ˁôlām.	lᵉdōrōt	ˀitkem		ˀăšer	ḥayyā	nepeš

The nailed Aleph-Tav

In Genesis 9:12, in the Hebrew word for "token," we see the *Aleph-Tav* with another letter in the center. This Hebrew letter is *vav*.

- Vav = nail

The token of covenant with God was the nailed *Aleph-Tav*. Could we have ever imagined that Jesus was in the story of Noah and the Ark? Isn't it interesting that we find, in the book of Revelation, that no flesh would have survived if it were not for the return of the *Aleph-Tav* that had been nailed to the cross? This is just another example of how amazing the Word of God is!

Lucifer Also in Genesis 1
(If You Can Read between the Lines)

In the beginning God created the heaven and the earth.
 And the earth was without form, and void; and darkness was upon the face of the deep. And the Spirit of God moved upon the face of the waters. (Genesis 1:1–2)

Genesis 1 is a complete statement in itself. Almighty God created the heavens (*shamayim* is in the plural form and should be translated "heavens") and the earth. Yet there is the possibility that something happened between Genesis 1:1 and 1:2. The Hebrew word for "was" in Genesis 1:2 is *hayah* (haw-yaw), which means "to be, become, come to pass, exist, happen, fall out."[18] Whether or not you ascribe to the concept between Genesis 1:1 and 1:2 that there was a pre-Adamic race (like Finis Dake postulated in both his *Annotated Reference Bible* and his book, *God's Plan for Man*), there is evidence that something did indeed happen.
 The Word tells us in 1 Corinthians 14:33 that:

For God is not the author of confusion, but of peace, as in all churches of the saints.

This statement by the apostle Paul is significant in light of the next Hebrew word used in Genesis 1:2. The Hebrew word for "without form" is *tohuw* (to'-hoo). This word means "formlessness, confusion, unreality, emptiness."[19] If God had created the world in a state of confusion, that would have made God the author of confusion. In the *Commentary Critical and Explanatory on the Whole Bible*, biblical scholars Robert Jamieson, A. R. Fausset, and David Brown make the following observation:

> **The earth was without form and void**—or in "confusion and emptiness," as the words are rendered in Is 34:11. This globe, *at some undescribed period, having been convulsed and broken up*, was a dark and watery waste for ages perhaps, *till out of this chaotic state*, the present fabric of the world was made to arise.[20] (Emphasis added)

We find further evidence of a gap between Genesis 1:1 and 1:2 in the writings of Isaiah:

> For thus saith the LORD that created the heavens; God himself that formed the earth and made it; he hath established it, *he created it not in vain*, he formed it to be inhabited: I am the LORD; and there is none else. (Isaiah 45:18, emphasis added)

Notice the phrase within this verse that says: "he created it not in vain." The Hebrew word translated as "vain" is the same word used in Genesis 1:2: *tohuw*. In fact, the New American Standard Bible (NASB) expresses the Hebrew somewhat clearer in this particular verse:

> For thus says the LORD, who created the heavens (He is the God who formed the earth and made it, **He established it *and* did not create it a waste place, *but* formed it to be inhabited**), "I am the LORD, and there is none else." (Isaiah 45:18, emphasis added)

We can also apply something that Jesus said to what we see here in Genesis 1:2:

And ye shall know the truth, and the truth shall make you free. (John 8:32)

The Greek word here for "truth" is *aletheia* (al-ay'-thi-a), which means "in truth, according to truth, and in fact."[21] But it also has another meaning: in reality.

Is it possible that there is a conspiracy that predates mankind, in which Lucifer intended to bring an **unreality** to God's creation that would manifest in confusion and emptiness? Is it possible that the solution to this eternal conspiracy is the *Aleph-Tav* who came to bring truth or divine reality to set us free? It is very possible. Lucifer came to disrupt Creation, to bring *tohuw* or confusion, chaos, and unreality. Within the nature of Lucifer is embedded the very essence of all conspiratorial history: to so mar God's creation that the fingerprints of the Creator can no longer be found.

The Fall of Lucifer in Light of Conspiratorial History

We find the fall of Lucifer in the writings of the prophets: Ezekiel 28:1–19 and Isaiah 14:12–17. Not all biblical commentators agree that the verses in Ezekiel are directly about Lucifer, since the king of Tyrus is referred to as well. In Ezekiel, God used the prophet to hit two birds with one written stone. To get an understanding of what God is doing here, I want to refer to *Dake's Notes* on the "Law of Double Reference":

The Law of Double Reference

Here we have the first occurrence of the law of double reference (cp. Isa. 14:12–14; Ezek. 28:11–17; Mt. 16:22–23; Mk. 5:7–16; Lk. 4:33–35, 41). In these and many other passages a visible creature is addressed, but certain statements also refer to an invisible person using the visible creature as a tool. Thus, two persons are involved in the same passage. The principle of interpretation in such passages is to associate only such statements with each individual as could refer to him. The statements of Gen. 3:14 could apply only to the serpent and not to Satan. The first part of Gen. 3:15 could apply to both the seed of the serpent and Satan. The last part of Gen. 3:15 could only refer to Satan and Christ. A simple example of this law is the case of Christ addressing Peter as Satan. When Peter declared that he would never permit anyone to crucify his Lord on the cross, Christ rebuked him saying, "Get thee behind Me, Satan" (Mt. 16:22–23). Both Satan and Peter were addressed in the same statement, and both were involved in the rebuke. Peter, for the moment, was unknowingly being used as a tool of Satan in an effort to keep Christ from going to the cross. Satan was the primary one addressed, and so it is in Gen. 3:15. A literal serpent is addressed, but the primary reference is to Satan. We have other examples in Isa. 14:12–14 and Ezek. 28:11–17 where the kings of Babylon and Tyre are addressed, but the statements mainly apply to Satan—the invisible king of Babylon and Tyre. There are some statements in these passages which could not possibly refer to an earthly man.[22]

So we can see the Law of the Double Reference in Ezekiel 28. We will do our best to separate that which directly speaks of the king of Tyrus from that which speaks of Lucifer.

To be truthful, an entire book could be developed by simply conducting an exhaustive study of these verses in Ezekiel and Isaiah. I would like to focus on some of the aspects revealed about Lucifer's fall, as well as examine his gifts and other characteristics. Once you begin to understand his nature and see his influence in Heaven's conspiratorial history, you will see more clearly his fingerprints in the history of the earth as well.

Son of man, take up a lamentation upon the king of Tyrus, and say unto him, Thus saith the Lord GOD; Thou sealest up the sum, full of wisdom, and perfect in beauty. (Ezekiel 28:12)

When God created Lucifer, he was the embodiment of the grand, finishing touch on the creation of all the angels. He was:

The Seal of Completeness and Full of Wisdom

The first thing God said about Lucifer was, "Thou sealest up the sum." To understand exactly what God was saying here, we need to look at the Hebrew word used for "sum." *Tokniyth* (tok-neeth') means "measurement, pattern, proportion."[23] Lucifer was the seal; the pattern of perfect measurement. Then God used the word "wisdom." In Hebrew, the word is *chokmah* (khok-maw'), which means "wisdom, skill in war, wisdom in administration, shrewdness, prudence in religious affairs, and wisdom in ethical and religious matters."[24]

We need a panoramic view to completely understand the enemy we are dealing with. He represented the **full completion** of:

- The skill of war
- The gift of administration
- Full understanding of religious affairs (how to operate in the spirit realm)
- Shrewdness

Friends, we must not approach spiritual warfare as novices. God must empower us, anoint us, lead us, instruct us, and guard us. If we move outside of these parameters, the ramifications will be severe! Thank God for the Holy Spirit, the blood of Jesus, and the written Word of God.

Perfect in Beauty

Lucifer was the perfection of beauty. We cannot derive any deeper meaning out of the original Hebrew text. When Lucifer was created, no other angel compared to his beauty; we will find out later that he covered the throne of God.

The Word tells us that Lucifer can also appear as an angel of light that will dazzle those who see him.

> And no marvel; for Satan himself is transformed into an angel of light. (2 Corinthians 11:14)

Freemasonry has been dazzled by his beauty and considers Lucifer the one to seek light from:

> Lucifer, the Light-bearer! Strange and mysterious name to give to the Spirit of Darkness. Lucifer, the Son of the Morning! It is he who bears the Light, and with its splendors intolerable blinds feeble, sensual or selfish Souls. Doubt it not! For traditions are full of Divine Revelation and Inspirations: and Inspiration is not of one Age nor of one Creed. Plato and Philo also were inspired.[25]

As we survey the Ark of the Covenant, we see that God changed the way He covered His throne after the fall of Lucifer (more on his ability to cover God's presence shortly). Now there are two identical angels over the throne of God. No matter how perfect, how wise, or how beautiful one angel is, there is an exact replica across the throne of God; there is no chance of one being lifted up in pride. The fall of Lucifer cannot happen again! As far as the angels are concerned, the matter is settled forever.

Anointed

We need to understand that Lucifer has an anointing! That anointing was originally given by God, and Lucifer perverted it for his own purposes.

This is one reason I prefer the word "Messiah" over the word "Christ." Messiah comes from the Hebrew word *haMashiach*. There is only one Messiah as promised by the Word of God. "Christ" comes from the Greek word *Christos,* which in the Greek culture can refer to Apollo or Zeus. In paganism, these **no-gods** can manifest an anointing, too. Not every anointing is from God, and not everything that is supernatural is the Holy Spirit! The charismatic church needs to wake up to this fact.

Cherub That Covers

Lucifer was anointed and given the ability to cover the manifested presence of God. He was the canopy over the top of the throne of God. Lucifer maintains his abilities (although perverted) today. He still seeks to cover God's presence in individuals; this may help explain how God can move through an individual and yet the stream of anointing in his or her life is contaminated; we have all been confounded by this mystery. A man or woman with open doors to the enemy can have a **double-stream**. The anointing of Lucifer can cover or ride right on top of the anointing of God if the enemy has a legal right. This is part of his end-time strategy; the enemy uses carnally minded preachers who declare, "Since sin was taken care of on the cross, you can now live as you please—Jesus overrode the commandments of the 'wrathful' God of the Old Testament, and you can now disregard all of that instruction." Lucifer can create quite the canopy over a life embracing such lies, and this is just a part of the fulfillment of the **great falling away!**

This has been a problem in the Church for years, because most people believe that once they are saved, the enemy can't gain access to them. A wounded heart, pride, unconfessed sin, and a host of other issues can open a door to the enemy. With the constant updates of revelatory information concerning victims of mind-control programming and their placement in the churches, the following list provides a crucial template for pastors. These qualities must be present with a man or woman of God:

- Broken and humble
- Consecrated and walking in holiness

- Quick to deal with his or her own inner world
- Complete in Christ (This is a sensitive issue, but we need to address it. If people need something besides the completed work of Jesus to feel whole, they have a vacancy in their soul that the enemy can use to contaminate the anointing God placed within them. When I see individuals who are driven to be used up front in services and driven for others to see that they are anointed and can be used of God, I see a wound that Lucifer will use against them. The enemy uses the entryway of that open wound [manifested through that driven need] to contaminate their anointing to affect ministries and all they minister to! Lucifer strategically wounded them because they had a calling and an anointing on their life. He wants to use that wound against them and render them ineffective in the kingdom. If this sounds like you, the best thing you can do is to become God's secret agent. Refuse to be up front and be seen. Stay in the background and intercede for others. Allow the time in the background to be a season for God to minister to you; many times, these types of wounds come from not having the affirmation needed as a child and may require some introspection. Find your worth in knowing Him. You will know when you are healed, because being seen, recognized, and up front will no longer be important to you. You will find peace by simply communing with Jesus and watching God bless those around you. Then you will be able to use your talents for God.)

Understanding that Lucifer has an anointing also enables us to spiritually contextualize such historical phenomena as Adolf Hitler. Hitler was trained by Dietrich Eckart, who was an influential member of the Thule Society, a wealthy publisher, and editor-in-chief of an anti-Semitic journal he called *In Plain German*. Hitler's training included esoteric knowledge (possibly dating all the way back to the fallen angels of Genesis 6) on how to flow in Lucifer's anointing to recruit followers in

Germany. Later, he tapped into this perverted anointing and utilized forms of mind control to sway the masses. The words used in his speeches, the rhythm and framework of his sentence structure, and the pageantry of the meetings he led were occult constructs in which Lucifer's anointing could flow unimpeded. Once you develop a basic understanding of how to set the stage for occult power to flow, as it did with Hitler, you will never look at a presidential campaign in the United States the same way again!

The Five "I Wills" of Lucifer

> How art thou fallen from heaven, O Lucifer, son of the morning! how art thou cut down to the ground, which didst weaken the nations!
>
> For thou hast said in thine heart, I will ascend into heaven, I will exalt my throne above the stars of God: I will sit also upon the mount of the congregation, in the sides of the north:
>
> I will ascend above the heights of the clouds; I will be like the most High.
>
> Yet thou shalt be brought down to hell, to the sides of the pit. (Isaiah 14:12–15)

Notice in this passage that Lucifer declares "I will" five times. As I have already shared in this chapter, five is the biblical number for **grace**. Out of pride, Lucifer attempted to use his anointing from God to create a false grace to empower his ascension into something else…something outside of the framework of God's design. This counterfeit grace was offered to Adam and Eve, and it was embodied within the fruit of the Tree of the Knowledge of Good and Evil.

The promise of luciferian **grace** is being heralded today in esoteric secret societies and manifests in the aspirations of the Transhumanist Movement. But their end goal will never be attained. As with Lucifer, their attempts to ascend into godhood will result in them being brought down into the very pits of hell itself!

On to Genesis 2 and 3

These are the generations of the heavens and of the earth when they were created, in the day that the LORD God made the earth and the heavens,

And every plant of the field before it was in the earth, and every herb of the field before it grew: for the LORD God had not caused it to rain upon the earth, and there was not a man to till the ground.

But there went up a mist from the earth, and watered the whole face of the ground.

And the LORD God formed man of the dust of the ground, and breathed into his nostrils the breath of life; and man became a living soul. (Genesis 2:4–7)

In Genesis 2, God reveals Himself for the first time as the LORD God (*YHVH-Elohim*). *YHVH* is considered in Scripture as the most sacred name of God. The theological term for this name of God is the Tetragrammaton. When God began dealing with mankind, He revealed part of His nature that Lucifer had never seen. Let's look at what the rabbis understand about God as *YHVH-Elohim*.

The divine appellation *Elohim*, translated "God," was understood to denote His aspect of judgment and YHVH, translated "Lord," His aspect of mercy (Gen. R. XXXIII. 3), and the combination of the two names in the verse, "These are the generations of the heaven and the earth when they were created, in the day that the Lord God (YHVH Elohim) made earth and heaven" (Gen. ii. 4) is explained as follows: "It may be likened to a kind who had empty vessels. The king said, 'If I put hot water into them they will crack; if I put icy water into them they will contract.' What did the king do? He mixed the hot with the cold and poured the mixture into the vessels, and they endured. Similarly said the Holy One, blessed is He, 'If I create the world only with the attribute of mercy, sin will multiply beyond all bounds; if I created it only with the attribute of justice, how can the world last? Behold, I will create it with both attributes; would that it might endure!" (Gen. R. XII. 15).

Indeed, it was only because the quality of mercy prevailed at Creation that the human race was allowed to come into being.[26]

In the creation of mankind, God balanced mercy and judgment together. This is very significant, and it took Lucifer by surprise. Notice how the serpent in the garden referred to God:

Now the serpent was more subtil than any beast of the field which the LORD God had made. And he said unto the woman, Yea, hath God said, Ye shall not eat of every tree of the garden? (Genesis 3:1)

The serpent only addressed God as *Elohim*. There was no mention of *YHVH* by the serpent. This is the part of God's nature that was never revealed to Lucifer. No redemption of Lucifer or those angels who fell with him is ever mentioned in the Word of God. The only thing reserved for them is the judgment that flows from *Elohim*. It is very possible that Lucifer believed that once man sinned, redemption would be impossible for him as well, and mankind would forever be under his control.

Now it is very easy to see Lucifer in the story of Genesis 3; he was the serpent that came to take God's family from Him. (We will look more into what he offered a little later.) But can we find Jesus in Genesis 2 and 3? Let's use our chart again to examine the most Holy Name of God: the Tetragrammaton.

- Yod = hand
- Hey = behold, reveal, window
- Vav = nail
- Hey = behold, reveal, window

The first thing that we see in the mercy side of God is that He has a nailed hand! The *Aleph-Tav* has now been revealed as YHVH! He is the same God that is revealed in the Old and New Testaments.

Another way of saying the Tetragrammaton is "I AM."

Jesus said unto them, Verily, verily, I say unto you, Before Abraham was, I am. (John 8:58)

Jesus is also the same God who was revealed to the earth in His First Coming and will be revealed in His Second Coming. Not only are the two revealments encoded into God's name as *YHVH*, but they are also found in His combined name of *YHVH-Elohim*.

- *YHVH:* In His First Coming, He did not come to judge the world (John 3:17) but to bring salvation and mercy. Another way of expressing this would be to call Him "Messiah ben Joseph" ("the Suffering Servant").
- *Elohim:* In His Second Coming, He comes to judge a world that has rejected Him and His sacrifice as Messiah ben Joseph. He comes as "Messiah ben David" ("the Conquering King"). Those who have not bowed before Him will be cut off and removed from the earth.

John understood this nature of God as revealed in *YHVH-Elohim* and saw both the Jesus he knew in the Gospels and the Jesus who was revealed to him in the Revelation. All of that was told from the very beginning!

The Serpent's Promise

The serpent's promise is at the heart of all true conspiratorial history on planet earth. It is the desire of the Luciferian Elite, every adept of the mystery religions, every Freemason (whether they know it or not—many at the lower levels never read their own materials), and those involved in the current Transhumanist Movement.

> Now the serpent was more subtil than any beast of the field which the LORD God had made. And he said unto the woman, Yea, hath God said, Ye shall not eat of every tree of the garden?
>
> And the woman said unto the serpent, We may eat of the fruit of the trees of the garden:
>
> But of the fruit of the tree which is in the midst of the garden, God hath said, Ye shall not eat of it, neither shall ye touch it, lest ye die.
>
> And the serpent said unto the woman, Ye shall not surely die:
>
> For God doth know that in the day ye eat thereof, then your eyes shall be opened, and ye shall be as gods, knowing good and evil. (Genesis 3:1–5)

Now let's spend a few minutes dissecting what the serpent was doing.

Questioning God's Motives

> And God blessed them, and God said unto them, Be fruitful, and multiply, and replenish the earth, and subdue it: and have dominion over the fish of the sea, and over the fowl of the air, and over every living thing that moveth upon the earth. (Genesis 1:28)

After blessing Adam and Eve, God began to speak words of empowerment over them. In the original Hebrew, it is clear that God was speaking commands over Adam and Eve the same way He had spoken them over creation to bring divine order to nullify Lucifer's chaos. But the commands do not stop there.

> And the LORD God took the man, and put him into the garden of Eden to dress it and to keep it.

And the LORD God commanded the man, saying, Of every tree of the garden thou mayest freely eat:

But of the tree of the knowledge of good and evil, thou shalt not eat of it: for in the day that thou eatest thereof thou shalt surely die. (Genesis 2:15–17)

The authority God had commanded into mankind is now more defined in chapter 2. Adam's task was to dress and keep the garden. Or, to put it another way, Adam was to work in the garden and protect it (that is what "keep" means in Hebrew). Then, finally, God instructed Adam to never eat of the Tree of the Knowledge of Good and Evil, because doing so would produce death. So, Adam had commandments before the Fall. Many are shocked to discover this truth. If Adam had been without commandments in the garden, it would have been impossible for him to have sinned, because sin is the violation of God's commandments (1 John 3:4). God's commandments were given to empower Adam for blessing and authority. The serpent then questioned God's motivation behind those very commandments, insinuating that God was keeping something important away from mankind: godhood!

Questioning the Consequences of Violating God's Commandments

The serpent moved from questioning the motives behind violating the commandments given to Adam to questioning the consequences: "Ye shall not surely die!" Our enemy has become a master of half-truths (required for any true conspiracy). In fact, two types of death were wrapped up in the violation of God's commandments:

- **Spiritual Death**: Biblically, death simply means "separation." It does not mean the "blinking out of existence." Spiritual death is separation from God, and it entered the spirits of Adam and Eve the moment they sinned. At that moment, they lost fellowship with God and entered a union with Lucifer.

- **Physical Death**: God told Adam that in the day when he ate of the fruit of the Tree of the Knowledge of Good and Evil in the garden, he would die. Peter reveals that, to God, a thousand years is as a day (2 Peter 3:8). Adam lived for 930 years (Genesis 5:5). Physical death is separation from one's physical body and this physical plane of existence. God kept His word; Adam never saw 1,001.

A Promise Worth Dying For?

The promise of the serpent was: He would provide knowledge that would allow man to ascend into godhood and become like *Elohim*. The darkened hearts of men have been hungering for this knowledge and its promise ever since the garden. Those who labor in the army of darkness seek to become like God, live forever, and evade the judgment of the Almighty. Gaining this knowledge and its transformative power is at the very heart of the beginning of Babylon and all mystery religions on earth! In fact, the mystery religions claim that their hero, Nimrod, achieved transformation into something other than human and finally realized *apotheosis*.[27]

chapter three

Conspiratorial History within the Bible

Part 2: Genesis 6

In the previous chapter, we discovered that there is a gold mine of information God encoded into the stories presented in the Torah (especially in the book of Genesis) just waiting to be unearthed. The sages of Israel have told us that it would take a faithful student of the Word a lifetime just to discover most of the secrets God presented to us in Genesis 1–3. Over the years, several of my students have attempted to develop an exhaustive study of the book of Genesis for their doctoral dissertations. As they examined the original language of the Hebrew text and discovered such a treasure trove of information, they concluded that their dissertations could only cover a fraction of what is available in just the first chapter. Even then, many of their papers far surpassed the required standard length of a doctoral dissertation. **What God can say in one sentence can become a lifetime of study for any serious student of the Word.**

The perfect example of the power of one sentence from God is when Jesus made a seemingly simple statement in Matthew 24:37:

But as the days of Noe were, so shall also the coming of the Son of man be. (Matthew 24:37)

Jesus was speaking of the last days. In the verse that preceded this statement, we find:

But of that day and hour knoweth no man, no, not the angels of heaven, but my Father only. (Matthew 24:36)

Since we have been so deprived of our Hebraic heritage, most students of the Bible miss the fact that Jesus had just used a Hebraic idiom that connected what He was sharing with the Feast of Trumpets. The language He continued to use in verses 40–42 confirms this fact for those who use the tools of hermeneutical[28] research to understand the cultural setting in which Jesus taught. Although the purpose of this chapter is not to teach on the importance of cultural idioms[29] and their proper use within our exegetical[30] exercises to glean truth from the Word of God, I hope I have sparked your interest enough to promote expansion of your hermeneutical toolbox. We need to realize that Jesus did not minister in the streets of Detroit or the country hills of Kentucky. He spoke to a culture that had a deep and enriched heritage cultivated by the God of Abraham, Isaac, and Jacob and nourished by a study of Torah. Biblical scholar Dr. John Garr makes this observation regarding our habitual dismissal of the cultural setting in our interpretative processes:

The problem is that practically all societies and people groups have read their own concepts and cultures into the Bible rather than drawing out of the Holy Scriptures the truths that have always been there. The church's approach to Holy Writ has been ignorant at best and disingenuous at worst. When interpreting the Bible, Christians have engaged in eisegesis rather than exegesis by injecting their preconceived notions into Scripture rather than extracting from the text what it clearly says.

Texts without context have become pretexts for proof texts! The grammar of the Scriptures (the Hebrew language of the first testament and the Hebrew thought underlying the Greek language of the second testament) has been largely minimized if not downright ignored. Likewise, the history and culture of the people through whom and to whom the sacred texts were committed have been virtually ignored. Entire theologies have been based upon a "criterion of dissimilarity" in which texts in the Apostolic Scriptures that have clear connections with the Hebrew Scriptures have been dismissed by some scholars as not being the authentic words of Jesus and the apostles but the work of subsequent redactors. It is as though Jesus had to have been born and lived in a vacuum and never influenced by his native language and culture. The very idea has given rise to a Christianity that has been wretched from its theological and historical moorings and set adrift in a maelstrom of nonbiblical—in far too many cases, anti-Biblical—traditions, including postmodernism, consequentialism, secular humanism, and even demonic perversion.[31]

If the cultural context within Scripture is so essential to the formation of the practics of our faith, is it not equally paramount in our understanding of Bible prophecy? Such casual dismissals caused prophecy teachers in the past century to declare anyone teaching that Israel would once again become a nation as a promoter of heresy. When Israel became a nation overnight in 1948, it shook the very foundations of many evangelical prophecy ministries worldwide. We need to learn from these mistakes and incorporate a Hebraic understanding into our hermeneutical process.

I said all of that to make a point: When Jesus spoke of the "days of Noah," it served as a memory trigger to all of the hearers who could tap into over one thousand years of teaching regarding every aspect of the Noah narrative. In the times of Jesus, there were not chapters and verses to Scripture; these would not be added until the twelfth century by Stephen Langton with the introduction of the Latin Vulgate Bible. The sages of Israel would use a word or phrase to take the hearers to the portion of Scripture they were referring to. This is especially true with the Torah. Thus, as diligent students of God's Word, we must labor to hear with Hebraic ears and dig deep into Noah's story to properly ascertain all that Jesus was referring to.

Abounding Evil and Giants and Watchers, Oh My!

[1]And it came to pass, when men began to multiply on the face of the earth, and daughters were born unto them,

[2]That the sons of God saw the daughters of men that they were fair; and they took them wives of all which they chose.

[3]And the LORD said, My spirit shall not always strive with man, for that he also is flesh: yet his days shall be an hundred and twenty years.

[4]There were giants in the earth in those days; and also after that, when the sons of God came in unto the daughters of men, and they bare children to them, the same became mighty men which were of old, men of renown.

[5]And GOD saw that the wickedness of man was great in the earth, and that every imagination of the thoughts of his heart was only evil continually.

[6]And it repented the LORD that he had made man on the earth, and it grieved him at his heart.

[7]And the LORD said, I will destroy man whom I have created from the face of the earth; both man, and beast, and the creeping thing, and the fowls of the air; for it repenteth me that I have made them.

[8]But Noah found grace in the eyes of the LORD. (Genesis 6:1–8)

So many things seem to jump off the page as I approach these verses. Before I fully dive into the story of Noah, I want to touch on a biblical conundrum for the Transhumanist Movement contained within these passages of Holy Writ. In verse 3, God declares that He is going to limit the lifespan of man to 120 years. As we examine the text, we find as a mission of grace to mankind, Noah spent 120 years preaching repentance and building the ark. It was only after the canopy over the earth was broken up by God that the Flood came, and with it the dynamic changing of earth's environment, which reduced man's lifespan. Prior to the Flood, according to biblical record, men would not even begin to have children until they approached their eighties or older! Now God sets the time limit to a man's life based on the number of years that Noah preached of the coming destruction and the need for repentance. (This also serves as a prophetic warning that there is a limit to how long God will extend His grace toward men.) The more time sinful man had to live and learn, the deeper he would become entrenched with the knowledge of the Tree of Good and Evil. If given enough time, man's insatiable appetite for dark knowledge would transform earth into a literal hell that God could not tolerate. Today, transhumanists[32] are endeavoring to circumvent God's restraints on our lifespan. From what I have read in their literature, this is one of their primary goals. Seventy, eighty, or even one hundred and twenty years are not enough for them. While they lament over global warming and the perils of overpopulation, they seek to provide only a chosen few the opportunity to live hundreds of years, if not obtain near immortality. With the exponential acceleration of knowledge in the last days and the possibility of extending the life span of the Luciferian Elite, they may well have the time needed to thwart God's intervention in Genesis 6! You see, God shortening man's lifespan to 120 years (and then later to seventy to eighty) was not a judgment against humanity; it was an expression of His grace toward all mankind.

Evil Imaginations

> And God saw that the wickedness of man was great in the earth, and that every imagination of the thoughts of his heart was only evil continually. (Genesis 6:5)

I want to examine verses 4 and 5 in a manner that is similar to a physician's diagnostic procedure: He would examine the presenting symptoms. Symptomology can be used in medicine and nutrition, and even in examining the health of a civilization. If certain symptoms are present in a patient, it will point toward the underlying disease that caused it. There is an intertwining aspect within the text of the corrupt Sons of God *(Bene Elohim)*, the development of hybrid offspring, and the explosive evil within men's hearts. This wickedness that manifested within mankind was declared as "great" by God. In Hebrew, the word for "great" is *rab* (rab). This word means "abounding, strong, exceedingly, and more numerous than."[33] When evil has become so strong that it abounds throughout humanity and its perpetrators are more numerous than the righteous, it is a presenting sociological symptom of interference by the fallen *Bene Elohim*. (More on this later in both this chapter and an upcoming chapter dedicated to the "Communion with Darkness.")

Dealing with the Fallen Angels in the Room

> That the sons of God saw the daughters of men that they were fair; and they took them wives of all which they chose. (Genesis 6:2)

There is great speculation regarding the identity of the Sons of God in Genesis 6:2. I prefer the traditional Hebraic view that these were angels and not men. Some would argue today that the sons of God represented the descendants of Seth. Dr. Chuck Missler explains the origin of the Sethite theory:

> The strange events recorded in Genesis 6 were understood by the ancient rabbinical sources, as well as the Septuagint translators, as referring to *fallen angels* procreating weird hybrid offspring with human women-known as the "*Nephilim.*" So it was also understood by the early church fathers. These bizarre events are also echoed in the legends and myths of *every* ancient culture upon the earth: the ancient Greeks, the Egyptians, the Hindus, the South Sea Islanders, the American Indians, and virtually all the others.
>
> However, many students of the Bible have been taught that this passage in Genesis 6 actually refers to a failure to keep the "faithful" lines of Seth *separate* from the "worldly" line of Cain. The idea has been advanced that after Cain killed Abel, the line of Seth remained separate and faithful, but the line of Cain turned

ungodly and rebellious. The "Sons of God" are deemed to refer to leadership in the line of Seth; the "daughters of men" is deemed restricted to the line of Cain. The resulting marriages ostensibly blurred an inferred separation between them. (Why the resulting offspring are called the *"Nephilim"* remains without any clear explanation.)

Since Jesus prophesied, "As the days of Noah were, so shall the coming of the Son of Man be," it becomes essential to understand what these days included.

Origin of the Sethite View

It was in the 5th Century A.D. that the "angel" interpretation of Genesis 6 was increasingly viewed as an embarrassment when attacked by critics. (Furthermore, the worship of angels had begun within the church. Also, celibacy had also become an institution of the church. The "angel" view of Genesis 6 was feared as impacting these views.)

Celsus and Julian the Apostate used the traditional "angel" belief to attack Christianity. Julius Africanus resorted to the Sethite interpretation as a more comfortable ground. Cyril of Alexandria also repudiated the orthodox "angel" position with the "line of Seth" interpretation. Augustine also embraced the Sethite theory and thus it prevailed into the Middle Ages. It is still widely taught today among many churches who find the literal "angel" view a bit disturbing. There are many outstanding Bible teachers who still defend this view.[34]

In my own personal research, I have concluded that Dr. Missler is correct. All of the sages of Israel and the early Church fathers concluded that the "sons of God" referred to some category of angel and not righteous men! It should also be noted that, in the rabbinical literature of today, these sons of God are still interpreted as fallen angels as well. The only deviation from this interpretation is within Catholic theology and the Protestant theology that was influenced by Rome. Any time a biblical theory stops at Rome and does not continue on to Jerusalem, I am convinced that it produces problems. Rome's universal Church tends to amalgamate pagan traditions and concepts rather than replacing them with biblical truth. It appears to me that the truth of fallen angels breeding with human women did not fit well into other areas of their developing theology, thus an alternative view was developed.

George H. Pember, in his classic work written in late 1800s, *Earth's Earliest Ages*, came to the same conclusion:

> These words are often explained to signify nothing more than the intermarriage of the descendants of Cain and Seth: but a careful examination of the passage will elicit a far deeper meaning.
>
> When men, we are told, began to multiply on the face of the earth, and daughters were born unto them, the sons of God saw the daughters of men. Now by "men" in each case the whole human race is evidently signified, the descendants of Cain and Seth alike. Hence the "sons of God" are plainly distinguished from the generation of Adam.
>
> Again; the expression "sons of God" (Elohim) occurs four times in other parts of the Old Testament, and is in each of these cases indisputably used of angelic beings.[35]

To me, the concept of producing giants by the marriage of godly men with corrupt women is far-fetched. If that were the case, we would have giants living among us today. It is obvious that something more was going on—something supernatural.

Finally, we find that the book of Genesis is not the oldest book in the Bible; the book of Job is. Moses wrote the book of Genesis after 1440 BCE, during the forty years in the wilderness. Most scholars believe Job was written between 2000 to 1800 BCE. In the book of Job, the angels that appeared before God, to include Satan, were called *Bene Elohim*. The Noah narrative perfectly matches the language already inspired by the Holy Spirit.

Communion with Evil

There was more than just sex going on in Genesis 6. At this juncture, I need to interject a couple of points for clarification:

1. Sex was not Satan's idea; it was God's. God meant for it to deepen the covenant relationship of marriage between a man and a woman. It was for pleasure, intimacy, and procreation.

2. Since God created sex, He also set boundaries for its proper use. These boundaries, as well as all others declared within the Word of God, were established because of God's love for us. The act of sex is more than just a physical union. Mankind was created in the image of God; this is exemplified in our tripartite design. Sex brings all three aspects of our being into play, so our spirits, souls, and bodies are affected. Sexual union outside of the boundaries established by God can open the doors of Hell to the lives of those individuals and within society as a whole.

It is interesting to note that all of the angels revealed in the Bible are presented as male. (I am concerned about some of today's ministers reportedly having visitations from female angels. This does not fit the biblical norm, and I believe deception is involved.) Their stories seem to deviate from the creation of mankind. God desired a helpmeet for Adam and created Eve from Adam's own flesh. This action not only gave Adam a companion, wife, and friend, but it enabled him to procreate. This ability corresponds with God's command for the two to "be fruitful and multiply." No such command was ever given to the angels. It would seem that they were all created as males, and God never intended for them to procreate. So we see, in Genesis 6, why both the concepts of sex and procreation were such an overwhelming temptation for them. This understanding allows us to correlate within our thinking: (1) Genesis 6; (2) the men of Sodom and Gomorrah wanting to have sex with the angels; and (3) what Jesus said about angels in Matthew 22:30.

For in the resurrection they neither marry, nor are given in marriage, but are as the angels of God in heaven. (Matthew 22:30)

The subject of these verses in Matthew is marriage and procreation. It is not that the angels (presented as male) cannot have sex; rather, it is not in the plan of God for them to enter marriage or to procreate. This might have been the sin that caused them to lose their first estate (Jude 6). In the same way, after the resurrection, there will be no need for the glorified saints to procreate.

I. D. E. Thomas, in his now-classic book on Genesis 6 entitled, *The Omega Conspiracy,* shared a quote from renowned theologian, Francis A. Schaeffer, regarding his belief that Genesis 6 revealed that the *Bene Elohim* were indeed angels and not descendants of Seth:

> More and more we are finding that mythology in general though greatly contorted very often has some historic base. And the interesting thing is that one myth which occurs over and over again in many parts of the world is that somewhere a long time ago supernatural beings had sexual intercourse with natural women and produced a special breed of people.[36]

The Masonic Hierarchy

The Palladium is level 9[37]

BRIEFING NOTE

The Sodom and Gomorrah Story

There is more to the story than just the homosexual desires of the men in the city; you have to understand occult practices to comprehend it. Dr. Bill Schnoebelen of One Accord Ministries has shared in his video, *Exposing the Illuminati from Within*,[38] his account of his promotion within the occult. To be accepted into the lower branches of the Illuminati, he was required to marry a fallen angel. In the ceremony, there was a requirement of drinking each other's blood, which is forbidden in Scripture, and the ceremony was concluded with the consummation of the marriage. In the thirteen levels of Masonic hierarchy revealed in the pyramid on the back of the US dollar, there is a level between memberships in the *Ordo Templi Orientis* (OTO) and the Illuminati: This level is known as the Palladium. (Entrance in the Palladium is where this marriage/sexual union with a fallen angel takes place. The combination of drinking blood and sexual union greatly expanded one's occult powers. In my own research, I found other references to this practice within advanced levels of the occult. The Sodom and Gomorrah story was about more than just homosexuality; it tells the tale of those individuals who were seeking to increase the power of evil within their lives through union with the angels who came to visit Lot.)

It is not specifically revealed in Scripture whether the Watchers fell away from God at the time of the fall of Lucifer or during the Genesis 6 account of the sin of mating with human females, but their falling away was alluded to twice in the New Testament:

For a man indeed ought not to cover his head, forasmuch as he is the image and glory of God: but the woman is the glory of the man.

For the man is not of the woman; but the woman of the man.

Neither was the man created for the woman; but the woman for the man.

For this cause ought the woman to have power on her head *because of the angels.* (1 Corinthians 11:7–10, emphasis added)

The Greek word used for power here is *exousia* (ex-oo-see'-ah), which speaks of authority. When a woman comes under the authority of her husband as a part of covenant relationship, it closes the door of temptation (or possibly access) by angelic beings.

BRIEFING NOTE

Male Covering

In our own congregational ministry, we have dealt with individuals who had obvious connections to the occult. Several unmarried women who attended our congregation voiced their desire to have a pastoral covering. Through the process of research and observation, we concluded that they were using the spiritual covering as protection from retaliation of demonic spirits sent from others involved in the occult as they practiced their devilish arts. Pastors are called to protect sheep, not to protect wolves in sheep's clothing. I have received reports from pastors (who extended such coverings) of how these demonic forces would attack them. Once the covering was renounced, the attacks would stop. Please let this serve as a warning to pastors who find themselves in similar situations.

And the angels which kept not their first estate, but left their own habitation, he hath reserved in everlasting chains under darkness unto the judgment of the great day. (Jude 1:6)

Jude tells us that certain angels did not keep their "first estate," but they left it for something else. He was connecting this, I believe, with Genesis 6. The sensual pleasures of sex and the power to procreate could have been what caused the angels to fall.

Jude 1:6 is a direct quote from the *Book of Enoch*. Although the *Book of Enoch* is not considered a part of biblical canon, it is within the Orthodox Ethiopian Church and was known and respected by the Jewish world in which the New Testament was written. An article on Wikipedia shares a possible reason it was never officially accepted as canon by the Jewish community at large:

> Although evidently widely known during the development of the Hebrew Bible canon, 1 Enoch was excluded from both the formal canon of the Tanakh and the typical canon of the Septuagint and therefore, also the writings known today as the Deuterocanon. One possible reason for Jewish rejection of the book might be the textual nature of several early sections of the book that make use of material from the Torah; for example, 1 En 1 is a midrash of Deuteronomy 33.[39]

There are several aspects of the *Book of Enoch* that I find interesting:

- In 1 Corinthinians, Paul seems to allude to an understanding drawn from the *Book of Enoch*.
- Jude quotes directly from the *Book of Enoch*.
- One of the angels (or Watchers, as described in the *Book of Enoch)* is notorious for his crimes against humanity. His name was Azazel. Here is what the *Book of Enoch* has to say about him: "The whole earth has been corrupted through the works that were taught by Azazel: to him ascribe all sin" (1 Enoch 10:8).

The *Book of Enoch* goes on to tell us regarding his judgment:

> And again the Lord said to Raphael: "Bind Azazel hand and foot, and cast him into the darkness: and make an opening in the desert, which is in Dudael, and cast him therein. And place upon him rough and jagged rocks, and cover him with darkness, and let him abide there for ever, and cover his face that he may not see light. And on the day of the great judgment he shall be cast into the fire." (1 Enoch 10:4–6)

It is interesting that the scapegoat of Leviticus 16 is connected to Azazel, and its fate is similar to his own.

> And Aaron shall cast lots upon the two goats; one lot for the LORD, and the other lot for the scapegoat. (Leviticus 16:8)

> And when he hath made an end of reconciling the holy place, and the tabernacle of the congregation, and the altar, he shall bring the live goat:
>   And Aaron shall lay both his hands upon the head of the live goat, and confess over him all the iniquities of the children of Israel, and all their transgressions in all their sins, putting them upon the head of the goat, and shall send him away by the hand of a fit man into the wilderness:
>   And the goat shall bear upon him all their iniquities unto a land not inhabited: and he shall let go the goat in the wilderness. (Leviticus 16:20–22)

The Hebrew word in Leviticus 16:8 for "scapegoat" is *azazel* (az-aw-zale').[40]

There was a possible trade agreement going on between the Watchers and mankind: the **trading of women for knowledge and technology.** In exchange for access to human women, the Watchers began teaching mankind knowledge drawn from the Tree of Knowledge of Good and Evil that polluted their minds. According to the *Book of Enoch*, that is exactly what Azazel did:

> And Azazel taught men to make swords, and knives, and shields, and breastplates, and made known to them the metals of the earth and the art of working them, and bracelets, and ornaments, and the use of antimony, and the beautifying of the eyelids, and all kinds of costly stones, and all colouring tinctures.
>
> And there arose much godlessness, and they committed fornication, and they were led astray, and became corrupt in all their ways. (1 Enoch 8:1–2)

> Thou seest what Azazel hath done, who hath taught all unrighteousness on earth and revealed the eternal secrets which were (preserved) in heaven, *which men were striving to learn.* (1 Enoch 9:5, emphasis added)

I also believe that the Watchers and their children, the Nephilim, introduced sexual perversions to mankind, such as homosexuality, pedophilia, and bestiality. Christian researcher Stephen Quayle, in his groundbreaking book, *Aliens & Fallen Angels: The Sexual Corruption of the Human Race,* shares the following:

> Ancient historians had a variety of horrors to tell about the Celtae giants, including the fact that they were homosexuals (another crime which dictated the death penalty under Mosaic Law). Athenaeus states that the giants were accustomed to sleeping with not one but two boys. The historian Diodorus also suggested that homosexuality was rampant among the giants when he wrote:
>
> Although their wives were comely, they have very little to do with them, but raged with lust in outlandish fashion for the embraces of males. And the most astonishing thing of all is that they feel no concern for their proper dignity but prostitute to oth-

ers without a qualm the flower of their bodies; nor do they consider this a disgraceful thing to do, but rather when anyone of them is thus approached and refuses the favor offered him, this they consider an act of dishonor.[41]

Quayle goes on to share the connection of the Watchers and the practice of bestiality:

While such a possibility is almost too repulsive to imagine, the bestiality of Sodom and Gomorra and the linkage of these two cities to the practices of the fallen angels elsewhere in the Bible suggest such hideous acts might be considered a possibility.

Interestingly, a Canaanite tablet contains several verses claiming that such matings took place between animals and the god Baal:

He loved a heifer in the pasture,

He lay with her seventy-seven times,

She made him mount eighty-eight times,

She conceived and gave birth to his likeness.[42]

From all the research I have completed over the past several decades, I have found a weaving of the sexual practices of the Watchers and Nephilim with the practice of many forms of ritual magic. One such practice combines homosexuality and pedophilia; it is known as Transyuggothian Magic. This horrific practice allows the male sorcerer to access other dimensions or galaxies to commune with supposed older and stronger entities than the God of the Bible through sex with young boys. Through this commune, spiritual, occult power is drawn through the young boy to empower the sorcerer. This defilement also serves as **sexual vampirism**, in which the sorcerer draws the life force of the young boy to extend his own life—a vain attempt to achieve immortality. Dr. Bill Schnoebelen reveals in his video series, *Exposing the Illuminati from Within,* that this was a common practice with Aleister Crowley (one of the most well-known sorcerers and Freemasons of the past century) and members of the Ordo Templi Orientis (OTO), and that it is also the royal secret of the 32nd degree of Freemasonry (the certificate of the 32nd degree declares that the Freemason holds the secret, but none are told what it actually is—a common practice in occult circles).

The list of connections between deviate sexual practices/lifestyles and the occult could easily become a book in itself. The link between the two is real and is manifested in many levels, from combining forces to change societal norms to ritualistic magic forbidden by Scripture. There is a correlation between the new sexual revolution being forced upon us worldwide today, the waning of the influence of Christianity in the Northern Hemisphere, and the expansion of all occult groups within our society. Truly, the days of Noah are unfolding before our very eyes.

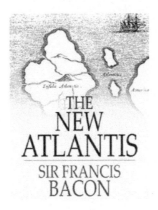

Then the *Book of Enoch* goes on to tell us that the Watchers began revealing eternal secrets that were preserved in Heaven, and that men were striving to learn them. Today, all esoteric societies are striving to once again discover and use these eternal secrets to enslave mankind and to return to the "old glory days" before Almighty God intervened! Rediscovering **Atlantis** is a theme that permeates occult literature to include the influential writings of H. P. Blavatsky, Sir Francis Bacon, and Masonic philosopher, Manly P. Hall, just to name a few. This desire was embedded within the Thule Society that groomed Adolf Hitler and was the goal of the Third Reich. The story of Atlantis, in which super humans lived and ultimate knowledge had been obtained, was destroyed by a catastrophic flood. Perhaps Atlantis (or some variation of its name within occult lore) was a city inhabited by the Watchers and their children, the Nephilim.

This legendary city might have served as the center of culture, power, and learning of the forbidden arts in the pre-antediluvian world. It would appear that the Luciferian Elite are striving to recreate their City of Gold.

We need to reevaluate our perspective of the times of Noah. This was not a time when barbarians wandered around in small groups that lacked any type of civilization. In fact, it was quite the opposite. Again, I refer to the research of George H. Pember. He provides the following observations regarding the Antediluvian Age:

1. Cain had taught them to settle in communities, and build cities; and the sons of Lamech—speedily followed, no doubt, by many others—had introduced the mechanical and fine arts, and had devised unlawful means of evading the labour imposed by the curse.[43]

2. And yet so great had been their intellectual power that the famous library of Agane, founded at the time by Sargon I, was stocked with books "which were either translated from Accadian originally, or else based on Accadian texts, and filled with technical words which belonged to the old language."[44]

3. We have evidence that in very early times there were well-known libraries at Erech, Ur, Cutha, and Larsa, to which observatories and universities were attached.

If, then, we give but their fair weight to these considerations, we seem compelled to admit that the antediluvians may have attained a perfection in civilization and high culture that has scarcely yet been recovered, much as we pride ourselves upon our own times.[45]

This exchange of women for advanced (forbidden) knowledge, technology, and civil advancement is not limited to the Antediluvian Age. This same theme of women producing offspring of the gods and the people receiving advanced information and technology is seen throughout the ancient world. Even many of the cultures of ancient Mesa America, to include both the Aztec and Mayan civilizations, are filled with such stories. It should be noted that both of their cultures possessed advanced knowledge that was impossible with their level of technology. Before Nazi Germany exploded on the scene with a progressive society that boasted of fluoridated water, complete gun control, a robust economy, and a desire to bring humanity to a new level of perfection through what they termed as the "Aryan Race," they were obsessed with reconnecting to the old gods and practicing something called transchanneling. Transchanneling was similar to the work of a medium who would speak with the dead, except their mediums would communicate with aliens (or beings from another dimension). The established communion with these otherworldly beings provided the technological superiority that Nazi Germany had at the beginning of World War II—from rockets to the first jet fighters. We also need to ask ourselves: Were all of the experiments conducted by Nazi scientists in the horrors of the concentration camps ideas of their own making, or were they inspired by the entities they were in communion with? Remember, the knowledge they gained was considered so valuable that the nations that conquered Germany divided up the scientists to tap into that vast, cutting-edge research. In our own country, under Operation Paperclip, scores of Nazi scientists were secretly brought to our nation. Many of these individuals were instrumental in the founding of US institutions that are in the forefront of influence in our society today: from the CIA to NASA.

BRIEFING NOTE

Nazi Aryan Race Connected to Nephilim

In Russ Dizdar's video entitled, *The Black Awakening: The Rise of the Satanic Supersoldier,*[46] he discusses how the mind-controlled victims of the Black Awakening Programming have German-speaking Nazi alter-personalities that believe the "Aryan Race" is the return to a pure Nephilim bloodline. These personalities are convinced that they are a superior breed of humans and are the super army of the Luciferian Elite.

I also find it interesting that there were UFO sightings during World War II. Our fighter pilots called them "Foo Fighters." Wikipedia provides the following information on this phenomenon:

> The term **foo fighter** was used by Allied aircraft pilots in World War II to describe various UFOs or mysterious aerial phenomena seen in the skies over both the European and Pacific theaters of operations.
>
> Though "foo fighter" initially described a type of UFO reported and named by the U.S. 415th Night Fighter Squadron, the term was also commonly used to mean any UFO sighting from that period. Formally reported from November 1944 onwards, witnesses often assumed that the foo fighters were secret weapons employed by the enemy.[47]

Did the pagan rituals practiced by the SS of Nazi Germany open portals into outer darkness and allow the very Watchers that God had cast out in the times of Noah to enter back into the earth? New revelations have come to light in the eye-opening documentary entitled *Blood Sacrifice— Cleansing the Soil for the Aryan Antichrist* by Cutting Edge Studios. The researchers of this documentary found eyewitnesses of Nazi movements right before the end of World War II. Trucks were loaded with the ashes of all those killed in the concentration camps (both Jews and Gentiles) to be used in occult rituals throughout Europe. The purpose of the rituals was to cleanse the land of the effects of Christianity and to rededicate it back to the old gods. (Christianity has been in decline in Europe ever since.)

After World War II, the United States began to experience numerous UFO sightings. At first, the military was concerned that these sightings were new secret weapons from the Soviet Union or another enemy. After the alleged Roswell crash, the attitude of the US government and the military changed drastically. They moved from worrying about secret weapons to actively discrediting their reality. From that point on, two things began to happen in the US: 1) Citizens were abducted and had sexual reproductive experiments conducted on them;[48] and 2) technological advancement exploded within our nation. Has America been exchanging access to our citizens for advanced knowledge since the end of WWII? Let's address this from the symptomological standpoint regarding the influence of the Watchers.

1. Has there been a great acceleration of knowledge that surpasses that of previous generations?
2. Has there been a refining of civilization and technology with a corresponding level of darkness released with it?
3. It there a move within our civilization to cast off all boundaries (restraints) set by God for a more enlightened view?
4. Has there been an increase in sexual perversion that far surpasses historical norms?

If you answered "yes" to these questions, the underlying disease in our society is the tacit influence of the Watchers from behind the closed doors of our government and the Luciferian Elite.

The Nephilim—Human 2.0?

> There were giants in the earth in those days; and also after that, when the sons of God came in unto the daughters of men, and they bare children to them, the same became mighty men which were of old, men of renown. (Genesis 6:4)

An important word I want to look at in this Scripture is "giants." In Hebrew, the word is *nephiyl* (nef-eel'), and it means "giants, the Nephilim."[49]

The *New American Commentary* provides the following insights regarding the usage of the term "Nephilim."

> "Nephilim" is a transliteration of the Hebrew, not a translation, **which indicates a group or class**. It is commonly related to *nāpal*, meaning "to fall"; thus the Nephilim are considered "the Fallen

Ones." If so, does this refer to their expulsion from heaven, their death as "fallen" in battle, or to their moral degeneracy? Another proposal is the related noun *nēpel*, meaning **"miscarriage"** (Job 3:16; Ps 58:8 [9]; Eccl 6:3), **suggesting that they were unusual in appearance since they were born by miscarriage.** The terms "fallen" and "warriors" occur repeatedly in Ezekiel's oracles against the nations (Ezek 32:20–27) whose armies fall in battle; this may have alluded to 6:1–4. Ezekiel's use of "fallen," however, is likely a sound play on the word "Nephilim" and not derived from an etymological association.

The traditional English rendering "giants" (AV) follows the LXX Septuagint (and ancient versions), which translates *gígantes* for Hebrew *nĕpilîm* (Nephilim). We can attribute this most likely to the influence of the later account recorded in Num 13:33. The frightened Israelite spies marveled at the exceptional height of the Nephilim, remarking that the Hebrews were no more than like "grasshoppers" before them. Later Jewish literature interpreted the Nephilim as giants and referred to their infamous pride and wickedness.[50] (Emphasis added)

A Commentary of the Holy Scriptures: Genesis also provides the confirmation that these Nephilim were the offspring of angels:

Delitzsch, nevertheless, together with Hofmann, prefers to explain it as *the fallen*, namely, from heaven, because begotten by heavenly beings. Here from *to falt*, would he make *to fall from*, and from this again, *to fall from heaven;* **then this is *made* to mean begotten of heavenly beings!** The sense, *cadentes, defectores, apostatæ* (see Gesenius), would be more near the truth. "There *were* giants" (הָיוּ), not, there *became* giants, which would have required וַיִּהְיוּ for its expression (see Keil). These giants, or powerful men, are already in near cotemporaneity with the transgression of these mesalliances (in those very same days), and this warrants the conclusion of Luther, that these powerful men were doers of violent deeds.[51] (Emphasis added)

Finally, Gesenius' *Hebrew and Chaldee Lexicon to the Old Testament Scriptures* adds another piece to our exegetical puzzle.

נָפִיל only in pl. נְפִילִים m. *giants*, Gen. 6:4; Nu. 13:33. So all the ancient versions (Chald. נְפִלָא the giant in the sky, i.e. the constellation Orion, plur. the greater constellations). The etymology of this word is uncertain. Some have compared نَبِيلٌ, نَبَيِلَةٌ, which Gigg. and Cast. render, great, large in body; but this is incorrect; for it means, excellent, noble, skilful. I prefer with the Hebrew interpreters and Aqu. (Ἐπιπίπτοντες) falling on, attacking, so that נָפִיל is of intransitive signification. Those who used to interpret the passage in Genesis of the fall of the angels, were accustomed to render נפילים *fallers, rebels, apostates.*[52]

From these three highly respected Christian references, we can deduce the following:

- The Nephilim were the offspring of angels (most likely a specific class of angels described in 1 Enoch as Watchers).
- The term "Nephilim" would seem to indicate a new classification or group of beings, separate for the normal human population.

The Nephilim possessed no godly characteristics. They were rebels against anything godly, representing those fallen from heaven, and were complete apostates (there was no hope for redemption). Violence and an insatiable appetite for every sinful practice were fully embodied within their nature.

These creatures were so unnatural that the women's bodies would reject them, and they would miscarry these abominations. The unearthly strength of these creatures was manifested in their ability to survive the miscarriages and continue to grow into adulthood.

I want to refer back to my quote from renowned theologian, Francis A. Schaeffer:

> More and more we are finding that **mythology** in general though greatly contorted very often has some historic base. And the interesting thing is that one myth which occurs over and over again in many parts of the world is that somewhere a long time ago supernatural beings had sexual intercourse with natural women and produced a special breed of people.[53]

Mythology is replete with stories of men who were half god or demigod, such as the legendary Hercules. We also find stories of beings that were half man and half animal that possibly fit the narrative of "Baal and the Heifer" referred to by Stephen Quayle from the ancient Canaanite tablet. Such legends seem to be derived from nothing more than the imaginations of primitive men, until recently when Russia announced that it discovered the ancient remains of a satyr in an archeological dig.[54]

It should be noted that both Christian researchers Stephen Quayle and Dr. L. A. Marzulli have discovered a planned, massive cover-up of such findings by the world's Elite, to include the Smithsonian Institute here in the US. While the Elite promote evolution in our schools (something they do not believe in themselves) and herald the benefits of the grand transhumanist endeavor to transform mankind into Human 2.0, they are actively hiding the evidence that this transformation has already occurred in human history. This transformation, referred to in Genesis 6, resulted in the unprecedented wrath of God, in which all mankind was destroyed except for eight souls. (Interestingly, eight is the biblical number for new beginnings.)

What is the end game for all of this? It is possibly found in the very name "Nephilim." Remember Gesenius' rendering of the Hebrew word "Nephilim" as "apostate"? There was no redemption possible for the Nephilim, only destruction and divine judgment. The Word also tells us in Isaiah 26:14:

> They are dead, they shall not live; they are deceased, they shall not rise: therefore hast thou visited and destroyed them, and made all their memory to perish.

Finis Dake, in his *Annotated Reference Bible*, shares from his research that this verse indeed refers to the Nephilim:

Giants Have No Resurrection

Hebrew: *rapha'* (HSN-<H7496>), translated dead (Isa. 26:19; 14:9; Job 26:5; Ps. 88:10–11; Prov. 2:18; 9:18; 21:16); deceased (Isa. 26:14); giants (Dt. 2:11, 20; 3:11,13; Josh. 12:4; 13:12; 15:8; 17:15; 18:16; 2 Sam. 21:16–22; 1 Chr. 20:4–8); and Rephaim (Isa. 17:5; Gen. 14:5; 15:20; 2 Sam. 5:18, 22; 23:13; 1 Chr. 11:15; 14:9). In the eight places where it is translated dead and deceased it should have been retained as a proper name— Rephaim, as follows:

1. Rephaim under waters.
2. Shall the Rephaim arise and praise You? (Ps. 88:10–11)
3. Her paths unto the Rephaim. (Prov. 2:18)
4. The Rephaim are there. (Prov. 9:18).
5. Congregation to the Rephaim. (Prov. 21:16)
6. It stirreth up the Rephaim for you. (Isa. 14:9)
7. They are Rephaim. (Isa. 26:14)
8. The earth shall cast out the Rephaim.

The Rephaim were the other lords of Isa 26:13; they shall not rise because God visited and destroyed them (Isa 26:14). This plainly teaches that the giants or Rephaim have no resurrection like the dead of Israel referred to in Isa 26:19. They were the offspring of fallen angels, not ordinary men who do have a resurrection.[55]

Regarding Genesis 6, I believe that the original intent of the kingdom of darkness was to accomplish two goals:

1. To so contaminate the human genome that there would be no pure human bloodline left for Messiah (the Seed of the women) to be born from. Note: Genesis 6:9 refers to Noah being "perfect in his generations," annotating him and his family as still being completely Human 1.0.

2. To replace the **image of God** within mankind with the **image of the Beast**. This would render mankind unredeemable. Although the image of God is marred within sinful man, it still provides a conscience. The conscience not only recognizes sin but the need for repentance. If that image could be replaced with another one (i.e., the image of the Beast), there would be no recognition of sin, and repentance would be impossible. This is possibly why there is no hope for those who receive the mark of the Beast and worship his image in the book of Revelation. (See my chapter entitled, "A New Theory on the Image of the Beast and the New Conscience," in the book, *Blood on the Altar: The Coming War between Christian vs. Christian,* Defender Publishing.)

The end game of the Elite is to completely remove the image of God from mankind through the so-called science of transhumanism. Through

Watcher-inspired technology, they are endeavoring to bypass the modification that Almighty God accomplished genetically within mankind (and animal kind) at the Flood to enable the cross-species hybridization once again. Their idea of a utopian society is a return to Atlantis. In this new Atlantis, humans and the God of the Bible would no longer be welcomed. Only those with genetically altered bodies and enlightened souls that have become **Nietzsche's New Man** (beyond good and evil) would be welcomed there. Their idea of Utopia is nothing more than Lucifer's promise of Hell on earth. No wonder the Word of God provides this end-time promise to the Remnant:

> And except that the Lord had shortened those days, no flesh should be saved: but for the elect's sake, whom he hath chosen, he hath shortened the days. (Mark 13:20)

In the next chapter, we will examine the continuation of this biblical conspiracy against God and mankind in the stories of Nimrod and the Tower of Babel.

Recommended References for the Serious Bible Student:

Dake's Annotated Reference Bible. Dake Publishing, Lawrenceville, Georgia.

Earth's Earliest Ages by George H. Pember. Defender Publishing, Crane, Missouri.

The Omega Conspiracy by I. D. E. Thomas. Hearthstone Publishing, Oklahoma City, Oklahoma.

Aliens and Fallen Angels: the Sexual Corruption of the Human Race by Stephen Quayle. http://www.stevequayle.com/

The Researchers Library of Ancient Texts Volume I: The Apocrypha. Defender Publishing, Crane, Missouri.

The Researchers Library of Ancient Texts Volume 3: The Septuagint. Defender Publishing, Crane, Missouri.

chapter four

The Conspiratorial History within the Bible

Part 3: Nimrod and Babylon

W hat started false religions? In the beginning, everyone knew Noah and believed in the One True God. The Scriptures call Babylon the mother of all false religions, because under Nimrod the original false religious system was successfully implemented. We learn from the Church fathers that the root of this madness started with the sons of Ham.

> Fallen angels taught men the use of magical incantations that would force demons to obey man. After the flood Ham the son of Noah unhappily discovered this and taught it to his sons. This became ingrained into the Egyptians, Persians, and Babylonians. Ham died shortly after the fall of the Tower of Babel. Nimrod, called Ninus by the Greeks, was handed this knowledge and by it caused men to go away from the worship of God and go into diverse and erratic superstitions and they began to be governed by the signs in the stars and motions of the planets. (*Recognitions of Clement* 4.26–29)

Nimrod turned the government into a tyranny and set up twelve idols of wood named after the twelve months of the year, each representing a sign of the Zodiac. He commanded everyone to worship each idol in its proper month. (Jasher 9:8–10; *Ancient Post-Flood History*—Ken Johnson, ThD)[56]

All Pagan Roads Lead to Babylon

To understand Nimrod fully, we need to go back a few generations in his family line.

> And the sons of Ham; Cush, and Mizraim, and Phut, and Canaan.
>
> And the sons of Cush; Seba, and Havilah, and Sabtah, and Raamah, and Sabtecha: and the sons of Raamah; Sheba, and Dedan. And Cush begat Nimrod: he began to be a mighty one in the earth. He was a mighty hunter before the LORD: wherefore it is said, Even as Nimrod the mighty hunter before the LORD. (Genesis 10:6–9)

As stated in the previous chapter, Noah and his family were selected by God to be saved from the Flood on the ark because they remained genetically pure (or still fully human). Unfortunately, the purity did not extend to all of their minds as well. Resting within the safety of the ark lay the seeds of the arcane knowledge given by the Watchers of Genesis 6. Ham became a sleeper agent of darkness, if you will, infected with the forbidden knowledge that resulted in the severe judgment of God upon humanity. Within the mind and heart of Ham were the foundational concepts upon which Babylon and Egypt were built (and upon which the kingdom of the Antichrist is being built today).

We find in Genesis 9:20–23 that the seeds of the Watchers already began to sprout within the heart of Ham.

And Noah began to be an husbandman, and he planted a vineyard:

And he drank of the wine, and was drunken; and he was uncovered within his tent.

And Ham, the father of Canaan, saw the nakedness of his father, and told his two brethren without.

And Shem and Japheth took a garment, and laid it upon both their shoulders, and went backward, and covered the nakedness of their father; and their faces were backward, and they saw not their father's nakedness. (Genesis 9:20–23)

There is much speculation as to the actual sin of Ham contained in these verses. Was this sin the great dishonor and disrespect that Ham had shown to Noah? Alternatively, was it possible that he had sexually violated Noah in some way? Over the centuries, Christian theologians and rabbinical scholars have debated these issues. *The New American Commentary* dives into the subject and provides a sensible conclusion:

What was Ham's sin? Why did Noah invoke curses against Canaan instead of the culprit, Ham ([Genesis 9]:25)? The meaning of the phrase "saw his father's nakedness" has been variously interpreted. Both Jewish and Christian interpretation speculated that Ham's deed was a sexual offense since the same language is found in the Pentateuch describing sexual transgressions. Further support was garnered from v. 25, which refers to what Ham "had done to him." Many suppose that the original story contained the sordid details but that they were excised for reasons of propriety when later placed in the Torah. Castration was thought to have been the crime by some Jewish and Christian interpreters, and others argued for a homosexual act. Jewish midrash explained that physical abuse by Ham answered why the curse was directed against Canaan; this act prevented Noah from having a fourth son, and thus Canaan as Ham's fourth son should suffer (*Gen. Rab57*. 36.7). This may have been fueled by the absence of any notice that additional children were born to Noah, since all the other patriarchs are said to have had "other sons and daughters" (5:3–32; 11:10–25). This lack of reference to other children, however, may be due to the author's desire to parallel the Sethite and Shemite lines, which both end with three sons (5:32; 11:26).

Concerning a homosexual desire or act, there is no indication that a sexual indiscretion occurred when Ham viewed his father or that Ham desired his father in an illicit way. Levitical language for the homosexual act is "to lie with a male," which we do not find here. "Saw"…is the common term for observing and does not convey necessarily the idea of sexual lust; the term can be used in this way (cf. 6:2; 34:2), but such meaning must be derived from the context and not the term by itself. On the contrary, the expressions "to see…nakedness" (Lev 20:17) and "to uncover…nakedness" are used of heterosexual actions, not homosexual encounters. The expression in our passage is not a figurative statement since the two sons actually cover up the exposed nakedness of their father, who was in a drunken stupor in the tent. This is reinforced by the description "their faces were turned." If in fact some lecherous deed occurred inside the tent, it is inexplicable why the covering of their father is in juxtaposition to Ham's act. On other occasions Genesis is straightforward in its description of sexual misconduct (e.g., 19:5, 30–35; 34:2). There is no reason to assume that homosexuality or, for that matter, heterosexual misconduct would be described euphemistically by the author.

Ham's reproach was not in seeing his father unclothed, though this was a shameful thing (cp. Hab 2:15), but in his outspoken delight at his father's disgraceful condition. The penalty against Ham's son may be thought too severe for mere sibling gossip, but this is because we fail to understand the gravity of Ham's offense. We have commented elsewhere (see 2:25; 3:7) that nakedness was shameful in Hebrew culture. In later Israel specific prohibitions guarded against the public exposure of the genitals and buttocks (e.g., Exod 20:26; 28:42), and nakedness was commonly associated with public misconduct (e.g., Exod 32:25). It is not surprising then that the euphemism "nakedness" was used for the shameful travesty of incest. Ham ridiculed the "old man's" downfall. In the ancient world insulting one's parents was a serious matter that warranted the extreme penalty of death. Mosaic legislation reflected this sentiment. This patriarchal incident illustrated the abrogation of the Fifth Commandment, "Honor your father and mother." To do so means divine retaliation, for the crime is not against parent alone but is viewed as contempt for God's hierarchical order in creation. Shem and Japheth, unlike Ham, treated Noah with proper respect. They refused to take advantage of him despite his vulnerable condition.[57]

The book of James warns us about wisdom that does not come from God. This dark wisdom produces specific effects within the souls of men.

This wisdom descendeth not from above, but is earthly, sensual, devilish.
    For where envying and strife is, there is confusion and every evil work. (James 3:15–16)

I believe that the dark wisdom of the Watchers was brewing within the mind of Ham. The result was that he became arrogant, boastful, and disrespectful (just to name a few). Instead of showing honor to his father and covering his nakedness, he mocked his father and made sure this disgrace was brought to everyone's attention. Once Noah realized what had happened, he uttered a curse that flowed through Ham to his son Canaan. The rabbis of old have debated why this curse was directed upon Canaan and not Cush. Some have concluded that he was an active participant in the disgrace and held the tent open for all to see. This, of course, would be mere speculation as the Scriptures are silent regarding it.

And he said, Cursed be Canaan; a servant of servants shall he be unto his brethren. (Genesis 9:25)

In the sad history of slavery in Great Britain and the United States, there were individuals who justified its practice by quoting Genesis 9:25. However, this misinterpretation does not bode well in the light of historical facts. Finis Dake provides us with a quick summary of the descendants of Ham and where they settled:

The Sons of Ham
1. **Cush** (Gen. 10:6–12; 1 Chr. 1:8–10; Isa. 11:11), progenitor of various Ethiopian tribes that settled south of Egypt and also overran Arabia, Babylonia, and India.

2. **Mizraim** (Gen. 10:6, 13–14; 1 Chr. 1:8–11), progenitor of various Egyptian tribes. Mizraim means "double." Tribes of the double Egypt (upper and lower Egypt), called the land of Ham, came from him (Ps. 78:51; 105:23–27; 106:22). The Philistines also came from Mizraim (Gen. 10:14).

3. **Phut** (Gen. 10:6; Ezek. 27:10), progenitor of the Libyans and other tribes in northern Africa (Ezek. 27:10; 30:5; 38:5; Jer. 46:9; Nah. 3:9).

4. **Canaan** (Gen. 10:6,15–19; 9:18–27; 1 Chr. 1:8–13), progenitor of peoples that settled mainly in Palestine, Arabia, Tyre, Sidon, and other parts of the land promised to Abraham. These nations are often mentioned in connection with Israel (Gen. 10:15–19; 15:18–21; Dt. 7:1–3; Josh. 12).[58]

Since Canaan's descendants stayed primarily in the Middle East, there was no validity to their claim that this referred to the Africans sold into slavery. What we do find is that Ham's children became major problems for God's people throughout history, both in ancient times and today.

From a mystery religion[59] point of view, we can examine how the Watchers' seeds of defiance spread like wildfire through Ham's children.

1. Cush

Cush is named in the Bible as the father of Nimrod. Ancient history tells us quite a bit more about this barely footnoted individual within the Word of God. Cush was a leading influence in both the formation of Babylon and in the construction of the Tower of Babel. As we begin to investigate Cush historically, it is obvious that the seeds of the Watchers had taken root and begun to spring forth. Alexander Hislop, in his classic work *The Two Babylons*, sheds light on both the activities of Cush and the various names he bore within ancient history:

> Now, assuming that Ninus is Nimrod, the way in which that assumption explains what is otherwise inexplicable in the statements of ancient history greatly confirms the truth of that assumption itself. Ninus is said to have been the son of Belus or Bel, and Bel is said to have been the founder of Babylon. If Ninus was in reality the first king of Babylon, how could Belus or Bel, his father, be said to be the founder of it? Both might very well be, as will appear if we consider who was Bel, and what we can trace of his doings. If Ninus was Nimrod, who was the historical Bel? He must have been Cush; for "Cush begat Nimrod" (Gen[esis] 10:8); and **Cush is generally represented as having been a ringleader in the great apostacy.** But again, Cush, as the son of Ham, was Hermes or Mercury; for Hermes is just an Egyptian synonym for the "son of Ham."
>
> Gregory attributes to Cush what was said more generally to have befallen his son; but his statement shows the belief in his day, which is amply confirmed from other sources, **that Cush had a preeminent share in leading mankind away from the true worship of God.** The composition of Her-mes is, first, from "Her," which, in Chaldee, is synonymous with Ham, or Khem, "the burnt one." As "her" also, like Ham, signified "The hot or burning one," this name formed a foundation for covertly identifying

Ham with the "Sun," and so deifying the great patriarch, after whose name the land of Egypt was called, in connection with the sun. Khem, or Ham, in his own name was openly worshipped in later ages in the land of Ham; but this would have been too daring at first. By means of "Her," the synonym, however, the way was paved for this. "Her" is the name of Horus, who is identified with the sun, which shows the real etymology of the name to be from the verb to which I have traced it. Then, secondly, "Mes," is from Mesheh (or, without the last radical, which is omissible), Mesh, "to draw forth." In Egyptian, we have Ms in the sense of "to bring forth", which is evidently a different form of the same word. In the passive sense, also, we find Ms used. The radical meaning of Mesheh in *Stockii Lexicon*, is given in Latin "Extraxit," and our English word "extraction," as applied to birth or descent, shows a connection between the generic meaning of this word and birth. This derivation will be found to explain the meaning of the names of the Egyptian kings, Ramesses and Thothmes, the former evidently being "the son of Ra," or the sun; the latter in like manner, being "the son of Thoth." For the very same reason Her-mes is the "Son of Her, or Ham," the burnt one—that is, Cush.

Now, Hermes was the great original prophet of idolatry; **for he was recognised by the pagans as the author of their religious rites, and the interpreter of the gods.** The distinguished Gesenius identifies him with the Babylonian Nebo, **as the prophetic god**; and a statement of Hyginus **shows that he was known as the grand agent in that movement which produced the division of tongues.** His words are these: "For many ages men lived under the government of Jove [evidently not the Roman Jupiter, but the Jehovah of the Hebrews], without cities and without laws, and all speaking one language. But after that Mercury interpreted the speeches of men (whence an interpreter is called Hermeneutes), the same individual distributed the nations. Then discord began."[60] (Emphasis added)

So Cush was known by many names throughout history and pagan mythology: Cush, Bel, Hermes, Mercury, and Nebo. Later on in *The Two Babylons*, Hislop links Cush to both Janus and to the releasing of chaos at the Tower of Babel as "Confounder."

It must have been in the sense of Bel the "Confounder." And to this meaning of the name of the Babylonian Bel, there is a very distinct allusion in Jeremiah 1:2, **where it is said "Bel is confounded," that is, "The Confounder is brought to confusion."** That Cush was known to Pagan antiquity under the very character of Bel, "The Confounder," a statement of Ovid very clearly proves. The statement to which I refer is that in which Janus "the god of gods," from whom all the other gods had their origin, is made to say of himself: "The ancients...called me Chaos."

Janus was so called in the most ancient hymns of the Salii. **Now, first this decisively shows that Chaos was known not merely as a state of confusion, but as the "god of Confusion."** But, secondly, who that is at all acquainted with the laws of Chaldaic pronunciation, does not know that Chaos is just one of the established forms of the name of Chus or Cush? Then, look at the symbol of Janus, whom "the ancients called Chaos," and it will be seen how exactly it tallies with the doings of Cush, when he is identified with Bel, "The Confounder." That symbol is a club; and the name of "a club" in Chaldee comes from the very word which signifies "to break in pieces, or scatter abroad."[61] (Emphasis added)

It would seem that Cush claimed the prophetic ability to channel the instructions and will of the now-banished Watchers to humanity (this will be important later on in our study of the Illuminati). His dark prophetic wisdom was the catalyst for both the establishment of Babylon and the building of the Tower of Babel.

I believe it is also interesting to note that Cush was called "the god of Confusion." This may give further insight into Paul's statement: "For God is not *the author* of confusion"[62] (1 Corinthians 14:33). Remember, both epistles to the Corinthians were written to a highly paganized population, in which a portion of the Gentiles had recently found Messiah. With all of the problems that Paul had to contend with, it seemed many of their members had one foot in biblical Christianity and the other foot solidly planted in the paganism of their fathers. In their pagan training, many times the influence of their gods produced chaos, as it did within the mythology of Janus—the god of gods. This would explain why Paul labored so hard in both of his epistles to separate, within their thinking, the concepts of the God of Abraham with the pantheon of pagan deities they were accustomed to.

God foretells His eventual judgment on the sons of Cush:

You too, Ethiopians, will be put to death by my sword. (Zephaniah 2:12, CJB [Complete Jewish Bible][63])

The Hebrew word here for "Ethiopians" is **Kuwshiy** (koo-shee'), which means "one of the descendants of Cush."[64] In fact, the *Anderson-Forbes Phrase Marker Analysis of the Hebrew Bible*[65] translates this as "Kushites" instead of "Ethiopians."

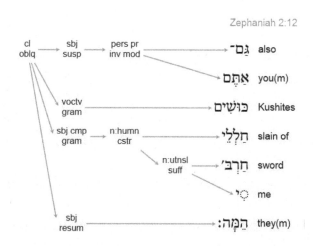

A Commentary: Critical, Experimental, and Practical on the Old and New Testaments shares insights into this prophetic word against the sons of Cush.

Whatever the reason for choosing Cush and whatever the process by which the oracle achieved this position in the book, Zephaniah made a strong statement about the day of the Lord as he used the oracle. The day of the Lord has a "three-fold 'no-escape': no escape for any people, no escape from the wages of sin, no escape from divine confrontation."[66]

I believe this signifies that when Jesus returns as Messiah ben David (the Conquering King), all of the esoteric knowledge that the Watchers provided this bloodline will not save them from God's judgment. No promise of godhood, immortality, or transcendence, whether offered by the Luciferian Elite or the evangelists of transhumanism, will save them. The "threefold" judgment of the trice Holy God will be poured upon their heads until they are no more.

Finally, we have an idea now of where Nimrod obtained the knowledge he used to enslave men, to cofound Babylon, to become its first worldwide king, and to develop a religious system designed to draw men away from the One True God. His father was a prophet of darkness and an interpreter for the old gods. Nimrod was raised to be an elitist—one illuminated with the forbidden knowledge that was promised by Lucifer in the garden and taught to mankind by fallen angels in Genesis 6. This proverbial apple did not fall far from the family tree. In fact, what he did eclipsed all of their occult endeavors.

2. Mizraim

Mizraim is identified as the founder of the nation of Egypt. In Hebrew, "Mizraim" is translated as "Egypt." All of the occult knowledge Egypt possessed stemmed from what Mizraim and his family brought to that area as they settled there. While Cush was busy working with Nimrod in the founding of Babylon, Ham was working with Mizraim in the development of Egypt. In *A Commentary: Critical, Experimental, and Practical on the Old and New Testaments* by Jamieson, Fausset, and Brown we find:

Sons of Ham—emigrated southward, and their settlements were: Cush in Arabia, Canaan in the country known by his name, and Mizraim in Egypt, Upper and Lower. **It is generally thought that his father accompanied him and personally superintended the formation of the settlement, whence Egypt was called "the land of Ham"** [Ps 105:23, 27; Ps 106:22].[67] (Emphasis added)

3. Put

In researching Put, I was underwhelmed by the data I was able to retrieve. He is not mentioned by either the name "Put" or "Phut" in *The Two Babylons*. I was, however, able to find several references to him; the first was in *Baker's Encyclopedia of the Bible*:

> Ancient nation, descended from a man of the same name. It is commonly identified as Libya, although it has been argued that it was the Punt of Egyptian records, somewhere along the northeast coast of Africa, perhaps Somalia. Its association with Egypt, Cush, and Canaan and the usage of the name in the Old Testament make the Libyan location probable. In the Old Testament the Libyan people are called Lubim, a name which always appears in the plural.[68]

And the second was in *Easton's Bible Dictionary*:

> **Put, Phut**—(1.) One of the sons of Ham (Gen. 10:6).
> (2.) A land or people from among whom came a portion of the mercenary troops of Egypt, Jer. 46:9 (A.V., "Libyans," but correctly, R.V., "Put"); Ezek. 27:10; 30:5 (A.V., "Libya;" R.V., "Put"); 38:5; Nahum 3:9.[69]

It would seem that Put and his descendants aligned themselves with Egypt and simply amalgamated into their system and society.

4. Canaan

Eerdman's Dictionary of the Bible provides the following on Canaan, son of Ham.

> **Canaan** (Heb. *kĕna ʿan*) **(PERSON)**
> A son of Ham and grandson of Noah (Gen. 9:18, 22); according to 1 Chr. 1:8 Ham's youngest son. He became the ancestor of the people later called the Canaanites (Gen. 10:15–19).
>
> For the impropriety of Ham's seeing the "nakedness" of Noah (Gen. 9:22–24), Noah cursed Canaan to be the "lowest of slaves" (Gen. 9:25) to his brothers. This curse, which applies more to his descendants than to Canaan himself, does not imply the slavery of a particular race (as some have held); rather, it suggests the inferior position of the Canaanites before the Conquest relative to the important role played by their neighbors, the Egyptians and the inhabitants of Mesopotamia.[70]

Canaan, like Put, is not mentioned by name in *The Two Babylons*, which would imply that he, too, was not mythologized into the pagan/occult belief systems of the mystery religions. Canaan's descendants did establish a civilization within the Promised Land, which God called Joshua and the children of Israel to displace. Israel's failure to completely eradicate the land of their influence proved to become a stumbling block for them spiritually. *Nelson's New Illustrated Bible Dictionary* provides the following regarding the Canaanites:

> Although both Canaanites and Amorites were established in Canaan before 2000 B.C., the Canaanites established their civilization as dominant during the Middle Bronze Age (about 2100 to 1550 B.C.). Their society had several classes, ranging from the ruling nobility to the peasants. The northern Canaanites used a particular Cuneiform script, featuring a wedge-shaped alphabet.

Their land was also dotted with walled cities. Several of these served as the centers of city-states, each having its own king, or mayor, and army.

The Canaanites, therefore, were a highly civilized people in many ways when Joshua led the Israelites across the Jordan River to conquer the people and settle the land. Canaanite history ended with the Israelite conquest. But certain segments of Canaanite culture remained to make both positive and negative impacts on the life of God's Covenant People.[71]

What segments of the Canaanite culture remained? The answer is: their gods and their religious practices. The *New Bible Dictionary* details the gods of the Canaanites.

The Canaanites had an extensive pantheon, headed by El. More prominent in practice were Baal (lord'), *i.e.* Hadad the storm-god, and Dagon, with temples in Ugarit and elsewhere. The goddesses Asherah, Astarte (Ashtaroth) and Anath—like Baal—had multi-coloured personalities and violent characters; they were goddesses of sex and war. Kothar-and-Hasis was artificer-god (*cf.* Vulcan), and other and lesser deities abounded.[72]

The worship of Dagon, Baal, and Astarte/Ashtaroth (the Queen of Heaven) continually infiltrated the cultural/religious beliefs of the Israelites. Almighty God warned them in Deuteronomy 12:29–32:

When the LORD thy God shall cut off the nations from before thee, whither thou goest to possess them, and thou succeedest them, and dwellest in their land;

Take heed to thyself that thou be not snared by following them, after that they be destroyed from before thee; and that thou enquire not after their gods, saying, **How did these nations serve their gods? even so will I do likewise.**

Thou shalt not do so unto the LORD thy God: for every

abomination to the LORD, which he hateth, have they done unto their gods; for even their sons and their daughters they have burnt in the fire to their gods.

What thing soever I command you, observe to do it: thou shalt not add thereto, nor diminish from it. (Emphasis added)

In all fairness, it should be noted that we cannot stand in history and fault the Israelites of old too harshly for adopting the pagan practices and celebrations of the Canaanites or any of the other pagan cultures that surrounded them. Many of these pagan practices were enfolded into the practices[73] and theologies of the Roman Catholic (Universal) Church. A good portion of these practices were originally rejected by the founders of the Protestant Movement; but with the passing of time, they were slowly adopted once again into many Protestant churches. In our generation, we need to ask ourselves: Am I still being influenced by the descendants of Ham, and has the leaven of their defiance before God infiltrated the practice of my own faith and service to God? To answer this question, you must do your own personal homework. Examine all of your traditions. Do they originate in the Bible or do they come from extrabiblical sources? If our traditions cannot be found in the Word of God and traced back to the faithful worship of God found in both the Old and New Testaments, we will need to renounce such practices and return to biblicity to prepare for the prophetic days ahead.

Another Link with the Sons of Ham

In our studies, we have been examining the establishment and flow of the doctrines given to mankind through the Watchers. We have called this occult stream "Mystery Babylon." After the Flood, giants began to appear on the earth again. What is interesting is that giants began to be born primarily through Ham's line. Nephilim researcher Rob Skiba has provided a very plausible theory to the reappearance of the Nephilim in his book, *Archon Invasion: The Rise, Fall and Return of the Nephilim.* The Word tells us that Noah was pure in his generations (100-percent human DNA).

Most researchers believe that Noah's wife was genetically pure, as well as their three sons: Shem, Ham, and Japheth. Before the wives of Noah's sons were mentioned, the Bible informs us that:

> The earth also was corrupt before God, and the earth was filled with violence.
>
> And God looked upon the earth, and, behold, **it was corrupt; for all flesh had corrupted his way upon the earth**. (Genesis 6:11–12, emphasis added)

It is quite possible that the wives of Noah's sons carried the DNA of the Nephilim within them. Many of the descendants of Ham and Japheth were born as Nephilim. Skiba goes on to postulate that the reason Noah cursed Canaan instead of Ham was that he saw characteristics of the Nephilim in his grandson.

Therefore, from the very foundations of the mystery religions, there has been a connection with the Nephilim. Whenever you add Nephilim influence (or even artifacts) to what the mystery religions teach, the darkest of black magic is released.

An Examination of Nimrod

Before I dive into what I have discovered about Nimrod, I want to share some of the basic information regarding the first king of Babylon that you will find in most Bible commentaries. For this task, I will refer to *The Pentateuch* by James E. Smith.

> The text furnishes scant information concerning Nimrod. He was a descendant of Cush, a Hamite. The Biblical record thus agrees with data from the ancient history of Mesopotamia which furnish evidence that the region was first ruled by a non-Shemitic people. Nimrod began to be (i.e., set out to be) a mighty one (*gibbor*) in the land (10:8). The term *tyrant* captures the intention of the

original. Nimrod's very name is an encapsulation of his lifestyle. His name means, "Let us revolt." He must have been a ruthless ruler who was opposed to all existing order.

Nimrod was especially noted as "a mighty hunter before Yahweh" (10:9). One of the royal responsibilities of kings in ancient times was to keep the wild animal population thinned out so that citizens would not be threatened. The text may refer to this function. The documents, however, also speak of ancient kings *hunting* the men of a city, capturing them, and carrying them off into slavery. Perhaps Nimrod hunted men. He did this "before (*liphne*) Yahweh," i.e., in opposition to Yahweh. The Septuagint rendered, "a mighty hunter against the Lord."

Nimrod was an empire builder. He started his rise to power in Shinar, in the lower Mesopotamian river valley. He gradually extended his influence over (or possibly built) Babel, Erech, Accad and Calneh. Nimrod eventually expanded his influence into Assyria where he built Nineveh, Rehoboth, Calah and the great city of Resen (10:10–12).[74]

To this basic understanding we can now add the perspective I have already shared regarding the knowledge of the Watchers that was embedded into Ham's family line. With this information, you can now have a better understanding of the family tree from which Nimrod sprang. He was not a strange spiritual anomaly within his family. He was the personification of all their hopes and dreams.

And Cush begat Nimrod: he began to be a mighty one in the earth.

He was a mighty hunter before the LORD: wherefore it is said, Even as Nimrod the mighty hunter before the LORD. (Genesis 10:8–9)

These two little lines of text within Holy Writ reveal a conspiracy that would change the world for the worse. The knowledge of the Watchers found its zenith in Nimrod. What he did and who he became would change the course of history and turn the hearts of men away from God. So powerful was its influence that it will continue through the currents of time until it abruptly halts at the return of the Lord Jesus.

What was the change that occurred in Nimrod that all of the occult Elite are working behind the scenes and using the resources of every advanced nation to rediscover? I have already hinted at it, but Dr. Tom Horn provides the answer with great clarity in his research.

> Nimrod, the original character who later was mythologized as the god Apollo prophesied by the apostle Paul in the New Testament (and by the occult elite on the Great Seal of the United States) as the ancient spirit that will return to earth to rule the *novus ordo seclorum*.
>
> The story of Nimrod in the book of Genesis may illustrate how this could happen through genetic engineering or a retrovirus of demonic design that integrates with a host's genome and rewrites the living specimen's DNA, thus making it a "fit extension" or host for infection by the entity. Note what Genesis 10:8 says about Nimrod:
>
> And Cush begat Nimrod: he began to be a mighty one in the earth.
>
> Three sections in this unprecedented verse indicate something very peculiar happened to Nimrod. First, note where the text says, "he began to be." In Hebrew, this is *chalal*, which means "to become profaned, defiled, polluted, or desecrated ritually, sexually or genetically." Second, this verse tells us exactly what Nimrod began to be as he changed genetically—"a mighty one" *(gibbowr, gibborim)*, one of the offspring of Nephilim. As Annette Yoshiko Reed says in the Cambridge University book, *Fallen Angels and the History of Judaism and Christianity*, "The Nephilim of Genesis 6:4 are always…grouped together with the gibborim as the progeny of the Watchers and human women." And the third part of this text says the change to Nimrod started while he was on

"earth." Therefore, in modern language, this text could accurately be translated to say: "And Nimrod began to change genetically, becoming a gibborim, the offspring of watchers on earth."[75]

Bible commentator Adam Clarke seems to agree with Dr. Horn's conclusions by quoting the Syraic Targum regarding Nimrod: "The Syriac calls him a warlike giant."[76]

Then Clarke continues to share about Nimrod and the building of the Tower of Babel and its connection to giants:

> On this point Bochart observes that these things are taken from the Chaldeans, who preserve many remains of ancient facts; and though they often add circumstances, yet they are, in general, in some sort dependent on the text. 1. They say Babel was built by the giants, because Nimrod, one of the builders, is called in the Hebrew text רובג *gibbor*, a mighty man; or, as the Septuagint, γιγας, a giant. 2. These giants, they say, sprang from the earth, because, in Genesis 10:11, it is said, He went, אוהה ץראה ןמ *min haarets hahiv*, out of that earth; but this is rather spoken of Asshur, who was another of the Babel builders. 3. These giants are said to have waged war with the gods, because it is said of Nimrod, Genesis 10:9, He was a mighty hunter before the Lord; or, as others have rendered it, a warrior and a rebel against the Lord. See Jarchi in loco. 4. These giants are said to have raised a tower up to heaven, as if they had intended to have ascended thither.[77]

Nimrod achieved something that only the Watchers of old had accomplished, yet he took it to a whole new level. In fact, no one has been able to reproduce this highly revered occult achievement. This cutting-edge breakthrough of Nimrod has been the goal of all secret societies, alchemists, wizards, sorcerers, warlocks, and Illuminati elite throughout the millennia. You see, he was a fully grown man who was able to become a *gibborim* (another type of Nephilim)—he was not born that way. It would appear that Nimrod took the arcane knowledge of his family line and pushed it beyond what the Watchers themselves could do: He was able to alter his DNA and become a Nephilim. This transmogrification must have thrilled the kingdom of darkness. The fallen angels of Genesis 6 required the use of women in their genetic breeding program. Nimrod accomplished this alchemical feat without the use of a woman's womb.

This is important to note, because the Word of God in Daniel gives us a hint that the Antichrist will be able to reproduce the dark magic of Nimrod.

> Neither shall he regard the God of his fathers, nor the desire of women, nor regard any god: for he shall magnify himself above all. (Daniel 11:37)

Some have speculated that this refers to the Antichrist being a homosexual. Although it is true that most within the occult are bisexual (for use in ritual magic), I believe this is a prophetic clue linking the coming man of sin with Nimrod. This powerful working of dark magic and esoteric wisdom will be reproduced one more time in human history. The coming transmogrification of a man will invite Lucifer himself to come and coinhabit this enhanced man-god. He will become the reincarnation of Nimrod—the Antichrist!

Babylonian and Egyptian mysticism are still the leading spiritual forces within the winding currents of the mystery religions today. **Egyptian Sex Magic,** a product of Egyptian mysticism, is prominent in the teachings of Aleister Crowley, as well as the *Ordo Templi Orientis* and the Golden Dawn. It is also interwoven in the esoteric teachings of Freemasonry. In his internationally acclaimed book, *Apollyon Rising 2012,* Dr. Tom Horn reveals the Lost Symbol of Freemasonry:

> Unrecognized by the vast majority of peoples around the world is the greatest conspiracy of all time, sitting right out in the open in Washington DC and at the Vatican. It is an ancient, magical, talismanic diagram—the Lost Symbol—which waits its final use by the hidden, occult hand guiding the Secret Destiny of America.[78]

It would seem that the Lost Symbol was designed utilizing ancient Watcher knowledge, handed down through the line of Ham, and was embedded in the occult religious practices of Egypt. Could the Lost Symbol be a Watcher-inspired spiritual/technological device designed to replicate the transformation of Nimrod? Will it one day produce a new man-god: *Gibborim/Nephilim* (Osiris made flesh)? The truth is that the physical occult symbols/devices have been in place for centuries, and practitioners of the occult have been going through the prescribed rituals with absolute devotion. Yet, through all of the centuries of faithful rehearsals, the equal to Nimrod has yet to be reproduced. Perhaps the realization of the next Nimrod will require intervention by the Watchers through a stargate (or dimensional portal) into our reality. On the other hand, maybe the last piece of the god-maker puzzle is still just waiting to be discovered in one of the world's pyramids or ziggurats.

The Elite of the world are working behind the scenes with secret government agencies around the globe and the Transhumanist Movement community to unlock the secrets of Nimrod.

Lost symbol at nation's capitol

Lost symbol at the Vatican

Dr. Horn continues detailing the mystic meaning of these ancient symbols of Babylon's mystery religion:

Undoubtedly the vast majority of people, when looking at Washington, DC, and at the Vatican, never comprehend how these cities constitute one of the greatest open conspiracies of all time. There, reproduced in all their glory and right before the world's eyes, is an ancient talismanic diagram based on the history and cult of Isis, Osiris, and Horus, including the magical utilities meant to generate the deity's return. The primeval concept—especially that of sacred Domes facing Obelisks—was designed in antiquity for the express purpose of regeneration, resurrection, and apotheosis, for deity incarnation from the underworld to earth's surface through union of the respective figures—the Dome (ancient structural representation of the womb of Isis) and the Obelisk (ancient representation of the erect male phallus of Osiris). This layout, as modeled in antiquity, exists today on the grandest scale at the heart of the capital of the most powerful government on earth—the United States—as well as in the heart of the most politically influential church on earth—the Vatican. Given this fact and the pattern provided by the apostle Paul and the Apocalypse of John (the book of Revelation) that the end times would culminate in a marriage between political (Antichrist) and religious (False Prophet) authorities at the return of Osiris/Apollo, it behooves open-minded researchers to carefully consider this prophecy in stone, as it defines the spiritual energy that is knowingly or unknowingly being invoked at both locations with potential ramifications for Petrus Romanus, the year 2012, and beyond. The US Capital has been called the "Mirror Vatican" due to the strikingly similar layout and design of its primary buildings and streets. This is no accident. In fact, America's forefathers first named the capital city "Rome." But the parallelism between Washington and the Vatican is most clearly illustrated by the Capitol building and Dome facing the Obelisk known as the Washington Monument, and at St. Peter's Basilica in the Vatican by a similar Dome facing a familiar Obelisk—both of which were, according to their own official records, fashioned after the Roman Pantheon, the circular Domed Rotunda "dedicated to all pagan gods." This layout—a Domed temple facing an Obelisk—is an ancient, alchemical blueprint that holds significant esoteric meaning.[79]

(Author's note: For more information on this and related topics, I encourage you to read Dr. Horn's updated version of his book entitled *Zenith 2016: The Revised and Expanded Edition of Apollyon Rising 2012*. This book is a must for any serious student of Bible prophecy.)

Nimrod also possessed the strength, cunning, and cruelty of the children of the Watchers before the Flood. This change within him supercharged his despotic desires. What were some of those despotic desires? Finis Dake provides some of the answers.

Nimrod comes from the Hebrew *marad* (HSN-<H4775>), "to rebel." It points to some violent and open rebellion against God. Nimrod began to be a mighty one in the earth **by bold and daring deeds. His rebellion is associated with the beginning of his kingdom and suggests that his hunting and mighty deeds were related primarily to hunting men by tyranny and force.** He lorded it over others, hunting and destroying all who opposed him in his despotic rule over people. This is the meaning understood by Josephus and writers of the Targums. **Josephus says that Nimrod persuaded people to ascribe their happiness to him rather than God.** He became a great leader, taught people to centralize, and defied God to send another flood. It is said that Nimrod hunted down wild beasts also, which were killing many people, and taught people to build walls around cities for protection against them.

The term "mighty hunter" (Gen. 10:9) could refer to a hunter of animals or of men to enslave them. Nimrod was a hunter of

both human beings and animals. The Hebrew *gibbowr* (HSN-
<H1368>), translated "mighty" here, means a powerful warrior,
tyrant, champion, giant, or strong one. It is used of giants who
were renown for wickedness (Gen. 6:4), and of other wicked men
(Ps. 52:1–3; 120:4; Isa. 5:22; Jer. 9:23). It could refer to Nimrod
as a tyrant and oppressive despot. **He established the first kingdom and the first universal false religion opposing God since
the flood of Noah.**... This was done "before the Lord," that is,
openly: in the presence of God with all defiance. That is why God,
when He came down to see Babel, took action to counteract the
rebellion of Nimrod (Gen. 11:1–9).[80] (Emphasis added)

Nimrod possessed both a demonic intelligence and a supernatural
strength that enabled him to enslave people through tyranny and force.
He demanded that everyone ascribe their happiness to him and him
alone. He became the first ruler of the known world (the first New World
Order) and established the first one-world religion. Nimrod is the perfect
type and shadow in the Old Testament of the Antichrist. The Antichrist
will be unstoppable as a warrior, his cruelty will know no bounds, he will
enslave the world as the new leader of the New World Order, and he will
establish a one-world religion to draw all men away from the True God
and Creator of mankind. No other figure in history or the Bible, not even
the pharaohs of Egypt, comes close to personifying the Antichrist the way
that Nimrod did.

A. W. Pink agrees with this analysis of Nimrod and Babylon. In his
classic work on the Antichrist, he writes:

In the first place, as Nimrod—the founder of Babel, that is, the
Tower of Babylon—a savage tyrant and cruel oppressor of men,
was the first person who declared open war against God; so it is
meet that there should arise from the selfsame Babylon, the last
and most atrocious persecutor of the saints—the Antichrist. Moreover, seeing that Nebuchadnezzar and Antiochus Epiphanes—two

monsters who bore down upon the people of God with an over-whelming power of destruction, and who were the antichrists of the old Testament and remarkable types of the Antichrist which is to come; seeing, I say, that these monarchs reigned in Babylon, it is fitting that the true Antichrist of the New Testament should arise from the same Babylon.

Besides, no place can be pointed out more meet for the nativity of Antichrist than Babylon, for it is the City of the Devil—always diametrically opposed to Jerusalem, which is deemed the City of God; the former city, that is, Babylon, being the mother and disseminator of every kind of confusion, idolatry, impiety—a vast sink of every foul pollution, crime, and iniquity—the first city in the world which cut itself off from the worship of the true God—which reared the city of universal vice,—which perpetually (according to the record of Holy Writ) carries on the mystery of iniquity, and bears imprinted on her brow the inscription of blasphemy against the name of God. The consummation, therefore, of impiety, which is to have its recapitulation in Antichrist, could not break forth from a more fitting place than Babylon.[81]

Needless to say, Nimrod set the standard for ruthlessness. In fact, his exploits were greater than all other despots in history combined. Even the practice of crucifixion did not originate in Rome; it all began in Babylon!

Understanding the Two Faces of Nimrod

Although his ruthlessness is well documented in most biblical resources, I do think they overlook the other side of Nimrod. He was able to inspire men to come under his leadership. He was genius in military tactics; he was a consummate politician; he developed cities, honed an entire civilization, and birthed a religion that is still spreading like a cancer in the world today. Nimrod's spiritual influence was so great that families would willingly offer their children on the fiery altars of Molech.

The Two Sides of Nimrod	
Sophisticated	Savage
Civilized	Barbaric
Intelligent	Demonically Twisted
A Builder	A Destroyer
Inspiring Leader	Betrayer
Religious	Full of Spiritual Darkness
Social Engineer / World Savior / Luciferian Messiah	Deceives the Masses for His Own Glory and Dark Purposes

Nimrod would be the perfect world leader for today. He would wear a Giorgio Armani suit, have a disarming smile, possess the personality perfect for TV, have a physique like that of the Greek gods, and have a wisdom drawn from the deepest well of the ascended masters of the New Age throughout time. His words would drop like honey from his perfect, genetically altered lips, and his transhuman-enhanced blue eyes would seem to look straight into your soul. He would be able to mesmerize the masses into following him without question, and he would engineer a society that reflects his true personality: the perfect blending of sophistication and savagery. High culture and blood would run through all the streets of the cities and nations that he would build and rule. Safety, security, health, pleasure, and prosperity would be extended to those who gave unquestioned loyalty. This is also a perfect description of the Antichrist—truly, the reincarnation of Nimrod.

Nimrod's Aspirations

As I began to research the Babylon that Nimrod labored to build, something began to dawn upon my soul: **Nimrod was the first to attempt to rebuild Atlantis**. He possessed a portion of the knowledge of the ancient Watchers; he was able to transmogrify himself into a gibborim; and he began to build cities that rivaled many of our own today! Here are some facts I discovered in my research of the Babylon of Nimrod.

The Size of Babel

Of the magnificence of Babel, the capital of the empire of Nimrod, "the mighty hunter," it is difficult to convey an adequate conception, without entering into details foreign to our purpose. *But some idea of it may be formed from its extent, which according to the lowest computation, covered no less than one hundred square miles, or about five times the size of London; while the highest computation would make it cover two hundred square miles, or ten times the* extent **of London**! Such was the world-city, the first "beginning" of which at least Nimrod had founded. No wonder that the worldly pride of that age should have wished to make such a place the world-capital of a world-empire, whose tower "may reach unto heaven! (Emphasis added)

—Alfred Edersheim[82]

The Walls to Keep Wild Animals and Perhaps Flood Waters Out

Babylonia and Assyria, once the granaries of Asia, the garden spots of that continent, enjoying a great civilization, are now in desolation and mostly unproductive deserts. The predictions of Isaiah and Jeremiah have been fulfilled. The judgments predicted to come upon Babylon were also fulfilled long ago. ["How utterly improbable it must have sounded to the contemporaries of Isaiah and Jeremiah, that the great Babylon, this oldest metropolis Of the world, founded by Nimrod, planned to be a city on the Euphrates much larger than Paris of today, **surrounded by walls four hundred feet high, on the top of which four chariots, each drawn by four horses, could be driven side by side**; in the center a large, magnificent park an hour's walk in circumference, watered by machinery; in it the king's twelve palaces, surrounding the great temple of the sun-god with its six hundred-foot tower and its gigantic golden statue—should be converted into a heap of ruins in the midst of a desert! Who today would have any faith in a similar prophecy against Berlin or London or Paris or New York?" (Prof. Bettex.)]

—Arno C. Gaebelein[83]

The Size of the Tower

> And they built it: forty and three years [1645–1688 A.M.] were
> they building it; its breath was 203 bricks, and the height (of a
> brick) was the third of one; its height amounted to 5,433 cubit
> and 2 palms, and (the extent of one wall was) thirteen stades (and
> of the other thirty stades). [**Note:** 5,433 cubits is 8,150 feet.]
> —*Book of Jubilees* 10:21[84]

It is almost impossible to wrap our minds around what Nimrod was
building in Babel—the capital of Babylon. Alfred Edersheim states that
the size of the city was one hundred to two hundred square miles. Arno
C. Gaebelein describes twelve palaces, watering systems, a six hundred-
foot-tall temple of the sun god that was surrounded by a four hundred-
foot-tall wall that was so large the Babylonians could have chariot races on
it. Was Nimrod attempting to recapture the splendor of the lost Watcher/
Nephilim city? I believe he was. He was building the first New Atlantis that would reestablish the secrets of the Watchers embedded within
a mystery religious system to turn men away from the Living God. And
just in case God loosed judgment by a flood against his endeavors, he surrounded the entire one hundred- to two hundred-square-mile city (either
ten miles times ten miles or twenty miles times twenty miles) with a wall
large enough to hold back significant flood waters. Just in case the walls
did not hold, the people could escape into the Tower of Babel that was
8,150 feet high.

All of these heights regarding Babel are significant. The only structure
to survive the Flood of Noah was the Great Pyramid of Giza. Its construction predates the Flood by 235 years. The height of the Great Pyramid is
455 feet. The walls around Babel were just 55 feet short of its height. But
the Tower, whether you go by the height of 600 feet as stated by Gaebelein
or the 8,150 feet as recorded in the *Book of Jubilees*, it would have provided
an additional refuge if the walls failed to hold back the only judgment of
God mankind had ever seen.

This concept of taking refuge in the tower was also confirmed by the
Jewish historian, Flavius Josephus:

[Nimrod] also gradually changed the government into tyranny,—seeing no other way of turning men from the fear of God, but to bring them into a constant dependence upon his power. He also said he would be revenged on God, if he should have a mind to drown the world again; for that he would build a tower too high for the waters to be able to reach! and that he would avenge himself on God for destroying their forefathers![85]

Nimrod's Religion

He was mighty in hunting (or in prey) and in sin before God, for he was a hunter of the children of men in their languages; and he said unto them, Depart from the religion of Shem, and cleave to the institutes of Nimrod.

—*Jerusalem Targum* on Genesis 10:9

Not less than two-thirds of the population of the earth at this hour are Pagan idolaters, drivilling under the same old intoxication which came forth from Nimrod and Babylon; …Infidel, or adherents of some tainted and anti-christian faith and worship. Nor is there a kingdom or government on the face of the whole earth at this hour which does not embody and exhibit more of the spirit of Nimrod than of the spirit, commandments, and inculcations of God. All the kings of the earth, and all the governments under heaven, have more or less joined in the uncleanness of that same old Babylonian Harlot who had defiled every spot and nook of the whole inhabited world, notwithstanding that God from the beginning set His seal of wrath upon it.

—E. W. Bullinger[86]

It would take an entire book to cover extensively all of the aspects of the cradle of all pagan religions. As Dake shared regarding Nimrod, his task was to draw men away from God. The concepts within the religion and practices (institutions) Nimrod developed are still bringing darkness into the world today. I would first like to highlight some of the practices that plague our world that were part of Nimrod's mystery religion.

Human Sacrifice—All of the most powerful occult practices require human sacrifice to gain or release spiritual power. One of the purposes of the shedding of blood by the occult is for the formation of dimensional portals or stargates (as coined by Dr. Tom Horn) into other realities or universes. (Note: Although human blood is not required for opening all portals, it will open the largest and most stable ones.) There are several occult holidays that require human sacrifice. Here is a quick overview of the occult's yearly festivals:[87]

1. **Winter Solstice**—Thirteen weeks; Minor sabbath
   a. December 21—Yule
   b. December 21–22—Winter Solstice/Yule. One of the Illuminati's human sacrifice nights
   c. February 1 and 2—Candlemas and Imbolg, aka Groundhog Day. One of the Illuminati's human sacrifice nights
   d. February 14—Valentine's Day
2. **Spring Equinox**—Thirteen weeks; Minor sabbath, but does require human sacrifice
   a. March 21–22—Goddess Ostara (Note: Easter is the first Sunday after the first new moon after Ostara. March 21 is one of the Illuminati's human sacrifice nights.)
   b. April 1—All Fool's Day, precisely thirteen weeks since New Year's Day!
   c. April 19–May 1—Blood sacrifice to the beast. Fire sacrifice is required on April 19.
   d. April 30–May 1—Beltaine Festival, also called Walpurgis Night. This is the highest day on the Druidic Witch's calendar. May 1 is the Illuminati's second most sacred holiday. Human sacrifice is required.
3. **Summer Solstice**—Thirteen weeks; when the sun reaches its northernmost point in its journey across the sky
   a. June 21–22—Summer Solstice

    b. June 21—Litha is one of the Illuminati's human sacrifice nights

    c. July 4, America's Independence Day, is thirteen days after Day of Litha and sixty-six days from April 30

    d. July 19—Thirteen days before Lughnasa

    e. July 31–August 1—Lughnasa, Great Sabbat Festival. August— One of the Illuminati's human sacrifice nights

  4. Autumnal Equinox—Thirteen weeks; Minor sabbath, but does require human sacrifice

    a. September 21—Mabon, one of the Illuminati's human sacrifice nights

    b. September 21–22—Autumnal Equinox

    c. October 31—Samhain, also known as Halloween, or All Hallows' Eve. This date is the Illuminati's highest day of human sacrifice.

BRIEFING NOTE

New Insights Regarding Human Sacrifice by Occult

We have discovered that deaths through disease, accidents, and even war can count spiritually as a human sacrifice as long as they were initiated by the occultist through either spell, incantation, or sabotage. If the Holy Spirit brings such events to your attention, pleading the Blood of Jesus over the shed blood and death will neutralize any occult powers gained through these events.

Child Sacrifice—The horrid practice of child sacrifice for the gaining of prosperity and sensual pleasure is connected with the worship of Molech. When you understand the concepts behind the worship of this Babylonian god, you realize we have turned the wombs of women worldwide into altars of worship for this bloodthirsty demonic entity. Our future generations are offered up for sexual pleasure for the masses and prosperity for the Elite. Each drop of blood shed in abortion clinics slowly falls upon satanic scales to open doors into outer darkness under its weight. When these doors are opened wide enough, the exiled Watchers will return (so we can return to a time similar to that of Noah).

Apotheosis—This is the ability to become a god. Nimrod became a demigod or Nephilim without killing himself in the process. In Freemasonry and Egyptian mythology, apotheosis only occurred after death, thus illustrating their pale accomplishments compared to him. Once Nimrod returns as the Antichrist, he will promise the Elite the final step in reincarnation: transcendence. They will step off the reincarnation cycle into apotheosis—godhood.

Ascension—This is passing from this physical plane to become a spiritual god or ascended master. In Babylonian mythology, after Nimrod's death, he ascended to become the sun god.

Reincarnation—After his death, Nimrod ascended to become the sun god, but later was reincarnated as Tammuz. This is also mythologized in Egypt as Osiris/Horus. Reincarnation became the chief mechanism of the occult and the Luciferian Elite. Their task to create a one-world, luciferian empire would be spread over many generations. To die in the pursuit of Lucifer's plans would ensure an elevated position on the next go-around on the reincarnation wheel. Doc Marquis also shared how this ideology justifies human sacrifice within the minds of the Illuminati. When an individual becomes a human sacrifice, he (or she) becomes a part of Lucifer's plan. This ensures that he will be promoted to a more enlightened state in his next life. It is just another version of "for the greater good" justification that has been claimed by dictators and despots throughout time.

Incestuous Relationships—In Babylon, Nimrod married Semiramis, his mother. Even when Nimrod supposedly returned as Tammuz, he remained her consort (lover). Not only was Semiramis the "Mother of God" twice over, but she was the continued lover of both. In the Egyptian version, Osiris (Nimrod) married Isis (his sister). It is interesting to note that Friedrich Nietzsche wrote extensively about the *übermensch*, or superman, which was beyond the concepts of good and evil (which inspired

Hitler). He had a hatred for the God of the Bible; this hatred stemmed from his burning desire for his own sister to become his sexual mate. The society of his time drew its moral compass from the Word of God, and he could never realize his own carnal desires. In the highest ranks of the Elite, incestuous sexual relationships are used to create greater spiritual power and enlightenment.

Pedophilia—Semiramis began her love affair with Nimrod while he was yet a baby. The origin of the cute flying baby with bow and arrow known as Cupid originated with the infant Nimrod. His sexual energies were so great that his own mother desired him, even while he was still feeding upon her breasts. Pedophilia is still an important aspect of occult sexual magic today. I have already shared about the use of Transyuggothian Magic (chapter 3). This practice was a vital part of the magical disciplines of Aleister Crowley, who became the herald of the "age of the fascinating child" (i.e., sexual fascination with children), which he proclaimed would replace Christianity. It has been reported that Crowley performed magical workings in Cairo, Egypt, and New York City and loosed the spirit behind this new age of pedophilia. It should be noted that an explosion of pedophilia occurred in New York after that time and spread across the United States from there. In many of the Middle Eastern cultures, pedophilia is also practiced. I have personally heard reports from some of my students that served in the military in Afghanistan that young boys are used for sexual pleasure, while women are used for having children by the men in that country.

Another symbol of Nimrod is the heart symbol we use today. This heart shape did not originate with the shape of the human heart; rather, its design came from the silhouette of a woman's backside while she is bent over. In other words, there was not a woman he could not seduce.

Bestiality—I have already shared from an ancient Canaanite tablet how a Watcher had intercourse with an ox and produced something similar to a Minotaur. Within occultism, this practice of sex with animals is both a way to honor the ancient gods and to achieve spiritual power. I have found several references to this practice in ancient Babylon and Egypt.

Bestiality in Babylon: Archaeological findings demonstrate that bestiality was practiced in Babylonia, the ancient Empire in Mesopotamia, which prospered in the third millennium BC. In his famous code of Hammurabi, King Hammurabi (1955–1913 BC) proclaimed death for any person engaging in bestiality. At other times, according to Waine, during the spring fertility rites of Babylon, dogs and other animals were used for maintaining a constant orgy condition for seven days and nights.[88]

Bestiality in Egypt: The ancient Egyptians worshiped Gods with animal shapes almost exclusively in the predynastic period before about 3000 BC. Animal-human sexual contacts are occasionally portrayed on the tombs, and bestiality was recorded in Egyptian hieroglyphics as far back as 3000 BC. Several kings and queens had a reputation of engaging in bestiality. Most famous was Cleopatra, who was said to have had a box filled with bees which she had placed against her genitals for stimulation, similar to a vibrator.

Egyptian men often had sexual intercourse with cattle or any other large domesticated animal, while the women resorted to dogs. Sexual contact with apes was further reported for both men and women, and, most interestingly, the Egyptians are reported to have mastered the art of sexual congress with the crocodile. This was accomplished by turning the creature onto its back, rendering it incapable of resisting penetration. This form of copulation was believed to bring prosperity and restore the potency of men. The Egyptians were also known to engage in worshipful bestiality with the Apis bull in Memphis, Egypt and with goats at the Temple of Mendes. The goats were further used as a cure for nymphomaniacs.[89]

From secular humanism to Freemasonry to every pagan religion, these concepts have been woven into their religious/philosophical DNA and have tacitly influenced their thoughts and actions.

Now you understand why the occult seeks to do things behind closed doors and requires initiation into their orders with terrifying oaths to keep their secrets. It is not only for the knowledge of how to build nations, sway populations to their will, and garner wealth and power; it is to hide from the general public these practices that create the spiritual empowerment for their endeavors.

The Tower of Babel

And the whole earth was of one language, and of one speech.

And it came to pass, as they journeyed from the east, that they found a plain in the land of Shinar; and they dwelt there.

And they said one to another, Go to, let us make brick, and burn them throughly. And they had brick for stone, and slime had they for morter.

And they said, Go to, let us build us a city and a tower, whose top may reach unto heaven; and let us make us a name, lest we be scattered abroad upon the face of the whole earth.

And the LORD came down to see the city and the tower, which the children of men builded.

And the LORD said, Behold, the people is one, and they have all one language; and this they begin to do: and now nothing will be restrained from them, which they have imagined to do.

Go to, let us go down, and there confound their language, that they may not understand one another's speech.

So the LORD scattered them abroad from thence upon the face of all the earth: and they left off to build the city.

Therefore is the name of it called Babel; because the LORD did there confound the language of all the earth: and from thence did the LORD scatter them abroad upon the face of all the earth. (Genesis 11:1–9)

In writing this portion of chapter 4, I really struggled with what aspects of the Tower of Babel story to examine. I could easily dive into the rich minutia contained within this story and miss the main points that we need to explore. So, before I examine this unfinished conspiracy, let's look at some basic information regarding the Tower of Babel.

1. **The gathering**: Nimrod gathered the people together in direct defiance to God's instruction for Noah to replenish the earth. Men working together also served as a mechanism to build a society in which men need not walk with the Creator to survive and thrive. They developed reliance upon one another (secular system) and developed gods most likely based upon the legend of the Watchers and the Nephilim.

2. **The construction**: This tower/altar was made of bricks (more on this shortly) and sealed with bitumen. Bitumen is asphalt in its natural state. This substance would have made the tower waterproof.[91] Again, this reinforces the concept that they were preparing themselves to withstand another judgment flood.

3. **Make a name and prevent scattering**: I will address the concept of making a name for the citizens of Babylon a little later in this chapter. Their refusal to scatter shows their absolute determination to defy the instruction of God.

4. **The symbolic meaning of the tower**: Dr. Edward F. Murphy, in his *Handbook for Spiritual Warfare,* states the following:

> Again this supports our spiritual warfare interpretation of the sin of Babel leading to God's judgment. Satan, "the god of this world," building on the corrupt flesh of man (his pride) and his worldly ambitions, was the spirit behind the Tower of Babel. Wenham says, "Throughout Scripture Babylon is seen as the embodiment of human pride and godlessness that must attract the judgment of almighty God." *It is also the symbol of the rejection of the true God and the creation of god systems which are created by men to meet their own selfish wants.*[91] (Emphasis added)

So the tower served as an occult symbol of the rejection of the Creator and the establishment of a god system that catered to the sinful/carnal desires of fallen man.

5. **The power of being one:** The people had a singular focus of building a civilization that would draw men from the Creator. God said that
the people had one language, and they were completely unified in their
Babylonian work. Because of their unity, God said that they could accomplish anything they envisioned.

An Uncompleted Occult Work

The Tower of Babel stands in the sands of time as both a prophetic and
occult lightning rod. God chose to include the story of this tower within
Holy Writ, because it will add to our understanding of the final days
before Jesus returns. When God confused the tower builders' language
and stopped the progress of the tower's construction, it also served as
an incomplete aspiration for all divisions within the occult world that
demanded the completion of the original work.

Most biblical commentators believe that the Tower of Babel was in
the shape of a *ziggurat*. The abrupt intervention by Almighty God would
also suggest that the structure was never completed. When you look at the
shape of a ziggurat and that of the unfinished pyramid on the back of the
US dollar bill, you will notice that they are very similar (especially since
Nimrod did not complete the tower).

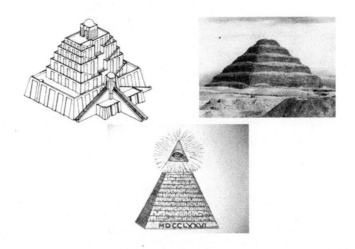

This shape is also known as a **trapezoid**. The trapezoid is a specific geometric shape used within the occult to attract both demonic energy and demons themselves. You will find this shape in old-style homes that were similar in design to the one used in the 1960s TV show, *The Munsters,* as it was associated with haunted houses. Another name for the trapezoid is the frustum. I believe this second term associated with this shape illustrates the frustration of all those associated with Babylon, because their great work remains unfinished. It is also interesting to note that the Masonic altar is trapezoidal in shape. Like all things within a Masonic temple, this could be a hidden identification to the work they are all laboring to accomplish.

Part of biblical conspiratorial history is that the spirit of Babylon is still laboring behind the scenes today to complete the work started by Nimrod at the Tower of Babel.

This Elite desire to finish what Nimrod started is seen in the poster developed for the European Union (EU) announcing its formation. This poster is filled will occult significance.

1. **The Tower of Babel chosen as a symbol for unifying Europe:** Isn't it interesting that the leaders of the European Union chose the only symbol within human history that caused intervention by God Himself? Not only is the symbol used, but the leaders declare that they have overcome the judgment of God (confusion of the languages) by providing one voice for the people of many tongues!

2. **Eleven Baphomets (upside-down stars):** First, the star is a symbol of Nimrod. Within the occult belief system and use of symbols, the star is used for many purposes. In the *Dictionary of Mysticism*, we find that the star "is considered by occultists to be the most potent means of conjuring spirits. When a single point of the star points upward, it is regarded as the sign of good and a means to conjure benevolent spirits; when the single point points down and a pair of points are on top, it is a sign of evil and is used to conjure powers of evil."[92]

So the EU poster is announcing a working of dark magic for evil. The numbers eleven, twenty-two, and thirty-three are important in Masonic endeavors. The number eleven announces the beginning of the work, the number twenty-two then adds action to the undertaking, and the number thirty-three declares its completion. This poster was announcing the beginning of a work of dark magic to complete the unfinished Tower of Nimrod.

BRIEFING NOTE

About Bricks

While the Tower of Babel was made of bricks, their use for an altar to God is forbidden in Scripture (Deuteronomy 27:5). God requires uncut stones for His altar because it represents the body of Christ and the power of our sanctified uniqueness in its construction. Nimrod and the spirit of Babylon demand conformity, uniformity, and interchangeability. With this in mind, you can now better understand many of the current political winds within the Progressive and Socialistic Movements worldwide—from wealth redistribution to removing the distinction of the sexes toward a unisex philosophy. We must all conform and be interchangeable, so we can serve as bricks in the new Tower of Babel that the Illuminati Elite are building.

3. The People in the Poster: Notice the people in the poster. (If you cannot see them well, you can simply do an Internet search for "EU Tower of Babel Poster" to get a better look.) The people are brick shaped. This is the declaration that the end-time Tower of Babel will not be made from physical bricks, but from people who have been conformed to the Babylonian mindset.

The symbolism of the Tower of Babel did not just stop with the poster announcing its formation. The EU's Parliament also reflects this same concept.

The Tower of Babel Connected to a Mark

In his work, *The Apocalypse: A Series of Special Lectures on the Revelation of Jesus Christ,* Joseph Seiss provided a possible connection to the Tower of Babel and the mark of the Beast.

The Bible says that it was further arranged for the people to make for themselves *"a name,"*—a *Sem,* token, sign, banner, ensign, or **mark of confederation**, fellowship, and organized unity, as an undivided people, lest they should become dispersed over the earth into separate societies. (Compare Jer. 13:11; 33:9; Ezek. 39:13; Zeph. 3:20.) **Against God they had determined to hold together, and they wished to have a badge, standard, something by which they could be known, and in which they could all glory and rejoice as the centre and crown of their unity.** That *Sem,* or *Sema,* was to be a mark of consolidated greatness, a loftiness and pride to them; that is, in the language of the time, a *Sema-Rama.* Thus we have the name of the mythic *Semiramis,* the Dove-Goddess, which was the ensign of all the Assyrian princes, and which figures so largely as Ashtaroth, Astarte, the heavenly Aphrodite, and Venus. Semiramis is said to have been the wife of Nimrod; so that the *Sem,* or **token**, of the Nimrodic confederation was probably the image of his wife, with a dove upon her head, **with wings spread like the horns of the new moon**. This, in the language of the time, would be called *Sema-Rama,* because the great *Sem,* name, or token, of the combination against being scattered abroad. The symbol of such a name or confederation would naturally and almost necessarily take the place of a god, and become the holy mother, the great heavenly protectress, the giver of greatness and prosperity to those rallying under it.[93] (Emphasis added)

Over time, this symbol for Semiramis was reduced to the horn-shaped crescent moon. In occultism, the crescent moon always represents Semiramis or the goddess, and the star represents Nimrod or the hunter god. The crescent moon is also connected to the religion of Islam and its use of the name "Allah." Biblical researchers in Australia have found the following in their research of the origins of the moon god known as Allah:

According to Middle East scholar E. M. Wherry, whose translation of the Koran is still used today, in pre-Islamic times Allah-worship, as well as the worship of Baal, were both astral religions in that they involved the worship of the sun, the moon, and the stars

In ancient Arabia, the sun-god was viewed as a female goddess and the moon as the male god. As has been pointed out by many scholars as Alfred Guilluame, the Moon god was called by various names, one of which was Allah.

The name **Allah** was used as the *personal* name of the Moon god, in addition to the other titles that could be given to him.

Allah, the Moon god, was married to the sun goddess. Together they produced three goddesses who were called "**the daughters of Allah.**" These three goddesses were called **Al-Lat, Al-Uzza**, and **Manat**.

The daughters of Allah, along with Allah and the sun goddess were viewed as "high" gods. That is, they were viewed as being at the top of the pantheon of Arabian deities.[94]

Today in America, Christians are being told that Allah is simply the Arabic name for the God of the Bible, but, when examined properly, these claims are clearly false. I believe that Islam (with its explosive growth worldwide) is a part of the end-game plans of the Elite to complete Nimrod's unfinished work.

A Prophecy Established in Europe's Name

Europe draws its name from the mythological story of the seduction of Europa by the Greek god Zeus. Wikipedia provides an overview of this story:

The mythographers tell that Zeus was enamored of Europa and decided to seduce or ravish her, the two being near-equivalent in Greek myth. He transformed himself into a tame white bull and mixed in with her father's herds. While Europa and her helpers were gathering flowers, she saw the bull, caressed his flanks, and eventually got onto his back. Zeus took that opportunity and ran to the sea and swam, with her on his back, to the island of Crete. He then revealed his true identity, and Europa became the first queen of Crete. Zeus gave her a necklace made by Hephaestus and three additional gifts: Talos, Laelaps and a javelin that never missed. Zeus later re-created the shape of the white bull in the stars, which is now known as the constellation Taurus. Some readers interpret as manifestations of this same bull the Cretan beast that was encountered by Heracles, the Marathonian Bull slain by Theseus (and that fathered the Minotaur). Roman mythology adopted the tale of the *Raptus*, also known as "The Abduction of Europa" and "The Seduction of Europa," substituting the god Jupiter for Zeus.[95]

There are many versions of this myth. In some, Zeus raped Europa and she gave birth to this union while still in the water. I found it interesting that, in most renditions of this myth, the horns on the bull formed a crescent moon very similar to the bulls of Egyptian mythology. Could the Elite and their guiding spirits be planning to bring down Western civilization in Europe through the religion whose sign is the crescent moon? Can the same thing be planned for America?

Infectious Seed of the Watchers throughout History

Babylon becomes a symbol of a fallen world power, exemplified in Nimrod, later in Nebuchadnezzar, and finally in the sea beast of the book of Revelation.

—Robert James Utley[96]

The rebuilding of Babylon began around 612 BC, after the defeat of the Assyrian empire by Nebuchadnezzar. I endeavored to find Nebuchadnezzar's family tree, but my research turned up little. I was able to find one reference by Alfred Edersheim: "Similarly, when Nebuchadnez-zar proposed to ascend into heaven, and to exalt his throne above the stars, and be like the Most High, the Bath Qol replied to this grandson of Nimrod."[97]

It is very possible that Nebuchadnezzar was a descendant of Nim-rod—a direct line to the family business of Ham. He was also the high priest of the mystery religion in Babylon and its king. (The same was true for the emperors of Rome.) He had full access to the knowledge passed on to mankind through the Watchers.

With the reconstruction of Babylon by Nebuchadnezzar, the capital city became one of the Seven Wonders of the Ancient World. During his reign, he was used by Almighty God to bring judgment on Judea for refusing to honor God by observing the seventh-year Sabbath rest for the land. The southern nation of the divided kingdom missed seventy Sab-bath years, and God exiled it to Babylon for exactly seventy years.

While Daniel was exiled in Babylon, the king had a dream but could not remember it. He demanded that his wise men tell him both the dream and the interpretation. Here is Daniel's interpretation:

> This is the dream; and we will tell the interpretation thereof before the king.
>
> Thou, O king, art a king of kings: for the God of heaven hath given thee a kingdom, power, and strength, and glory.
>
> And wheresoever the children of men dwell, the beasts of the field and the fowls of the heaven hath he given into thine hand, and hath made thee ruler over them all. Thou art this head of gold.
>
> And after thee shall arise another kingdom inferior to thee, and another third kingdom of brass, which shall bear rule over all the earth.
>
> And the fourth kingdom shall be strong as iron: forasmuch as iron breaketh in pieces and subdueth all things: and as iron that breaketh all these, shall it break in pieces and bruise.
>
> And whereas thou sawest the feet and toes, part of potters' clay, and part of iron, the kingdom shall be divided; but there shall

be in it of the strength of the iron, forasmuch as thou sawest the iron mixed with miry clay.

And as the toes of the feet were part of iron, and part of clay, so the kingdom shall be partly strong, and partly broken.

And whereas thou sawest iron mixed with miry clay, they shall mingle themselves with the seed of men: but they shall not cleave one to another, even as iron is not mixed with clay.

And in the days of these kings shall the God of heaven set up a kingdom, which shall never be destroyed: and the kingdom shall not be left to other people, but it shall break in pieces and consume all these kingdoms, and it shall stand for ever.

Forasmuch as thou sawest that the stone was cut out of the mountain without hands, and that it brake in pieces the iron, the brass, the clay, the silver, and the gold; the great God hath made known to the king what shall come to pass hereafter: and the dream is certain, and the interpretation thereof sure. (Daniel 2:36–45)

The picture here is generally the way Protestant theologians have interpreted this vision with the alignment of history:

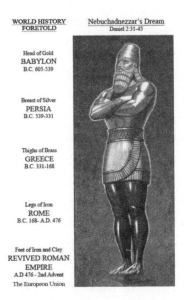

WORLD HISTORY FORETOLD   Nebuchadnezzar's Dream
Daniel 2:31-45

Head of Gold
BABYLON
B.C. 605-539

Breast of Silver
PERSIA
B.C. 539-331

Thighs of Brass
GREECE
B.C. 331-168

Legs of Iron
ROME
B.C. 168- A.D. 476

Feet of Iron and Clay
REVIVED ROMAN EMPIRE
A.D 476 - 2nd Advent
The European Union

Nebuchadnezzar built his empire upon the esoteric knowledge (or knowledge of the Watchers) that resided on the ark with Ham and his family line. Alfred Edersheim alluded to the fact that he was a descendant of Nimrod. So, it was not just the flowing of various kingdoms throughout human history, but the historical stream of the doctrines of the Watchers that empowered the development of those physical kingdoms.

Historically, our Protestant theologians and ministers have interpreted the "Revised Roman Empire" as an expression of the end-time ascension of the Roman Catholic Church, with the Pope as the Antichrist. My personal research library is filled with classic works, from Charles Spurgeon to B. H. Carroll, that take this position.

What I want to do next is not establish prophetic doctrine, but a thought process that allows the development of an academic/theological discussion. In the tracing of these empires, the Christian community has completely left out the Ottoman Empire. The Ottoman Empire was a Turkish Islamic kingdom established in AD 1299 and that lasted until AD 1922. How does this calculate into the vision?

Breast of silver: We look at the "breast of silver" on the statue and just see the "Persian Empire" title. Yet this empire or mystery religion-based civilization was made of up two peoples: the Medes and the Persians. The arms could have represented these two peoples working together under one esoteric vision.

Legs of iron: Is it possible that the two "legs of iron" represent two peoples with one esoteric flow—the Roman Empire and the Ottoman Empire? After the falls of both empires, their principles continued in religious institutions: for Rome, it was the Roman Catholic Church and for the Ottoman Empire, it was the continuation of Islam (the Ottoman Empire was Sharia-based). Once you understand the mystery religions, you clearly see currents of it in both institutions.

With Europe (the territory included in the Revised Roman Empire) quickly becoming Islamic, we may need to revisit our historical eschatological positions to include the dynamic changes that are occurring worldwide.

In 2009, Joel Richardson released his ground-breaking book, *The*

Islamic Antichrist: The Shocking Truth about the Real Nature of the Beast.
He took the unique position of studying the last-days teachings of Islam.
He approached his study with integrity and wanted it to accurately represent the full body of teaching within this religion. From a Christian point
of view, it was shocking. If you take the book of Revelation and turn it
upside down, you would have the Islamic theology of the end times.

Islam is looking for the Mahdi to come and bring the world under
the banner of Islam and Sharia law. This Mahdi will appear after a great
conflict that threatens to set the world on fire (perhaps World War III).
But the Mahdi will not come alone. Richardson shares:

The Unholy Partnership of the Mahdi and the Muslim Jesus

Likewise, in the Islamic narrative of the last days, we do not find a
lone character coming to rescue the world, instead we find a team.
We find both the Mahdi and the Muslim Jesus. And, as in the case
of the Antichrist and the False Prophet, we find that one clearly
fills a supporting role while the other leads. While the Mahdi is
clearly described as "the vice regent (caliph) of Allah," Jesus is
described as one who will "espouse the cause of the Mahdi" and
"follow him." The partnership between the Mahdi and Jesus is
one of a leader and his subordinate. And as we have already seen,
and will continue to see, the partnership of the Mahdi and Jesus is
indeed an unholy partnership—particularly if you are not a Muslim and have no intention of becoming one. If this is the case,
then you are marked for death—plain and simple.[98]

The Luciferian Elite are positioning Islam to become the next favored
religion to influence the world. I believe they are convinced that they can
contain and control Islam the same way they have historically controlled
much of Christianity. But Daniel tells us that it does not work out so well.

I considered the horns, and, behold, there came up among them
another little horn, before whom there were three of the first horns

plucked up by the roots: and, behold, in this horn were eyes like the eyes of man, and a mouth speaking great things. (Daniel 7:8)

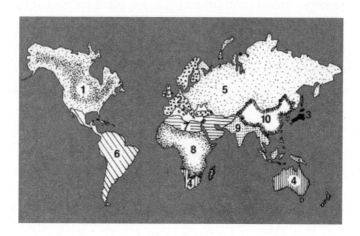

When you connect this to Revelation 13, you realize that the horns of Daniel 7 are the ten horns with crowns or ten kings. In my own personal study, I have come to believe that these represent the presiding leaders/kings the Elite have set up over the ten financial regions on our planet. As Doc Marquis has said many times, "They are looking for the final great despot king" to bring them the final information for ascension off the reincarnation wheel into godhood. They will be betrayed by the very one to whom they have lent their financial and occult powers. Three of them will be utterly destroyed by the Antichrist/Mahdi, and the rest will fall in line with his plans.

In the next few years, we could see the fusion of the Roman Catholic Church and Islam. The mythology of Europa may play out before our very eyes. The crescent-moon-horned bull (Islam) will either seduce or rape Europa (formerly under Catholic control) to give birth to something new: The Revised Roman Empire with a horrific version of Islam-Christianity, with the Pope (who is the regent of Christ, according to Catholic doctrine) serving as a False Prophet and new herald of Islam who will perform miracles like those found in the Gospels. He will team with the Islamic messiah (the Mahdi) to bring the entire world under the banner of Islam. Those who refuse will be beheaded.

Somehow in this mix, the Nephilim will return as an expression of power within this blending of Islam and apostate Christianity. The Mahdi himself will be the return of Nimrod to fulfill his work at the Tower of Babel. He will be the transhumanists' dream and the biblical Christians' nightmare.

So we end up with two legs of iron representing two streams of esoteric wisdom that began with Nimrod, reached a certain zenith with Nebuchadnezzar, and will resurface as the power behind the Revised Roman Empire. Each foot is mingled with the clay of Nephilim influence and each foot has five toes—a false grace that leads to damnation rather than salvation. (Note: The total of ten toes can also represent the ten regions into which the Elite have divided the world.)

Conclusion

Why do the heathen rage, and the people imagine a vain thing?
The kings of the earth set themselves, and the rulers take counsel together, against the LORD, and against his anointed, saying,
Let us break their bands asunder, and cast away their cords from us. (Psalms 2:1–3)

With all that we have covered in the last three chapters, I hope you can better understand the first three verses of Psalm 2. The heathen and the kings counsel were established in Babel, the original capital of Babylon. While they reach for the knowledge the serpent promised in the garden, they seek to break asunder (or destroy) the commandments of God and the salvation that can only come through His Anointed One. As the work continues through the efforts of the Luciferian Elite today, the attacks on God's Word and the gospel will increase dramatically.

chapter five

The Unfinished Work of Nimrod

Part 1: A Basic Primer

"Listen carefully, Feyd," the Baron said.
"Observe the plans within plans within plans."
—Sci-fi novel *Dune*, Frank Herbert

I n the last chapter, I hinted at the fact that the objective of the Luciferian Elite (to include all aspects of the mystery religion and its systems) is really all about completing the work that Nimrod began. Only when they reach a certain advanced point within this Babylonian working will the great despotic King Nimrod return to put the final pieces into place, complete his work, and reward his faithful with the knowledge of godhood. This work flows through the currents of history. Its polluted stream runs from Babylon to the pharaohs of Egypt, to the emperors of Rome, to the kings of Europe, and even to the presidents of the United States. For the work to build progressively within society, it must control every facet of civilization: from finances to politics to religion. Nothing must be overlooked.

Frank Herbert had insights on how the Elite operate and encoded this belief in his sci-fi novel, *Dune*.[99] Several times throughout the novel, when the plans for the emperor and some leaders of the noble houses are revealed, he refers to them as "plans within plans within plans." I think the apostle Paul provides the same insight regarding Lucifer:

> Finally, my brethren, be strong in the Lord, and in the power of his might.
> Put on the whole armour of God, that ye may be able to stand against the wiles of the devil. (Ephesians 6:10–11)

Paul uses the Greek word *methodeia* (μεθοδεία; meth-od-i'-ah), which can be defined as "cunning arts, deceit, craft, and trickery."[100] The *Theological Lexicon of the New Testament* expands on this basic definition:

> This noun is unknown in Greek before Eph 4:14; 6:11. It is derived from the verb *methodeuō*, "follow closely," then "pursue by devious means," hence "capture, trick, seduce." The noun *methodos* is also used in both positive and negative senses. In the papyri, *methodeia* does not appear before AD 421, and it is always used in the administrative and financial sense of "method" of collecting taxes. But in Eph 4:14, it refers to the shrewdness (*panourgia*) of the false teachers, whose "devices" lead people into error (*planē*), and in Eph 6:11 it has to do with the devil's ambushes or ensnaring maneuvers. **So this *methodeia* can be defined as the well-thought-out, methodical art of leading astray, what we would call "machinations."**[101] (Emphasis added)

We could also add to this definition the term "stratagems."[102]

Therefore, the wiles of the devil are defined as methodically planned and implemented machinations or stratagems to first lead astray and then entrap the world. In other words, "plans within plans within plans."

The Luciferian Elite's system of occult philosophy consists of many layers (similar to an onion) within the organization, within its planning, and even within the meaning and purposes behind its beliefs. Grand Commander Albert Pike shares this truth regarding the Masonic Lodges:

Masonry, like all the Religions, all the Mysteries, Hermeticism, and Alchemy, conceals its secrets from all except the Adepts and Sages, or the Elect, and use false explanations and misinterpretations of its symbols to mislead those who deserve only to be misled; to conceal the Truth, which it calls Light, from them, and to draw them away from it.[103]

I have referred to this onion analogy many times with my students over the years. Its outer layer is pure white, but as you peel off each of the layers, they gradually become darker. The center is completely black and is pure evil; only a few individuals know the complete plan.

You may ask: Why do the Elite use such secrecy and hidden levels? I think we find the answer in the demise of Nimrod. In the traditional history of Nimrod, his uncle Shem had gathered just men to kill Nimrod for his war against Almighty God. It is said that Shem cut Nimrod into pieces (similar to the death and killing of Osiris) and sent pieces of his body to the major cities of Babylon as a warning not to follow his idolatry. Alexander Hislop continues this narrative in his book, *The Two Babylons:*

Now when Shem had so powerfully wrought upon the minds of men as to induce them to make a terrible example of the great Apostate, and when that Apostate's dismembered limbs were sent to the chief cities, where no doubt his system had been established, it will be readily perceived that, in these circumstances, if idolatry was to continue—if, above all, it was to take a step in advance, it was indispensable that it should operate in secret. The terror of an execution, inflicted on one so mighty as Nimrod, made it needful that, for some time to come at least, the extreme of caution should be used. In these circumstances, then, began, there can hardly be a doubt, that system of "Mystery," which, having Babylon for its centre, has spread over the world. In these Mysteries, under the seal of secrecy and the sanction of an oath, and by means of all the fertile resources of magic, men were gradually led back to all the idolatry that had been publicly suppressed, *while new features were added to that idolatry that made it still more blasphemous than before.*[104] (Emphasis added)

As horrific as circumstances were under the leadership of Nimrod in Babylon, I cannot imagine how new features were added that were even more blasphemous. But I believe that, historically, Reverend Hislop is correct.

Mystery Babylon and Government Secrets

The system the military and governments use to keep secrets is based on the esoteric layering of the mystery religions. When I served in the military, one of my posts required a secret security clearance. After the vetting process was finalized, I had to sign documentation that I would keep all information secret, would only reveal the information to those of secret clearance or higher, and only to those who had a need to know. I had to learn about the various clearances, the compartmentalization of those secrets, and the levels "above top secret." One of the more interesting concepts was **compartmentalization**. A select few men and women with "above top secret" clearance reviewed information within a briefing room. The information could be discussed freely within the room, as long as everyone had clearance and a need to know. Once the men and women left that room, the information could not be discussed for any reason—not even with each other. When they left the room, the project and information ceased to exist. This is the way the Game of Thrones is played and how secrets are kept. For many in government and the military (as well as the occult), few have the big picture. They are only provided the piece of the puzzle they are required to implement.

The Devil in the Details

The enemy loves complicated things—"plans within plans within plans." In his plan's complexity, only a demonically charged mind can make sense of it, while the average person is left clueless. But thank God for the Holy

Spirit, who can shed light on Lucifer's tactics and empower the believer to step beyond those traps. This is why the apostle Paul calls for believers to be strong in the LORD and the power of His might before he reveals the devil's wiles.

Here is a mind map that includes *some* of the layers of control Lucifer has built upon this planet. (Notice multiple overlapping on the various plans of the Elite.)

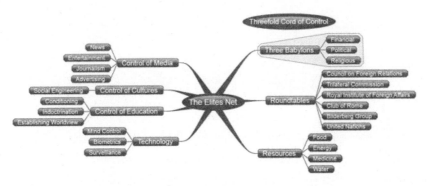

The "Three Babylons" (financial, political, and religious) serve as the main structure that oversees all other aspects of the Elite machinery for absolute control of mankind.

The Three-Cord Approach to Nimrod's Work

> He was mighty in hunting (or in prey) and in sin before God, for he was a hunter of the children of men in their languages; and he said unto them, Depart from the religion of Shem, and cleave to the institutes of Nimrod.
> —*Jerusalem Targum* on Genesis 10:9

To understand the above statement from the *Jerusalem Targum* regarding the plans of Nimrod, we need to understand how God and His kingdom works. God never meant for us to compartmentalize our lives into personal, religious, financial, etc. The concept of compartmentalization of life was first invented within Babylon and then embedded into the Greco-Roman mindset. Western civilization (to include most of the Church's worldview) is based on the Greco-Roman mindset that first flowed from Babylon, and it was as much a part of the statue in Daniel's interpretation of Nebuchadnezzar's vision as the kingdoms were.

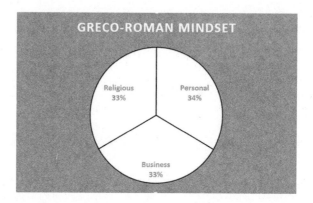

The Greco-Roman mindset divides all aspects of our lives and compartmentalizes (or separates) them, never allowing them to bleed over and affect another part or section. In fact, the unconstitutional concept of the separation of church and state (which is interpreted as "there is no room for religious practice in public life") is drawn from this pagan mindset. This philosophical divide exists within all Western civilization, and it is not an American phenomenon.

When this concept is brought into Christian practices, it creates a philosophical barrier between God in our religious life and that of our personal and business life. When God is excluded from the other areas of our lives, by default, Babylon exerts the influence that only God should have in the life of a believer.

The Hebraic mindset is a model of life built upon the stories and teachings of the Torah in the Old Testament. This model was taught by God to Abraham, Moses, and the prophets. Instead of the various aspects of our lives being divided into compartments that do not influence the others, the Hebrews viewed them as ingredients to be blended together and harmonized with God and His kingdom.

The religion of Shem was later expressed in the call of Abraham.

And when Abram was ninety years old and nine, the LORD appeared to Abram, and said unto him, I am the Almighty God; walk before me, and be thou perfect.

And I will make my covenant between me and thee, and will multiply thee exceedingly. (Genesis 17:1–2)

God called Abram out of Babylon to walk with Him, much the same way that the Holy Spirit calls us to salvation through the preaching of the gospel. To see verse 1 of Genesis 17 through Hebraic eyes (so we can understand our calling, too), we will need to examine the original Hebrew text.

"Almighty God": God reveals an aspect of Himself in the name He shares with Abraham: *El Shaddai*. Dake provides some insights into this powerful name.

[**Almighty God**] Hebrew: *'El* (HSN-<H410>) *Shaddai* (HSN-<H7706>), Almighty God. It is found 218 times. *'El* (HSN-<H410>) signifies "Strong One" and *Shaddai* (HSN-<H7706>), "the Breasted One." This pictures God as the Strong-Nourisher, Strength-Giver, Satisfier, and All-Bountiful, the Supplier of the needs of His people. Its first occurrence here reveals God as the Fruitful-One who was to multiply Abraham abundantly; the Life-Giver who was to restore life to Abraham and Sarah who were as good as dead where offspring was concerned. Through Him, they would have future offspring as the dust (Gen. 13:16), stars (Gen. 15:5), and sand in number (Gen. 22:17).[105]

We need to understand how important it was for Abram to realize, at that time, that God was going to be his complete source of strength and the bountiful supplier in his life. God had called him to leave Babylon spiritually, financially, and in every other area. God was calling him to leave behind the "Institutes of Nimrod" to walk in something completely new and different.

"Walk Before Me": This phrase is derived from one Hebrew word: *Halak* (haw-lak'), which means "to walk, to depart, to live."[106] There are two important things here to note: (1) God was restoring something Adam lost in the garden—he walked with God in the cool of the evening; and (2) this walking with God would include departing from Babylon into something greater in God and His kingdom (we must walk away from something before we can walk into something new).

"Be Thou Perfect": In English, this part of the promise of God sounds almost frightening. Our American ears hear it as "you better straighten up and fly right!" However, the Hebrew phrase means something completely different. This phrase comes from the Hebrew word *tamiym* (taw-meem'), which is a powerful promise. *Tamiym* means, "to be complete, entire, whole, unimpaired, having integrity, to be according to truth, and to be healthful."[107] The first time I saw this I thought, "WOW Lord, sign me up!" Then the Holy Spirit reminded me that every believer already has this calling and promise. This is why the apostle Paul used the example of Abraham so many times in teaching salvation to Gentiles. Like Abraham, we have a shared calling to hear the voice of God instructing us to depart from Babylon and walk with Him. This calling happens at the point of salvation. After we are born again, we must depart from the Babylonian system and learn to walk with God in a new and entirely different kingdom. As we mature in our walk with Him, He begins the process of making us "complete, entire, whole, unimpaired, having integrity, to be according to truth, and to be healthful." If we are not experiencing that, we have either not left Babylon or we have not been taught how to walk with God. When I see what God tells the Church in the book of Revelation, I have come to believe that both are true.

And I heard another voice from heaven, saying, Come out of her, my people, that ye be not partakers of her sins, and that ye receive not of her plagues.

For her sins have reached unto heaven, and God hath remembered her iniquities. (Revelation 18:4–5)

It would appear that the influence of Babylon so permeates society in the last days that God must warn His people to come out of it before He judges it. It is my prayer that this "Kingdom Intelligence Briefing" will serve as both a call to "come out" and an eye salve to clear your vision for differentiation between God's kingdom and Babylon.

The Institutes of Nimrod

Nimrod developed systems to replace man's walk with God in every aspect of life with absolute dependence upon those systems of control (system vs. relationship). I believe there are three basic facets of Babylon or, as many prophecy teachers have designated, the "Three Babylons."

In the last days, God will judge these three interlocking Babylons (or Babylonian systems). They are:

- Financial Babylon
- Political Babylon
- Religious Babylon

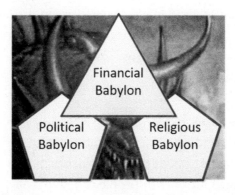

Let's define each of these for the sake of clarity.

Financial Babylon: Financial Babylon controls not only the finances of the world, but any resource that can translate into wealth: precious metals, gems, energy (oil, electric, nuclear power, etc.), water, food, medicine, illegal drugs, media, education, and even people (remember, in Babylon, people are considered a resource).

This financial control is established through an international, centralized banking system operated solely by the Elite. Nations no longer manage their currencies; they are handled through this central banking system. The Federal Reserve is no more controlled by the government than is Federal Express. Doc Marquis points out in his video series, *The Secrets of the Illuminati,* that all the nations involved in the War on Terror or those that are part of the Arab Spring (i.e., Iraq, Afghanistan, Libya, Syria, etc.) refused to become a part of the international, centralized banking system of the Rothschild dynasty. The turmoil within those nations is designed to change the governmental regimes to ones that will be more compliant to the control of their finances by Financial Babylon (with the side benefit of inflating the price of oil, another control mechanism). Usually, the first part of nation building that the US assists with, after the change in regimes, is the establishment of a centralized banking system.

I also believe that Financial Babylon is the most powerful of the three. Finances build political parties, fuel elections, sway politicians' votes, control who gains media coverage, and even control which ministries move into prominence and whose messages are suppressed (although the Internet is currently giving voice to many faithful ministries today). This influence is so pervasive in the United States that, in a study published by Princeton University, researchers declared that our nation was no longer a democracy: it is now an **oligarchy.**[108] Wikipedia defines an oligarchy as follows:

> **Oligarchy** (from Greek Ὀλιγαρχία *(oligarkhía)*; from Ὀλίγος *(olígos)*, meaning "few", and ἄρχω *(arkho)*, meaning "to rule or to command") is a form of power structure in which power effectively rests with a small number of people. These people could be dis-

tinguished by royalty, wealth, family ties, education, corporate, or military control. Such states are often controlled by a few prominent families who typically pass their influence from one generation to the next, but inheritance is not a necessary condition for the application of this term.[109]

How has America moved from a democracy to an oligarchy? The answer is: Through the riches and control of Financial Babylon. Without the proper financial backing, few candidates have any chance of winning elections.

This control of finances has answered so many questions for me, even beyond politics.

- Why are there no real differences in our political choices when it comes time to vote? Not only is there little difference anymore in the philosophical beliefs of the candidates, but the same agendas continue to move forward regardless of which party is in control. The only variation is the speed in which they are accomplished.
- Why has education been on a downward spiral over the past hundred or so years in the US? Secularization has transformed education from training students how to obtain knowledge and use critical thinking to indoctrinating them to serve in the New Babylon, as dumbed-down bricks in Nimrod's wall. This was achieved through control of secondary schools by federal mandates and funding. Control of postsecondary schools was accomplished through secular accreditation and the Title IV Guaranteed Student Loan Program.[110]
- Why is there always some type of shortage of resources worldwide? The resources of our planet (to include the food supply) should easily accommodate nearly fourteen billion people. (Scarcity inflates prices, causes civil unrest, and can control which nations thrive and which ones decline.)
- Why do many good ministries and ministers often struggle, while other ministries with questionable doctrines and practices

explode on the scene and become the new standard? Financial Babylon initially funds them, while Religious Babylon trains them to sway the masses through media and Christianized mysticism (more on this later in our study).

The list can go on and on. When you open your eyes to the reality of the influence of the threefold cord of Babylon, you see it in every aspect of our lives, from politics to the supermarket to your local church!

Babylon always uses riches to entrap and to control. God's blessings are outside the control and influence of Babylon. The only way to gain God's blessings is to walk out of Babylon (to depart) and to start walking with Him in all areas of your life so He can make you whole.

Political Babylon: The Founding Fathers in American politics viewed government as a necessary vice. When government works, it is small and provides some basic safeguards. This is true in a nation all the way down to the local church. When Babylon infects any type of governmental structure, it begins to grow like a cancer that swallows up everything around it. One of the telltale signs of any political system infected by Babylon is revealed in the following statement about Nimrod:

Now it was Nimrod who excited them to such an affront and contempt of God. He was the grandson of Ham, the son of Noah, a bold man, and of great strength of hand. He persuaded them not to ascribe it to God, as if it was through his means they were happy, but to believe that it was their own courage which procured that happiness. He also gradually changed the government into tyranny, seeing no other way of turning men from the fear of God, but to bring them into a constant dependence on his power.[111]

When government insists that true happiness (source of supply and well-being) can only come through its hands (i.e., socialism or communism) and it begins to oppress anyone or anything that does not align with its agenda, then you are dealing with the influence of Political Babylon.

There are only two real positions in life: dependence upon the Babylonian system or dependence upon the kingdom of God. Over the past few decades, it has appeared that many ministries and believers have prospered by standing with one foot in both kingdoms—straddling the fence. In the days ahead, the servants of Nimrod will spring their trap and all of these compromising ministries will be confronted by the proverbial fence post.

In the history of America over the past hundred years or so, we have seen the ebbs and flows of Political Babylon. As the influence of the Church increased, the power of Political Babylon decreased. When the salt nature of the Church decreased within society, the influence of Political Babylon increased. Today, Financial and Religious Babylon have teamed up against the Church at large. They have created a pseudo-spiritual system that makes us think we are walking with God and making huge impacts upon society. All the while (or in reality), the influence of Political Babylon grows within our culture and true spiritual holiness is lost within the Church.

Religious Babylon: To understand Religious Babylon, we need to understand several things. At the time of Shem and Nimrod, there were only two religions on the planet. The religion of Shem was to walk with the God of Creation, submit completely to Him, and walk in His ways (i.e., follow His commandments). The Institutes (religion) of Nimrod were exactly the opposite. Nimrod opposed all of the commandments of God (lawlessness) and set up a demonically inspired program of walking within a system rather than walking with God. When the languages were confused at the Tower of Babel, the people scattered and the names changed, but the concepts of the Institutes of Nimrod stayed the same.

When Abraham was called out of Babylon (contained within his bloodline), a departure from the Institutes of Nimrod occurred. Abraham and his descendants walked with God and learned His ways (commandments). Eventually, the children of Israel found themselves in bondage as slaves in Egypt—another version of Babylon.

When Moses brought the Hebrews out of Egypt by God's grace and they became a nation, Israel stood within history as the only religion that was the antithesis to the religion of Nimrod. All other religions on the planet were some variation of what started in Babylon. In fact, if you go to the Intertestamental Period during which Antiochus IV Epiphanes entered Jerusalem, erected a statue of Apollo, sacrificed a hog on the altar of God, and established the Institutes of Nimrod over Judea, these practices would have worked perfectly in any other nation. All other nations were based on the same concepts; they would just change the names of their gods. Within Judea, such things were an abomination. Antiochus found himself hunting down and killing all of the faithful who refused to bow to his demands. (I am sure he was not prepared for such resistance.) Eventually, the Maccabees rose up and drove him out of Judea three years to the day from when he started his war on the ways of God. (By the way, this war began on December 25, 168 BC—the birthday of the sun god of Babylon. He was driven out on December 25, 165 BC. This is the reason Christmas and Hanukkah overlap many years.)

After the death, burial, and resurrection of Christ, Christianity began as a new branch of Judaism: Christ's followers were known as the Nazarenes. Jews and Christians stood together in unity against the Institutes of Nimrod. Rome began its persecution of the Jews in both the first revolt in AD 70 that resulted in the destruction of the Temple and the second revolt in AD 132. That resulted in the complete destruction of Jerusalem; all Jews were forbidden to even travel through the area. With this persecution, Gentile believers began separating themselves from their Jewish counterparts. There was also a great deal of animosity against both Jewish and Gentile believers, because they would not fight in the second revolt. At the beginning of the second revolt, Rabbi Akiva declared Simon bar Kakhba the Messiah. Because of this action, believers in Jesus felt that if they fought, they would be endorsing Simon as Messiah and would be denying Jesus.[112]

This drift away from our Hebraic heritage continued over the next several centuries. Church leaders such as Origin declared that God gave Greek philosophy to lead Gentiles to Jesus, while the Torah was solely for the purpose of leading Jews to Jesus. (Note: in Origin's history with the church, he was declared a heretic many times.) This separation of Gentile believers from their Hebraic heritage was completed under the leadership of Constantine.

It was, in the first place, declared improper to follow the custom of the Jews in the celebration of this holy festival, because, their hands having been stained with crime, the minds of these wretched men are necessarily blinded....

Let us, then, have nothing in common with the Jews, who are our adversaries.... Let us...studiously avoiding all contact with that evil way....

For how can they entertain right views on any point who, after having compassed the death of the Lord, being out of their minds, are guided not by sound reason, but by an unrestrained passion, wherever their innate madness carries them....lest your pure minds should appear to share in the customs of a people so utterly depraved....

Therefore, this irregularity must be corrected, in order that we may no more have any thing in common with those parricides and the murderers of our Lord.... no single point in common with the perjury of the Jews.[113]

Constantine's goal was to create a catholic (universal) religion based upon the power of Rome and its stream of the mystery religion. Following the occult "onion" principle, the outer wrap was a veneer of Christianity, but within, it was completely the Institutes of Nimrod. Therefore, the Feasts of the LORD (which are all about Messiah) and the commandments of God had to be replaced with new universally understood pagan holidays and new catholic commandments.

We now stand in a period of human history in which the religions that are various versions of the Institutes of Nimrod are beginning to realign. Exactly how that will play out is yet to be seen—although, I must add, they will surely be seen very shortly. The only ones who resemble the faith of Shem, Abraham, Moses, and Paul are the Remnant—those who have purged themselves of the influence of the Great Whore and are walking in the power of covenant with Almighty God.

This is why we must be faithful Bereans and carefully examine our ways. We must cleanse ourselves from the leaven of Babylon and adhere to a pure faith that is based on the completed work of Jesus and the Word of God. To quote the Reformers of old, our cry must be *sola Scriptura* ("only Scripture")!

I believe this prophetic cry is being renewed by the Holy Spirit again in our generation. With the level of spiritual warfare in the last days, we cannot fight against something we are still plugged into and depend upon. We must separate the **clean** from the **unclean** in our lives, from sinful acts and attitudes to polluted ways of living. The apostle Paul reminds us about this dynamic relationship with the trice Holy God of Creation:

> Be ye not unequally yoked together with unbelievers: for what fellowship hath righteousness with unrighteousness? and what communion hath light with darkness?
>
> And what concord hath Christ with Belial? or what part hath he that believeth with an infidel?
>
> And what agreement hath the temple of God with idols? for ye are the temple of the living God; as God hath said, I will dwell in them, and walk in *them*; and I will be their God, and they shall be my people.
>
> Wherefore come out from among them, and be ye separate, saith the Lord, *and touch not the unclean thing*; and I will receive you,
>
> And will be a Father unto you, and ye shall be my sons and daughters, saith the Lord Almighty. (2 Corinthians 6:14–18, emphasis added)

We need the Holy Spirit to dwell in us **fully**; we need Almighty God to walk among us in the days ahead. In fact, we're talking survival here. Survival supplies and dehydrated food will only take you so far. It is the manifested presence and leadership of God in your life that will tip the balance in your favor! Please understand that Paul was writing to believers in these verses, and he wasn't merely referring to marriage. This Jewish rabbi named Paul, who was from the School of Hillel and trained by the famous rabbi, Gamaliel, was discussing how important it was for these formerly pagan Gentile believers to completely leave the Institutes of Nimrod behind and to walk completely with the God of Abraham, Isaac, and Jacob. Notice the affirmation of Abraham's call in verse 17: "Come out from among them, and be ye separate, saith the Lord, and touch not the unclean." Notice that I did not include "thing" in this quote. In the KJV, the word "thing" is in italics. This means that it did not occur in the original Greek text. (In 1611, these dedicated and faithful translators were not well versed in their Hebraic heritage.) When the apostle Paul used the term "unclean," he was using a Torah term that included everything the commandments of God declared as "unclean"—from items to practices. He expected his readers to open up their Bibles (which at that time only included Genesis through Malachi), study what God said was **unclean,** and separate it from their lives. In theological terms, we would call that "sanctification" (both a lost truth and a lost art these days within the body of Christ).

Over the years, I have found that when I write out explicitly all of the Institutes of Nimrod and its concepts for believers, the first thing they do is get upset...with me. It is not my fault that so much of what we do and accept, as common practices, did not originate in the Word of God; but the truth is that the carnal nature loves Babylon and most everything associated with it. Satan has done a great job of Christianizing his concepts over the centuries, turning them into big warm fuzzies and wrapping them in a big red bow. It takes two things for you to overcome: (1) sensitivity to the convicting power of the Holy Spirit, and (2) honest research. Some of my students, who were originally so upset with me for pointing these things out, eventually became the greatest advocates for biblical holiness—once they did their own research. (Although a good number spent many days arguing with themselves over their conclusions.) Never accept anything at face value. The enemy of our soul has become adept at deceiving righteous men into accepting unrighteous practices. Research extensively, dig deep, and do not go for the easiest answer, what is popular, or the path of least resistance. Be like Jacob, who dared to wrestle with

God over his pending confrontation with Esau. It was during the action of wrestling that Jacob's walk changed and he became Israel. There is a transformational wrestling match waiting for you; it will free you from the influence of Babylon and prepare you to become a world overcomer as we witness firsthand the unfolding of end-time prophecy.

chapter six

The Unfinished Work of Nimrod

Part 2: Communion with Darkness

Now, Hermes was the great original prophet of idolatry; **for he was recognised by the pagans as the author of their religious rites, and the interpreter of the gods**. The distinguished Gesenius identifies him with the Babylonian Nebo, **as the prophetic god**; and a statement of Hyginus **shows that he was known as the grand agent in that movement which produced the division of tongues**. His words are these: "For many ages men lived under the government of Jove [evidently not the Roman Jupiter, but the Jehovah of the Hebrews], without cities and without laws, and all speaking one language. But after that Mercury interpreted the speeches of men (whence an interpreter is called Hermeneutes), the same individual distributed the nations. Then discord began."[114] (Emphasis added)

As you recall from chapter 4, the above statement from *The Two Babylons* regards Cush, the father of Nimrod. One of the foundational elements of the establishment, as well as the continuation, of Babylon was *communion with dark spirits*—whether these spirits were fallen angels or chief demonic entities. In this chapter, we will define these spirits and examine their fellowship with the Elite, which empower all of their endeavors with dark, satanic energies.

Fallen Angels

1. Lucifer

The first scriptural reference regarding Lucifer that we will be looking at is in Ezekiel 28:

> Moreover the word of the Lord came unto me, saying,
> Son of man, take up a lamentation upon the king of Tyrus, and say unto him, Thus saith the Lord GOD; Thou sealest up the sum, full of wisdom, and perfect in beauty. (Ezekiel 28:11—12)

Ezekiel 28 is vital to understanding who Lucifer is and what he can do. Regarding these verses in Ezekiel, many have argued that they are not really about Lucifer at all; they believe these verses only pertain to the king of Tyrus. First, there are elements within these Scriptures that cannot be applied to a human being. There is no possibility that this king visited Eden (verse 13), dwelt on the holy mountain of God, or walked up and down in the midst of the stones of fire (verse 14). I would suggest that the king of Tyrus was an individual whom Lucifer was mentoring/utilizing at the time this prophecy was given by Ezekiel. Also within Bible prophecy, there is a law of interpretation called the Law of Double Reference. Finis Dake provides us with a solid working definition of the hermeneutical law:

The Law of Double Reference

Here we have the first occurrence of the law of double reference (cp. Isa. 14:12–14; Ezek. 28:11–17; Mt. 16:22–23; Mk. 5:7–16; Lk. 4:33–35, 41). In these and many other passages a visible creature is addressed, but certain statements also refer to an invisible person using the visible creature as a tool. Thus, two persons are involved in the same passage. The principle of interpretation in such passages is to associate only such statements with each individual as could refer to him. The statements of Gen. 3:14 could apply only to the serpent and not to Satan. The first part of Gen.

3:15 could apply to both the seed of the serpent and Satan. The last part of Gen. 3:15 could only refer to Satan and Christ. A simple example of this law is the case of Christ addressing Peter as Satan. When Peter declared that he would never permit anyone to crucify his Lord on the cross, Christ rebuked him saying, "Get thee behind Me, Satan" (Mt. 16:22–23). Both Satan and Peter were addressed in the same statement, and both were involved in the rebuke. Peter, for the moment, was unknowingly being used as a tool of Satan in an effort to keep Christ from going to the cross. Satan was the primary one addressed, and so it is in Gen. 3:15. A literal serpent is addressed, but the primary reference is to Satan. We have other examples in Isa. 14:12–14 and Ezek. 28:11–17 where the kings of Babylon and Tyre are addressed, but the statements mainly apply to Satan—the invisible king of Babylon and Tyre. There are some statements in these passages which could not possibly refer to an earthly man.[115]

Therefore, we can clearly see that the Law of Double Reference is in operation in Ezekiel 28. Now let's examine what the prophet reveals regarding Lucifer.

In this particular set of verses, the Amplified Bible (AMP) paints a clearer picture from the Hebrew of what the prophet had in mind when he said, "Thou sealest up the sum."

Son of man, take up a lamentation over the king of Tyre and say to him, Thus says the Lord God: You are the full measure and pattern of exactness [giving the finishing touch to all that constitutes completeness], full of wisdom and perfect in beauty. (Ezekiel 28:12, AMP, emphasis added)

In the statement "sealest up the sum," two Hebrew words are used. "Sealest up" comes from the Hebrew word *chatham* (khaw-tham'), which means "to seal, to seal up, to fasten up by sealing."[116] The second Hebrew word translated as "full of wisdom" is *chakmah* (khok-maw'), which provides powerful insights into the abilities of Lucifer and the level of spiritual warfare he can release. Here is what this Hebrew word means:

The skill of war
The gift of administration
Full understanding of religious affairs [i.e., operating in the spirit realm and how spirituality can affect individuals]
Shrewdness
Wisdom[117]

A basic understanding of each of these subjects would have made Lucifer a formidable foe. However, the Holy Spirit reveals that he has far more than that: Lucifer seals up the sum of perfection in each area! The average human being would have no chance of standing against such an opponent unless he was in covenant with Almighty God! In addition to being in covenant, we must also mature in that covenant and develop a proficiency in the spiritual disciplines of our Christian walk. The flippant and lackadaisical attitudes displayed in various portions of the body of Christ regarding spiritual warfare must stop. Immature believers focus on the moment while the enemy can plan over generations. He is patient and absolutely unforgiving. He will take your verbal, powerless tirades now, slowly implement a planned attack to get you spiritually off track over time, and then destroy you years down the road. For this reason, we must return to the Word of God, be led continually by the Holy Spirit, and discipline ourselves to walk in biblical holiness. The mature walk of a believer will defuse any plot the enemy can orchestrate against you. Obedience is truly better than sacrifice!

Ezekiel's description of Lucifer indicates that Lucifer possessed angelic perfection. Nevertheless, we need to remember that his perfection cannot come close to that of Almighty God. The phrase in Ezekiel is "perfect in beauty." Again, regarding angels, there was none more beautiful (and I have already explained the mystery revealed on the Ark of the Covenant, concerning Lucifer and his pride).

The Word tells us that Lucifer can also appear as an "angel of light."

Those to whom he reveals himself can be dazzled with a blinding brilliance. This dazzling first occurred in Heaven, when he was able to convince one-third of the angels to rebel against God with him (Revelation 12:3–4). Then his twisted logic, half-truths, and promise of illumination caused the Fall of mankind in the garden. This bedazzlement occurred again in the life of Cush, who became the prophet for Lucifer, and then this "dazzle effect" embedded itself into the esoteric streams that flow from Babylon. Everyone seduced by the mystery religions seems to resemble a deer caught in the headlights of an approaching eighteen-wheel truck! Listen to how Grand Commander Albert Pike refers to Lucifer in *Morals and Dogma:*

> Lucifer, the Light-bearer! Strange and mysterious name to give to the Spirit of Darkness. Lucifer, the Son of the Morning! It is he who bears the Light, and with its splendors intolerable blinds feeble, sensual or selfish Souls. Doubt it not! For traditions are full of Divine Revelation and Inspirations: and Inspiration is not of one Age nor of one Creed. Plato and Philo also were inspired.[118]

Those initiated into Freemasonry appear before a trapezoid-shaped altar (representing the unfinished work of Nimrod) and ask the god of the Lodge for light. Albert Pike has identified this god as Lucifer, the "light-bearer." Those caught up within that light believe this knowledge has created a supernatural **superiority** within them. At the beginning degrees of Freemasonry, this attitude will manifest itself more on an unconscious level. As the Mason develops a true expertise in his craft (only a select few really do, even at the higher degrees), this attitude moves into a more conscious level displayed in all areas of their lives. This would explain the arrogance seen in many political, public, and international figures—especially when they are caught off guard or believe the camera or mic is not on.

As I was researching to gain understanding of what happens within the minds of those who are mesmerized by the dazzling light of Lucifer, I found the testimony of Dr. Bill Schnoebelen—in his book, *Lucifer Dethroned*—very informative. He shares a pivotal, mystical experience he refers to as the "Cathedral of Pain." During this experience, he appeared before Lucifer. Here is an excerpt from his book:

The room into which I entered was a kind of temple, perhaps as large as a good-sized church. There was nowhere to sit, and only a trapezoid-shaped altar on a raised platform in the center. The altar itself was made of concrete—rough concrete. It had twisted steel girders projecting from it at all angles, and it was evidently stained with blood. One such girder reared up from behind it to form a rude, upside-down cross. Behind the altar was a raised throne which looked much larger than life. The throne was black, absolutely smooth, and unoccupied. I somehow felt relieved that it was unoccupied. However, it was the only thing about the room which was reassuring. My distinguished guide turned to me and gestured expansively at the room, rather like an orchestra conductor. He said, quite without fanfare: "Welcome to the Cathedral of Pain." With those words, darkly brilliant lights came on silently behind the walls of the huge place and I was so startled by what I saw that I nearly [retched]. The walls, which had appeared to be inward leaning smooth black stone, were starkly revealed to be clear glass holding back a transparent green fluid. Floating within the fluid were dozens, if not hundreds of naked human bodies! They were all dead, most with expressions of exquisite terror etched in a rictus on their frozen faces. Many of them were mutilated in manners which sickened even me. For the most part, this grotesque aquarium-like display consisted of young people. All but a few seemed barely adult, and there was a poignantly large number of infants and toddlers floating among the rest. It was like they were preserved, floating in formaldehyde or some other God-forsaken substance, like a butterfly collection from hell. This ghoulish diorama glared out at me from all but one of the sides of what I now perceived to be a nine-sided room. Nine is one of the most highly prized numbers among Satanists, for it is the only number which reduces into itself, always. Only the wall behind the throne was still black stone.

"These are the Master's children," proclaimed my guide, a strange kind of pride in his voice. "Are they not beautiful?"

"You have tasted of the illumination of our Master, the Light-Bearer, and have been found worthy to receive the Light," my guide told me. "Do you surrender yourself to the Light?" My head felt as if it was buzzing, and yet I felt oddly placid and relaxed. I managed to say, "Yes" and the chanting grew louder. Abruptly, the being on the throne arose. I was astonished at how tall he was. He effortlessly straddled the large altar like an adult might tower over a tricycle. He reached out his left hand and placed it on my forehead. I had to shut my eyes for the light which glared forth. It seemed my eyeballs were turning to molten steel. My forehead was about to explode. I felt a claw tear into my brow, right between but slightly above my eyebrows and insert itself into my brain like a white-hot poker. I tried to scream, but could not. My entire body felt like it was going to burst from being filled with roaring, flaming hot light. Another claw touched me, and I felt a stinging pain. Then both hands withdrew. A voice spoke, the same voice I had heard booming from within me on numerous ritual occasions. "Now, you are mine forever." The entire vast chamber suddenly rumbled with a hundred voices chanting: "Glory and Love for Lucifer! Hatred! Hatred! Hatred! to God accursed! accursed! accursed!" It felt as if the talon was burning into my very mind. My body shook on the altar with the power of the chanting. I felt like a fish on the end of a hook being hauled out of the water by my very brain. I screamed in pain, but it came out: "Glory and Love for Lucifer! Hatred! Hatred! Hatred! to God accursed! accursed! accursed!" A deafening thunderclap shook the cathedral. I was swept off the altar at incredible speed and carried into the awful wall of corpses. For a second I thought I was going to be placed among them, and I finally managed a scream. But before the scream was finished, I was through the wall and traveling on what seemed to be a lightning bolt crashing through clouds and hurtling toward the earth.[119]

It is at that moment that what Schnoebelen identifies as a "meta-mind" was released into his consciousness. He began to think differently. This difference manifested its influence the most when he would cast spells as a sorcerer. It was as if this **meta-mind** within him would become almost machine-like. He would be able to speak in twilight languages fluently, and would be able to speak them backwards, to add more spiritual power in spell casting. The part of his testimony that stood out to me the most was how he began to view the humans around him: They became like mere insects to him (a common theme of Nephilim and despots). To those illuminated by Lucifer, all unenlightened humanity is viewed as insects, and those insects must be controlled on planet earth. In science, one would have no problems with experimenting on, splicing the DNA of, or exterminating vast populations of insects (or in the luciferian mindset, an inferior subspecies of humans). This also explains the mentality of the scientists within the Third Reich in Nazi Germany. All the experiments in the concentration camps were conducted on the insects of humanity for the good of those who contained the illumination to transcend into the new supermen (*übermensch*). Because these Nazi scientists were embedded within the secret programs throughout the Allied nations, so was this dangerous mindset. The Elite have used the secret projects of world powers today to turn the entire planet into a concentration camp of sorts, with a multitude of ongoing experiments to advance their overall plan to complete Nimrod's work.

Lessons for the Charismatic Movement

There is so much in Ezekiel 28 that I would love to dissect theologically for you, but I need to stay within the topics needed for our current discussion. I do believe, in the days ahead, that we need to understand the revelations regarding Lucifer as revealed by the prophet in Ezekiel 28:14:

> Thou art the anointed cherub that covereth; and I have set thee so: thou wast upon the holy mountain of God; thou hast walked up and down in the midst of the stones of fire.

Lucifer Has an Anointing

Those within the Charismatic Movement need to realize that Lucifer has an anointing! He is called "the anointed cherub." That anointing did not leave him when he fell; it was perverted right along with him! In occult rituals, an anointing is released to empower the diabolical workings. Lucifer's counterfeit anointing can simulate an anointing released by the Holy Spirit for divine purposes. Remember, when it was time for the people of God to build the tabernacle in the wilderness, the anointing of the Holy Spirit came upon them and supercharged their natural abilities for their work. Lucifer's anointing can be released into the lives of his servants and supercharge their efforts to complete the work of Nimrod in the earth today. Manly P. Hall speaks about this energizing anointing and the need for Masons to learn to properly apply it in his book, *The Lost Keys of Freemasonry.*

> When the Mason learns that the key to the warrior on the block is the proper application of the dynamo of living power, he has learned the mystery of his Craft. **The seething energies of Lucifer are in his hands**, and before he may step onward and upward, he must prove his ability to properly apply energy.[120] (Emphasis added)

Therefore, not everything that is supernatural is of God. Not every anointing is from God. In addition, not every spiritual manifestation is from God. All things must be diligently compared to the Bible. If it is not clearly defined as a manifestation of God's Spirit in the Bible, then it is not of God. If you cannot see Jesus, Paul, or the apostles doing it in the Word, then it should not be done today. If it does not bear the fruit of true deliverance and moving into biblical holiness, it is not of God. We need to stop worrying about drawing a crowd, as if we are a part of some spiritual circus, and get back to the real preaching/teaching of the Word and true biblical ministry.

Years ago, my wife and I went to a large, international, charismatic conference that included leaders from all over the world. It was at a time in my life when I really needed a touch from God. (My wife, Mary, knew this too and made sure I was right down front for most of the meetings.) During the conference, I also attended several seminars for educators. I was completely disappointed. The presenters all spoke of this new move of God, but could not give any answers relevant to education (much less on how this move applied to our Christian walk). When the time came for one of the leaders of this new move of God to speak, I sensed in my spirit that something was wrong. I noticed that a national leader (a man I have great respect for) got up and left the auditorium the moment this man was introduced. (Having been on many platforms in my life, I took notice of this action.) So there I was, sitting in front, and I began to pray under my breath, "Lord, I want everything that You have for me, but I also stand in my authority in Jesus and bind up anything from the enemy." The moment I prayed this, the energy in the room began to wane. The speaker noticed the change but continued his sermon. From that moment on, he began to stare directly at me. Those stares were not stares of love, either; they were death stares. It became obvious that he had a real problem with me, but he went on with his sermon. His staring became so intense that people began to move away from me, as if I would explode into flames at any moment. The good news is that I did not burst into flames, and the false anointing of this man did not affect me. However, I did learn a valuable lesson that day: Those in the occult were actively taking over portions of the Charismatic Movement, and many of the old guards of leadership were completely unaware of it. In fact, Russ Dizdar revealed, in his lectures on the *Black Awakening*, that there was a charismatic minister who was actually a "chosen one" with satanic and Nazi alter personalities. May God help us and give us true spiritual discernment!

The apostle Paul encourages believers to "prove all things; hold fast that which is good" (1 Thessalonians 5:21).

Why is it that the occult can have such an influence on something that was originally started by God? I have come to believe that part of the answer lies in our disenfranchisement from our Hebraic heritage and our theological jaundice to the Torah. The Torah was given to a people who were slaves in bondage in Egypt for four hundred years (another division of the mystery religions). Encoded within the stories and commandments of the Torah are both instructions and an anointing to separate the working of Nimrod from the things of God. Without the foundation of the Torah, nearly anything from Satan's camp can be accepted—if it is given the proper PR spin and produces a crowd or a bigger offering! No wonder Constantine wanted to separate Christianity from the Torah and anything remotely Jewish! I love what A. W. Tozer said regarding the Word: "The Word of God well understood and religiously obeyed is the shortest route to spiritual perfection. *Nothing less than a whole Bible can make a whole Christian.*"[121]

Lucifer Can Cover the Manifested Presence of God

Lucifer not only has an anointing, but part of his gifting was to serve as a covering. You might ask, "A covering to what?" He formed the covering over the top of the throne of God. The throne of God is the only place in all of existence where God's presence is fully manifested—He holds nothing back. Lucifer had the ability to cover the full manifestation of the presence of God in Heaven! He did not lose that ability when he fell. In fact, we find him in the book of Job appearing before the throne of God. He is also referred to in the New Testament as a prosecuting attorney[122] who accuses the saints before God's throne (Revelation 12:10). He will continue to appear before the throne of God until the time is reached in which God keeps His promise in Ezekiel 28:16: "therefore, I will cast thee as profane out of the mountain of God." I believe this will happen during the Tribulation period. Lucifer will realize that he has a short time left to complete his plans and will go forth with great wrath (Revelation 12:12).

So many times Christians expect the presence of God to drive out the enemy, but the Word tells us that God gave us the authority to bind him and cast him out. We must always stand firmly in that authority to confront the enemy when he rears his ugly head. This is the role God has assigned to us, not to His Spirit or His angels. Now, God's angels and His Spirit will back us up with power and assistance when we faithfully execute our authority on the earth. We must also learn to live and stand sanctified (or free) from the enemy's influence. Only then can we properly exercise kingdom authority over him.

If Lucifer covered the manifested presence of God in Heaven itself, it is logical that he would seek to cover God's presence on the earth, both in the lives of believers and in our services. The understanding of the anointing that Lucifer has and his ability to cover the presence of God has led me to understand a phenomenon I've witnessed many times in the body of Christ. Have you ever seen a preacher minister under the anointing of the Holy Spirit when a change occurs and something takes over for a few moments or rides on the top of his ministerial anointing? I have even seen men and women begin to give a true prophetic word, but a deviation causes the prophetic word to veer off course. In the past, I have always attributed this to immaturity or a fleshly moment. However, the information I've gleaned over the past couple of decades regarding spiritual warfare, coupled with the realization that there was a negative spiritual flow with these abrupt changes, finally helped me understand this phenomenon. I use the phrase, "the double stream," to describe this mystery. A double stream occurs when there are bondages within the life of the individual or areas in his or her life that he or she refuses to submit to Almighty God. These violations of kingdom laws provide a legal right for the enemy to piggyback his anointing on top of the anointing of the Holy Spirit within the individual's life. Once you become aware of this possibility and understand how the occult works, you can sense the ebbs and flows at times in services and on Christian TV.

This is why personal holiness is paramount in the life of ministers today. As the enemy declares from pulpits that grace is a license to sin, the Holy Spirit is reaffirming His call to return to true biblical holiness. The kingdom of darkness operates according to spiritual law, just like the kingdom of God. Repentance, deliverance, and the sanctifying influence of both the Word and the Holy Spirit systematically nullify the legal rights Satan uses to affect our lives and ministries, thereby breaking his power to form a canopy of his perverted anointing and maintaining a pure stream of God's anointing. It is time that we stop playing church and become a mature army for the Living God!

Lucifer's False Grace

Another prophetic view of the fall of Lucifer is found in the writings of Isaiah:

How art thou fallen from heaven, O Lucifer, son of the morning! how art thou cut down to the ground, which didst weaken the nations!

For thou hast said in thine heart, **I will** ascend into heaven, **I will** exalt my throne above the stars of God: **I will** sit also upon the mount of the congregation, in the sides of the north:

I will ascend above the heights of the clouds; **I will** be like the most High.

Yet thou shalt be brought down to hell, to the sides of the pit. (Isaiah 14:12–15, emphasis added)

Why does the Holy Spirit go to all the trouble to divide the five statements of "I will" regarding Lucifer's fall? Repetition is important in the Bible, and multiple occurrences of text have meanings. Biblically, five is the number of grace. Lucifer used his anointing to create a self-centered false grace in an attempt to ascend into godhood. He imitated God by attempting to speak his desires into existence. Lucifer did not become like the Most High God, but this false grace did produce a perverted power.

Thou wast perfect in thy ways from the day that thou wast created, till iniquity was found in thee. (Ezekiel 28:15)

The Bible identifies that perverted power as "iniquity." This new perverted power was so great that it caused angels to fall. Iniquity (and the pride that flows from it) is still the major weapon in Lucifer's arsenal in his fight against mankind. With that in mind, it is time to examine the theological definition of "iniquity."

The word used most often in the Old Testament for iniquity is *avon* (aw-vone'), which is used 230 times. *Avon* means "perversity, depravity, iniquity, guilt or punishment of iniquity."[123] *The Theological Wordbook of the Old Testament* provides a more detailed picture on Lucifer's new weapon:

1577 עָוָה (*ʿāwâ*) *bend, twist, distort.*

DERIVATIVES

1577a †עָוֹן (*ʿāwōn*) *iniquity, guilt, punishment.*

1577b †עַוָּה (*ʿawwâ*) *ruin.*

1577c םִעְוֶה (*ʿiwʿîm*) *distorting, warping* (Isaiah 19:14).

1577d עִי (*ʿî*) *ruin, heap of ruins.*

1577e יְעָמֹ (*meʿî*) *ruin* (Isaiah 17:1).

Cognates to Hebrew *ʿāwâ* include Arabic *ʿawaya* "to bend," "to twist" and/or *gawaya* "to deviate from the way"…and Biblical Aramaic *ʿawaya* "offense, iniquity" (Daniel 4:24).

Its main derivative is the masculine noun *ʿāwōn* (occurring 231 times against the verb found 17 times), an abstract nominal pattern with the ān > ôn ending…. BDB conjecture two roots: *ʿāwâ* I "bend" "twist" related to Arabic *ʿawaya* and *ʿāwâ* II "to commit iniquity" a denominative from *ʿāwōn* which in turn is related to Arabic *gawaya*. But KB [L. Koehler and W. Baumgartner] and GB [W. Gesenius and F. Buhl] with more probability see only one Hebrew root related either to *ʿawaya* "alone" (so KB) or to both roots (so GB). For convenience we shall follow this procedure.

The basic meaning of the verb, "to bend, twist, distort," can be seen in its concrete, nontheological uses: "I am bent over" (Niphal) (Psalm 38:7); "the LORD lays the earth waste, devastates it; and he ruins (Piel) it" (Isaiah 24:1). From this primary notion it derives the sense "to distort, to make crooked, to pervert": "He has made my paths crooked (Piel)" (Lament. 3:9); "I have…perverted (Hiphil) what is right" (Job 33:27); "a man of perverse (Niphal) heart will be despised" (Proverbs 12:8). When the distortion pertains to law it means "to sin, to infract, to commit a perversion/iniquity."[124]

This twisting or bending became associated with **lawlessness**. In the New Testament, the Greek word used is *anomia* (an-om-ee'-ah), which means "to be without law, to have contempt toward the law, and to violate the law."[125] This product of Lucifer has been a consistent empowering theme of the mystery religions from Babylon to Constantine, to even modern preaching in churches today. God's law does several things:

- Reveals sin
- Defines holiness and acts of righteousness
- Serves as a pedagogy to lead its students to Messiah
- Instructs the believer in the ways of righteousness, and how to function within God's kingdom
- Separates Mystery Babylon from the kingdom of God

In other words, God's law goes against the very twisted nature that Lucifer created (or perverted) when he fell. Those who are a part of the Babylonian system will have a hatred for the law of God. In fact, one of the leading occultists of the past century, Aleister Crowley, channeled a book from his spirit guide entitled *The Book of the Law*. This book did not show reverence for God's law, but desired to have the law replaced by something else. The teaching of this damnable book can be summarized in the Law of Thelema: "Do what thou wilt shall be the whole of the Law. Love is the law, love under will."[126]

This occult law sounds like a lot of the hyper-grace preaching today, doesn't it? This statement embodies both the nature of Lucifer and the Antichrist: to replace God's Law with "I will" and then call it "love."

Everything within Lucifer's kingdom of darkness and his mystery religions will bear this anointing toward iniquity and hatred for God's law. The apostle Paul had the opposite opinion toward the Torah:

Wherefore the law is holy, and the commandment holy, and just, and good. (Romans 7:12)

For we know that the law is spiritual. (Romans 7:14a)

The saints of God, during the Reformation, had the utmost respect for the commandments of God. It is only recently, in historical terms, that elements of the Protestant Church have developed such a negative view of God's law. I believe this negative view grew right along with the influence of the mystery religions. Today, the Church is less holy and less powerful than it was a hundred years ago, and it is filled with far too much showmanship. Carefully crafted sound bites wrapped in the proper emotional garments have become the new doctrines of the carnally religious of today.

2. Fallen Angels

Christians many times confuse fallen angels with demons. Theologically, they are two separate classes of beings. Angels were created by God to serve Him. When Lucifer fell, one-third (33.3 percent) of the angels fell with him. I believe the number thirty-three is important within Freemasonry, because it reveals the unseen army that empowers their work: the angels who fell with Lucifer.

Paul reveals in his writing to the Ephesians that these fallen angels have levels of power and authority:

> Finally, my brethren, be strong in the Lord, and in the power of his might.
>
> Put on the whole armour of God, that ye may be able to stand against the wiles of the devil.
>
> For we wrestle not against flesh and blood, but against principalities, against powers, against the rulers of the darkness of this world, against spiritual wickedness in high places. (Ephesians 6:10–12)

These were not new offices of power in which these angels operated. Originally, God created these positions (except for rulers of darkness and spiritual wickedness) to operate within His kingdom.

> For by him were all things created, that are in heaven, and that are in earth, visible and invisible, whether they be thrones, or domin-

ions, or principalities, or powers: all things were created by him, and for him. (Colossians 1:15–16)

When these beings fell, along with Lucifer, the perverting and twisting anointing of iniquity affected them and their positions of power.

Paul uses the Greek word *epouranois* (ep-oo-ran'-ee-os) for "high places." *Epouranois* is defined as "existing in heaven, the heavenly regions, heaven itself, the lower heavens."[127]

As with all kingdoms, there are levels of authority, governors of territories or regions, and so on. These beings operate within a region of the lower heavens. Although I want to save our discussion of the reality of a multiverse (as revealed within Scripture) for a later time, I do want to point out that there are three Heavens:

> I knew a man in Christ above fourteen years ago, (whether in the body, I cannot tell; or whether out of the body, I cannot tell: God knoweth;) such an one caught up to the third heaven. (2 Corinthians 12:2, emphasis added)

Although the Kabbalah (this Jewish book contains many of the concepts within the mystery religions and is esteemed by Freemasons and the occult) teaches that there are seven Heavens, the Word of God only refers to three. Each is contained within its own dimensional reality but can affect lower subrealities. I believe it looks something like this:

- **Third Heaven**—This is the home of Almighty God.
- **Second Heaven**—This is a dimensional reality between God's dwelling and our universe. Angels—both God's angels and fallen angels—work to assist in the governing of nations and people from within this region. Occultists have referred to this as the "astral plane."
- **First Heaven**—This is our universe.

The Second Heaven is alluded to in the book of Daniel, when an angel was delayed in bringing a message to Daniel:

> And, behold, an hand touched me, which set me upon my knees and upon the palms of my hands.
>
> And he said unto me, O Daniel, a man greatly beloved, understand the words that I speak unto thee, and stand upright: for unto thee am I now sent. And when he had spoken this word unto me, I stood trembling.
>
> Then said he unto me, Fear not, Daniel: for from the first day that thou didst set thine heart to understand, and to chasten thyself before thy God, thy words were heard, and I am come for thy words.
>
> **But the prince of the kingdom of Persia withstood me one and twenty days: but, lo, Michael, one of the chief princes, came to help me;** and I remained there with the kings of Persia. (Daniel 10:10–13, emphasis added)

The prince of the kingdom of Persia was a fallen angel who ruled over and empowered the kingdom of Persia.

A Modern Guide to Demons and Fallen Angels provides powerful insights into roles of certain angels in the affairs of nations:

Dr. Michael S. Heiser has argued that the Greek translation of Deuteronomy 32:8 sheds some added light on this arrangement, in his paper "Deuteronomy 32:8 and the Sons of God"; his work is where I first learned of this topic.

> Deut. 32:8–9 (with LXX and DSS)—When the Most High gave the nations their inheritance, when he divided all mankind, he set up boundaries for the peoples according to the number of the sons of God.
>
> The Hebrew reads "When the most High divided to the nations their inheritance, when he separated the sons of Adam, he set the bounds of the people according to the number of the

children of Israel." However in place of "children of Israel" the Greek reads "ἀγγέλων θεοῦ", "angels of God."

If the Greek is correct, then what we are looking at is a specific event and time, in which God divided the nations of mankind according to the number of the angels of God. This is specified to have occurred when God divided all mankind. When did God divide all mankind? God divided mankind right after the tower of Babel incident, which was not long after the Flood.[128]

Deuteronomy hints at the fact that the nations were divided under the leadership of angels and that men were driven to worship them instead of God.

And lest thou lift up thine eyes unto heaven, and when thou seest the sun, and the moon, and the stars, **even all the host of heaven**, shouldest be driven to worship them, and serve them, which the LORD thy God hath divided unto all nations under the whole heaven. (Deuteronomy 4:19, emphasis added)

Dr. Heiser has postulated that the angels in Deuteronomy 4:19 and 32:8–9 were a part of a ***divine council*** and that God will eventually judge them for leading men away from God and perverting justice. We find this reference in Psalm 82:

God standeth in the congregation of the mighty; he judgeth among the gods.

How long will ye judge unjustly, and accept the persons of the wicked? Selah.

Defend the poor and fatherless: do justice to the afflicted and needy.

Deliver the poor and needy: rid them out of the hand of the wicked.

They know not, neither will they understand; they walk on in darkness: all the foundations of the earth are out of course.

I have said, Ye are gods; and all of you are children of the most High.

But ye shall die like men, and fall like one of the princes. Arise, O God, judge the earth: for thou shalt inherit all nations. (Psalms 82:1–8)

Let's examine a short section of Dr. Heiser's work.

Psalm 82 has long been a nuisance for Jewish and Christian interpreters. As Morgenstern noted in his lengthy study of the psalm, "Although its text is in almost perfect condition and better far than the text of the vast majority of the Psalms, scarcely any psalm seems to have troubled interpreters more or to have experienced a wider range of interpretation and a more disturbing uncertainty and lack of finality than Psalm 82." Morgenstern is correct, but as I will suggest in this paper, the reason for the confusion stems from several defects in our own thinking and methods, not the clarity of the text. For the ancient orthodox Israelite, there was no conundrum.

To begin, the very first verse assaults our theological sensitivities:

אֱלֹהִים נִצָּב בַּעֲדַת־אֵל בְּקֶרֶב אֱלֹהִים יִשְׁפֹּט׃

God (אלהים) stands in the divine assembly; in the midst of the gods (אלהים) he passes judgment.

The first occurrence of םיהלא is correctly translated "God" obviously to be taken as singular for reasons of grammatical subject-verb agreement (נִ צָ ב). The second םיהלא is equally obvious as a plural since it is the object of the preposition (בְּ קֶ רֶ ב). One cannot be in the midst of one (and for anyone thinking of the Trinity here, as we will see, that presumption in this verse leads to heretical theology no one in this room would embrace). The grammar and syntax are crystal clear. The God of Israel is, in Psalm 82, presiding over a group—a council (עֵ דָ ת)—of םיהלא. The plurality point is also echoed in verses 6–7 where the םיהלא suffer the loss of their immortality:[129]

אֲנִי־אָמַרְתִּי אֱלֹהִים אַתֶּם וּבְנֵי עֶלְיוֹן כֻּלְּכֶם׃   6

אָכֵן כְּאָדָם תְּמוּתוּן וּכְאַחַד הַשָּׂרִים תִּפֹּלוּ׃   7

I said, 'You are gods (אלהים), even sons of the Most High (בני עליון), all of you;

nevertheless, like humans you will die, and fall like any prince.'

Men cannot be threatened with loss of their immortality, but angels can. When will this happen? We will get into that topic as we wind up our teaching on completing the unfinished work of Nimrod.

The point I am trying to make is that angels do not desire to inhabit human bodies. The spiritual bodies God gave them work perfectly fine, and they can manifest their presence in the earth without the need of a human host. In fact, on many occasions in the Word of God, angels take human form.

The angels of Psalm 82 assist in the governance of nations from the Second Heaven. For those who have aligned themselves with Lucifer, these angels prefer to be the puppet masters who pull the strings that sway nations. We must never underestimate the intelligence or power of these supernatural beings. Today, modern spiritual warfare is littered with destroyed ministries and lives of those who arrogantly assaulted principalities and powers without a direct assignment from the throne of God. We have failed to understand the difference between a demon and a fallen angel. Although this truth is contained within most systematical theologies, its application is rarely transferred into spiritual warfare practices. (We will address the proper model of spiritual warfare against principalities in chapters 10–12 on "Preparing the Remnant.")

3. Demons

There are distinct differences between demons and angels. Demons desire human hosts to experience carnal pleasures and manifest their influence on our dimensional plane. Although the Word of God is silent regarding their origin, a biblically endorsed book explains their origin: the *Book of Enoch*.

First, we find a specific class of angels the *Book of Enoch* calls "Watchers," who came to earth and had children with the daughters of men. (**Note:** this corresponds to Genesis 6 in the Bible.)

> And it came to pass when the children of men had multiplied that in those days were born unto them beautiful and comely daughters.
>
> And the angels, the children of the heaven, saw and lusted after them, and said to one another: "Come, let us choose us wives from among the children of men and beget us children."
>
> And Semjaza, who was their leader, said unto them: "I fear ye will not indeed agree to do this deed, and I alone shall have to pay the penalty of a great sin."
>
> And they all answered him and said: "Let us all swear an oath, and all bind ourselves by mutual imprecations not to abandon this plan but to do this thing."
>
> Then sware they all together and bound themselves by mutual imprecations upon it.
>
> And they were in all two hundred; who descended in the days of Jared on the summit of Mount Hermon, and they called it Mount Hermon, because they had sworn and bound themselves by mutual imprecations upon it. (1 Enoch 6:1–6)

> And the Lord said unto Michael: "Go, bind Semjaza and his associates who have united themselves with women so as to have defiled themselves with them in all their uncleanness.
>
> "And when their sons have slain one another, and they have seen the destruction of their beloved ones, bind them fast for seventy generations in the valleys of the earth, till the day of their judgment and of their consummation, till the judgment that is forever and ever is consummated." (1 Enoch 10:11–12)[130]

The judgment of God for their actions was swift. First, God caused the Watchers to be bound, then He required them to watch as the Nephilim (or giants) went to war with one another until they killed each other off. The imprisonment of the Watchers was for seventy generations (that means they would be released at a future date).

Pure-blooded, first-generation Nephilim can only be created through the mating of the Watcher class of angels with human women. Other types of Nephilim were created after the imprisonment of the Watchers through the blending of the DNA of various species. Rob Skiba has done an outstanding job of creating a synchronization of Genesis with the Apocrypha books of *Enoch, Jasher,* and *Jubilees,* as well as the mythologies of the ancient world. Skiba's timeline has connected the event of the original Nephilim killing each other with the clash of the Titans that occurred in Greek mythology.

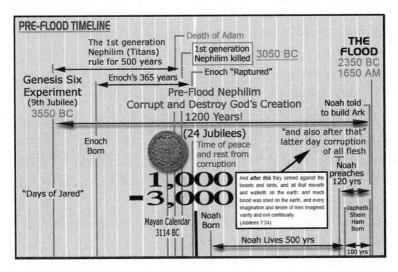

Chart by Rob Skiba. Used by permission.

Enoch goes on to describe what happened to the spirits of the Nephilim after they died.

> And now, the giants, who are produced from the spirits and flesh, shall be called evil spirits upon the earth, and on the earth shall be their dwelling.
>
> Evil spirits have proceeded from their bodies; because they are born from men and from the holy Watchers is their beginning

and primal origin; they shall be evil spirits on earth, and evil spirits shall they be called.

[As for the spirits of heaven, in heaven shall be their dwelling, but as for the spirits of the earth which were born upon the earth, on the earth shall be their dwelling.] And the spirits of the giants afflict, oppress, destroy, attack, do battle, and work destruction on the earth, and cause trouble: they take no food, but nevertheless hunger and thirst, and cause offences.

And these spirits shall rise up against the children of men and against the women, because they have proceeded from them. (1 Enoch 15:7–10)[131]

Demons are the disembodied spirits of the Nephilim. These spirits long to have physical bodies again and have insatiable appetites for the things of the flesh (from food to sex and everything in between). Although they require a host body, they have absolute hatred for their human host and Almighty God. This hatred drives them to destroy the very host bodies they are using to manifest themselves. They know there will be a time when God will judge them, and they will be cast into the Lake of Fire. This is why demons always seemed to ask Jesus if He was going to judge them before their appointed time.

Like their angelic fathers, demons (Nephilim spirits) have levels of authority and power. I believe the ground-troop Nephilim spirits are what most deliverance ministers confront in ministry. These are lesser demonic forces (or, to borrow a military term, the enlisted and noncommissioned officers). The generals within the Nephilim spirits prefer to commune with the Elite and to empower their work worldwide.

Possible Connection with Powerful Nephilim and the House of Rothschild

Any student of the Bible is familiar with the names "Gog" and "Magog." These names are referenced in both the Old Testament and in the book of Revelation. However, most Bible students are not familiar with the fact that Gog and Magog are connected to "The City" within London.

The City is the international banking district within the township of London. Referred to simply as "The City," it has its own Lord Mayor and its own police force (at near-military strength). In my research, I discovered that whenever the Queen of England visits The City, she must have permission from the Lord Mayor; she also must walk several steps behind him (showing her position is subordinate to his). The patron spirits or guardians, if you will, of The City are Gog and Magog. We find this reference to Gog and Magog in Wikipedia:

> Despite their generally negative depiction in the Bible, Lord Mayors of the City of London carry images of Gog and Magog (depicted as giants) in a traditional procession in the Lord Mayor's Show. **According to the tradition, the giants Gog and Magog are guardians of the City of London**, and images of them have been carried in the Lord Mayor's Show since the days of King Henry V. The Lord Mayor's procession takes place each year on the second Saturday of November.[132] (Emphasis added)

The City pays homage to these Nephilim spirits every November. Here is a photo from its 2011 parade.

Do members of the House of Rothschild commune with these guardian spirits, and do these spirits aid them in building and protecting their financial empire? With what I know about luciferian practices, I believe so. These particular disembodied Nephilim spirits prefer to commune with the Elite to build a financial empire to finance the continued work of Nimrod in the earth today. We even find their influence after Lucifer is released from the bottomless pit at the end of the millennial reign:

> And when the thousand years are expired, Satan shall be loosed out of his prison,
>
> And shall go out to deceive the nations which are in the four quarters of the earth, Gog and Magog, to gather them together to battle: the number of whom is as the sand of the sea.
>
> And they went up on the breadth of the earth, and compassed the camp of the saints about, and the beloved city: and fire came down from God out of heaven, and devoured them. (Revelation 20:7–9)

Those who have come out of the Illuminati, such as Doc Marquis, claim the Rothschilds are the most powerful family within the thirteen bloodlines that comprise the ruling class. Their alliance with Gog and Magog could be a key to their overwhelming power and wealth.

Occult Power and the Demonic Hive Mind

It also appears that demons can work together over groups of people as a hive mind in concert with a principality that governs that region or nation. This hive mind produces an energy called *egregores* that can take on a life of its own within its directed movement. Dr. Tom Horn comments on this energy the hive mind can create:

> Metaphysicians who do not rely solely on the Bible for authority often agree that powerful non-human energies, including evil ones, can emanate from symbols and, once released, take on a mind of their own. Writing about the Masonic involvement in the French Revolution, Gary Lachman makes an extraordinary and important observation about immaterial destructive forces—which had unseen plans of their own—released as a result of occult politics:
>
> Cazotte himself was aware of the dangerous energies unleashed by the Revolution....

Although Cazotte didn't use the term, he would no doubt have agreed that, whatever started it, the Revolution soon took on a life of its own, coming under the power of an egregore, Greek for "watcher," a kind of immaterial entity that is created by and presides over a human activity or collective. According to the anonymous author of the fascinating Meditations on the Tarot, there are no "good" egregores, only "negative" ones....

True or not, egregores can nevertheless be "engendered by the collective will and imagination of nations." As Joscelyn Godwin points out, "an egregore is augmented by human belief, ritual and especially by sacrifice. If it is sufficiently nourished by such energies, the egregore can take on a life of its own and appear to be an independent, personal divinity, with a limited power on behalf of its devotees and an unlimited appetite for their future devotion." If, as some esotericists believe, human conflicts are the result of spiritual forces for spiritual ends, and these forces are not all "good," then collective catastrophes like the French Revolution take on a different significance.[133]

I believe this type of manifestation happens when the minds of the people are influenced by occult power and become one—not only with each other, but with the demonic forces at work. This demonic power will take men and women to some very dark places, places where they would have never considered going before. Since those in esoteric circles believe such energy can be released from symbols, the *egregore* may be a precursor to the dark force that will possess those who receive the mark of the Beast.

Fellowship with Principalities, Nephilim, and Watchers

Ever since the idea of Babylon began to germinate in the hearts Cush and Nimrod, communing with ancient malevolent spirits has been quintessential. These spiritual agents of darkness and chaos have been mentoring generations of the Elite throughout the millennia. Through their counsel and energies, wars have been waged, kingdoms conquered or built, and thirteen bloodlines have become so powerful that they rule the entire world.

Preparation for the Return of the Watchers

I have noticed an explosion in technology, an accelerated corruption of mankind, and an unprecedented movement away from the things of God since the turn of the twentieth century. I believe the Watchers of the Prediluvian Age have returned.

> And the Lord said unto Michael: "Go, bind Semjaza and his associates who have united themselves with women so as to have defiled themselves with them in all their uncleanness.
>
> "And when their sons have slain one another, and they have seen the destruction of their beloved ones, **bind them fast for seventy generations** in the valleys of the earth, till the day of their judgment and of their consummation, till the judgment that is for ever and ever is consummated." (1 Enoch 10:11–12, emphasis added)

The *Book of Enoch* tells us that this special class of angel was bound for seventy generations. After making my own calculations, I determined that their release would have occurred around AD 1900. To verify my estimate of the time of their release, I contacted Nephilim researcher Rob Skiba. Here is a section of his email reply to my request:

> Assuming this timeline is correct, I believe the Watchers were judged, bound, and buried by about 3000 BC. Assuming the lesser number of 70 years for a generation according to Psalm 90:10, we end up with a 4,900-year prison sentence. Of course, 4,900 years from 3000 BC brings us to the end of the 19th Century/beginning of the 20th. In my mind, this helps explain the MASSIVE increase in technology and transportation in a VERY short period of time. I'm speculating of course, but it seems to

make sense that the Watchers may have been/are being released. When you look at what they taught men in the book of Enoch, it fits well with our current advancements.

This time frame is important. Although the body of Christ is still arguing about whether the information contained in the apocryphal books of *Enoch, Jasher,* and *Jubilees* should even be considered, the Elite take the information they provide very seriously. When I began researching the occult back in the 1990s, I noticed that these books were esteemed in many esoteric libraries. Therefore, the Elite have been waiting all of these millennia for the seventy generations to be completed. Preparations had to be made for the arrival of the Watchers. The groundwork was laid by the Darwin family in the mid 1880s.

Charles Darwin published his book, *Origin of the Species by Means of Natural Selection or Preservation of Races in the Struggle for Life* (I always prefer to include the entire title of his book, as it reveals his own prejudice), in 1859. Around the same period, Sir Francis Galton was pioneering **eugenics**. Similar to the family line of Ham, Darwin and Galton were half cousins. They shared the same grandfather, Erasmus Darwin. Some researchers believe the concept of evolution did not originate with Charles Darwin, but with Erasmus. I believe the concept of evolution was formulated by the Luciferian Elite and promoted through the mentoring of the Darwin family. This connection can be illustrated by the fact that the Darwins, Galtons, and several other families (to include H. G. Wells) began to marry only within that group (a selective inner breeding program), similar to how the thirteen bloodlines intermarry. Unfortunately, for this new group, the selective breeding program only produced inferior results.

During Dr. Tom Horn's first prophecy conference in Branson, Missouri, I was able to spend some time chatting with Doc Marquis. Doc was gracious and took time out of his busy schedule for our extended conversation. During that conversation, he explained that the Illuminati believe in the occult version of reincarnation. They introduced evolution as a smoke screen to pull men away from God. I agree with his summary, and I have also concluded that more is involved.

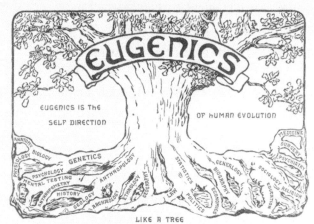

Evolution and eugenics were the foundational concepts that would lead humanity back into the Genesis 6 experiments of blending species to create a hybrid Nephilim army.

Evolution and eugenics worked dynamically together to accomplish several things:

- Pull men away from God and the Bible and toward a paradigm suitable for both the Watchers and the return of Nimrod
- Prepare the groundwork for the grand luciferian experiment in Nazi Germany
- Prepare the world for transhumanism and the corruption of the human genome

We need to realize that America embraced eugenics well before Germany did. In fact, the concepts were taken into Germany from both Great Britain and the United States. Hitler just accelerated the advancement of eugenics to its ultimate conclusion with religious zeal: selective breeding, eliminating the inferior genetics, and conducting experiments to find new ways of helping evolution are in its next quantum leap. After World War II, the atrocities committed by the Nazis were brought to light. Eugenics was covertly brought into all other branches of science under various names; the eugenics centers were closed down only to be opened later under their new name, "Planned Parenthood," and the repackaged science was eventually called the Genome Project.

This was all for the purpose of preparing the world for the return of the Watchers. I am convinced that their return commenced around the start of the twentieth century. Within the first forty years of the new century, mankind had already suffered through two world wars. Then, there was the advancement of technology in Germany. Was Germany, like the civilizations in the Prediluvian Age, trading access to their people for advanced knowledge? There is evidence that this was the case.

Hitler was a product of the Thule Society. As I shared in chapter 2, Hitler's mentor was Dietrich Eckart, a prominent member of this occult secret society. Both the Thule and Vril societies had a profound influence on Hitler and the Third Reich. Trance channeling was a common practice among both groups; it was their version of communing with the old gods, ascended masters, and yes, even powerful beings from another dimension. I believe the Nazis were communing with both principalities and Watchers. These spirits began providing advanced technology to Nazi scientists. One of the reasons Nazi Germany hosted the Olympics in 1936 in Berlin was to showcase their superior technology and advanced genetics. Nazi Germany also entered World War II with superior technology, from the V rockets to the first jet fighters.

Little did Germany know that it was never meant to win World War II. Long before World Wars I and II, the Illuminati planned out both wars. A researcher at the University of Virginia provides the following insights regarding the Illuminati:

In the 1780s, the Bavarian Government found out about the Illuminati's subversive activities, forcing the Illuminati to disband and go underground. For the next few decades, the Illuminati operated under various names and guises, still in active pursuit of their ultimate goal. According to the Illuminati, the Napoleonic Wars were a direct result of Illuminati intervention, and were intended to weaken the governments of Europe. One of the results of these wars was the "Congress of Vienna", supposedly brought about by the Illuminati who there attempted to form a one world government in the form of a "League of Nations." However, Russia held out and the league of nations was not formed, causing great animosity towards the Russian government on the part of the Illuminati.

Their short-term plan foiled, the Illuminati adopted a different strategy. The Illuminati say that they achieved control over the European economy through the International Bankers and directed the composition of Karl Marx's Communist Manifesto and its anti-thesis written by Karl Ritter in order to use the differences between the two ideologies to enable them to "divide larger and larger members of the human race into opposing camps so that they could be armed and then brainwashed into fighting and destroying each other."

Under new leadership by an American general named Albert Pike, the Illuminati worked out a blueprint for three world wars throughout the 20th century that would lead to a one world government by the end of the 20th century. According to the Illuminati, the First World War was fought to destroy Czarism in Russia (the Illuminati had held a grudge against the Czarist regime since Russia had thwarted its plans for a one world government after the Napoleonic Wars) and to establish Russia as a stronghold of Communism.

Likewise, the Illuminati claim that the Second World War pitted the Fascists against the "political Zionists" so as to build up International Communism until it equaled in strength that of the United Christendom. According to Illuminati plans, the Third World War, which is to be fought between the political Zionists and the leaders of the Moslem world, will drain the international community to the extent that they will have no choice but to form a one world government.[134]

This information agrees with the information presented in the documentary from Antiquities Research, *Eye of the Phoenix: Secrets of the Dollar Bill.*

Germany was never meant to win World War II. Several things were to be accomplished:

- To get the attention of world powers and show the technology that the Watchers could bestow
- To see how quickly a nation or people would surrender their belief in the God of the Bible for something they perceived as superior
- To establish a medium in which the influence and technology of the Watchers could be seeded into all the nations of the world
- To spread socialism/communism throughout Europe (WWI was to replace the czars of Russia with a communistic nation)

Operation Paperclip in the United States and similar operations by other Allied nations ensured that the top Nazi scientists and superspies were brought into those nations. In the US, you can trace the foundation of the Central Intelligence Agency and NASA to those brought over under Operation Paperclip. Untold off-book black projects in the US were the continued experiments or programs of Nazi Germany. We did not just receive the technology; we received an embedded philosophy that was drawn from the Watchers. Shortly after WWII, Roswell may have been the first contact with the Watchers in the United States.

It was after America was infected with the Watcher virus (if you will) that prayer was taken out of school, abortion became legal, a sexual/occult revolution occurred, the fairy tale regarding the constitutional separation of church and state was introduced, our schools became battle zones, and the church slowly became spiritually comatose. Similar things have happened within every nation that accepted the Nazi specialists. This is not a coincidence; it was a planned, occult work that spanned several hundred years.

Since World War II, America became the technological giant on the earth. However, this was to create a desire within the other nations for communion with the Watchers. Today, Russia and China have supercomputers, space programs, advanced weaponry, and (as recently revealed on a Hagmann and Hagmann report [June 2014] with Stephen Quayle and Henry Gruver) new energy weapons that can circumvent the technology of our military.[135]

All of these plans and accomplishments of the Elite happened because of their absolute devotion to their sacred, esoteric texts and communion with these spirits of darkness. I am speaking of a devotion that changed every aspect of their lives: from basic paradigms to lifelong goals. They will dedicate their fortunes and future generations to accomplish the plans of those they are in communion with.

Further Evidence of the Return of the Watchers

Many ancient names are associated with the Illuminati; here are just a few:

- Rothschild
- DuPont
- Collins
- Reynolds

One of the more recent additions to the Illumaniti's ranks is the Rockefellers.

John D. Rockefeller made his fortune in the oil industry in the late 1800s. As his wealth and influence began to grow, he got the attention of the Elite. The Rothschilds bought interest in the Rockefeller empire here in the US, and a new partnership was forged. Both families began working together toward a New World Order.[136] Here is a statement from John Rockefeller's memoirs:

> Some even believe we are part of a secret cabal working against the best interests of the United States, characterizing my family and me as "internationalists" and of conspiring with others around the

world to build a more integrated global political and economic structure—one world, if you will. If that's the charge, I stand guilty, and I am proud of it.[137]

In our discussion, I want to concentrate on the guiding force for the Rockefeller family that allowed them to build such wealth and enabled the alignment with the Rothschild dynasty. I believe the Rockefellers gave us a clue in front of their center in New York City: Prometheus.

Prometheus was judged by the gods for both making men more godlike and giving them fire from the gods. His punishment involved him being taken to the Caucasus Mountains and being chained there with unbreakable, adamanite chains. There he was tormented day and night by a giant eagle tearing at his liver.[138]

The story of Prometheus comes closer to that of the Watchers than the Nephilim. The Watchers were bound with unbreakable chains and tormented by watching their children kill each other in the war of the Titans. Prometheus gave the fire of the gods to mankind. Within the occult, this fire is not thought of as a physical fire. It refers to forbidden knowledge. Former president George W. Bush referred to this fire in his second inaugural speech:

Today, I also speak anew to my fellow citizens:
    From all of you, I have asked patience in the hard task of securing America, which you have granted in good measure. Our

country has accepted obligations that are difficult to fulfill, and would be dishonorable to abandon. Yet because we have acted in the great liberating tradition of this nation, tens of millions have achieved their freedom. And as hope kindles hope, millions more will find it. By our efforts, **we have lit a fire as well—a fire in the minds of men**. It warms those who feel its power, it burns those who fight its progress, and one day this untamed fire of freedom will reach the darkest corners of our world.[139]

I believe our president was announcing to the world that the fire of the Watchers had returned and was flowing from the United States into other parts of the world.

Therefore, I believe, the alliance between the houses of the Rothschilds and Rockefellers was more than just about creating and managing wealth. The Rockefellers had proven on the world stage that they were in communion with a Watcher. This communion not only created their wealth but their desire for a New World Order.

The Rockefellers, the Federal Reserve, and a Nephilim Altar

A believer named Tim Bence has spent a number of years on a specific assignment from God: tearing down Canaanite/Nephilim altars around the world. He has done this, at the direction of the Holy Spirit, throughout the Middle East and in Germany. In an episode of *Revolutionary Radio* with Rob Skiba, Tim shares an extraordinary journey here in the US. This is a summary of his discussion on the show:

After returning from a three-month trip in the Middle East, God instructed Bence not to drive home from New York, but to drive to Jekyll Island in Georgia. He really wanted to drive home and see his family, but God assured him that there was an important reason for this trip. So, Bence called and made reservations with the hotel on the island, and began his journey there.

God supernaturally set up the lodging and a meeting with the curator of the museum on the island. Through his conversation with the curator, Bence discovered some interesting facts:

- A tribe of Indians called the Timucuas lived on the island. Skeletal remains of these Indians indicated that they were Nephilim (they were between eight and eight and a half feet tall).
- These Indians practiced child sacrifice over a stone altar that was exactly like the Canaanite altars of the Middle East.
- The houses on the island were built on top of the remains of the Indian village.
- John D. Rockefeller's house was built directly over the Timucuas altar.
- The men who formulated the secret plan of the Federal Reserve were sitting in a room directly over that altar during their meetings.

The Watcher who was leading John D. Rockefeller guided him to one of the few sites in America with a Nephilim altar to establish the Federal Reserve! Although the curator was not a spiritual man, he allowed Bence to pray in that very room to break the power of the dark energy that was released there. Within a very short period, the banks began to be judged by God, and the biggest government bailout in history began.[140]

Now you know the rest of the story.

The Progressive Return of the Watchers

As I prayed and researched the Watchers and their return, I believe they were not all released at one time. The Watcher identified as Prometheus may have been among the first to be released. In fact, it would appear that the final four Watchers will not be released until midway through the Tribulation period.

> And the sixth angel sounded, and I heard a voice from the four horns of the golden altar which is before God,

Saying to the sixth angel which had the trumpet, Loose the four angels which are bound in the great river Euphrates.

And the four angels were loosed, which were prepared for an hour, and a day, and a month, and a year, for to slay the third part of men. (Revelation 9:13–15)

Revelation 9 is an interesting chapter. Creatures resembling the genetic experiments of Genesis 6 are released. The Word identifies their commander.

And they had a king over them, which is the angel of the bottomless pit, whose name in the Hebrew tongue is Abaddon, but in the Greek tongue hath his name Apollyon. (Revelation 9:11)

Dr. Tom Horn has decoded the identity of this mysterious Apollyon:

In the New Testament, the identity of the god Apollo, repeat-coded in the Great Seal of the United States as the Masonic "messiah" who returns to rule the earth, is the same spirit—verified by the same name—that will inhabit the political leader of the end-times New World Order. According to key Bible prophecies, the Antichrist will be the progeny or incarnation of the ancient spirit, Apollo. Second Thessalonians 2:3 warns: "Let no man deceive you by any means: for that day shall not come, except there come a falling away first, and that man of sin be revealed, the son of perdition [Apoleia; Apollyon, Apollo]." Numerous scholarly and classical works identify "Apollyon" as the god "Apollo"—the Greek deity "of death and pestilence," and Webster's Dictionary points out that "Apollyon" was a common variant of "Apollo" throughout history. An example of this is found in the classical play by the ancient Greek playwright Aeschylus, The Agamemnon of Aeschylus, in which Cassandra repeats more than once, "Apollo, thou destroyer, O Apollo, Lord of fair streets, Apollyon to me."

Accordingly, the name Apollo turns up in ancient literature with the verb *apollymi* or *apollyo* ("destroy"), and scholars including W. R. F. Browning believe apostle Paul may have identified the god Apollo as the "spirit of Antichrist" operating behind the persecuting Roman emperor, Domitian, who wanted to be recognized as "Apollo incarnate" in his day. Such identifying of Apollo with despots and "the spirit of Antichrist" is consistent even in modern history. For instance, note how Napoleon's name literally translates to "the true Apollo."

Revelation 17:8 likewise ties the coming of Antichrist with Apollo, revealing that the Beast shall ascend from the bottomless pit and enter him:

The Beast that thou sawest was, and is not; and shall ascend out of the Bottomless Pit, and go into perdition [Apolia, Apollo]: and they that dwell on the Earth shall wonder, whose names were not written in the Book of Life from the foundation of the world, when they behold the Beast that was, and is not, and yet is.[141]

"Apollo" (Antichrist) is another name for Nimrod. With Nimrod commanding an army of Nephilim, the last four remaining Watchers are released from their captivity. The timing of all of this is divinely strategic. Remember what the *Book of Enoch* tells us regarding the Watchers:

And the Lord said unto Michael: "Go, bind Semjaza and his associates who have united themselves with women so as to have defiled themselves with them in all their uncleanness.

"And when their sons have slain one another, and they have seen the destruction of their beloved ones, bind them fast for seventy generations in the valleys of the earth, *till the day of their judgment and of their consummation, till the judgment that is forever and ever is consummated.*" (1 Enoch 10:11–12, emphasis added)

This also corresponds with Jude 1:6:

And the angels which kept not their first estate, but left their own habitation, he hath reserved in everlasting chains under darkness unto the judgment of the great day.

The last of the Watchers are released during the sixth trumpet in the book of Revelation. When the seventh trumpet sounds, the process of God judging the earth begins, and God's seven bowls of perfected wrath are poured out. The wrath of God does not begin until all of the Watchers have been freed to receive their part of this judgment.

What the Return of the Watchers Means

In the last days, we are facing an enemy the early Church never faced. The Watchers have been imprisoned since 3000 BC. As their release began around the turn of the twentieth century, socialism, communism, and liberalism weakened both Western society and the Church. Technology has redefined (or replaced) interpersonal relationships, and certain breakthroughs have created a false sense of humans wielding the power of the gods. The Watchers have joined ranks with the principalities, powers, rulers of darkness, spiritual wickedness, the demonic Nephilim spirits, and the Luciferian Elite. They are preparing for the greatest spiritual war of human history, while the Church at large is mesmerized, is enthralled with entertainment, and has taken up permanent residence in spiritual preschool!

We seldom pray, much less know how to commune with God. We use grace as an excuse for our immaturity and lack of responsibility before God instead of as a spiritual force to work out our salvation with fear and trembling (Philippians 2:12). Church services are no longer places where we are to be confronted with spiritual reality and the gospel; they are now places where we go to be entertained and presented psychobabble/New Age jargon to feel better about ourselves. No spiritual depth, no real, life-transforming power flows from the cross of Christ, and biblical illiteracy is at an all-time high! Today, the Church is NOT "Rapture ready" (regardless of which eschatological position you take). For the most part, the modern Church is wearing Babylonian garments and has forsaken the kingdom's robes of righteousness. We must awaken from spiritual slumber and change!

It is time to bring our spiritual "A" game. We need to get out of entertainment mode and get back to the basic spiritual disciplines of an authentic biblical faith. We need to turn off the TV more often (to include much of Christian TV that has been infected with Babylon) and learn spiritual devotion again, because it leads to a sanctified life filled with the power of God.

In chapters 10 through 12, we will examine in detail how the Remnant can prepare for the days ahead! Now, let's examine how the Elite have captured mankind in chapter 7.

chapter seven

The Unfinished Work of Nimrod

Part 3: The Capturing of Mankind

The best way to take control over a people and control them utterly is to take a little of their freedom at a time, to erode rights by a thousand tiny and almost imperceptible reductions. In this way, the people will not see those rights and freedoms being removed until past the point at which these changes cannot be reversed.

—Adolf Hitler, *Mein Kampf*

When God intervened at the Tower of Babel, He interrupted Nimrod's plan of hunting and enslaving all of mankind and turning every single person on the planet against God. Since that time, those within the mystery religions have been honing their crafts toward this ultimate goal. In this chapter, we will examine several of the principles they utilize in their endeavors and the systems they have put into place to implement their overall plan.

BRIEFING NOTE

Cursory Examination of Principles and Organizations

For the purpose of this briefing, I am only providing a cursory examination of the principles and organizations and highlighting how they apply to completing Nimrod's unfinished work. Entire books have been written on each principle or organization by other gifted authors.

The Five-Staged Principle of Adam Weishaupt

Adam Weishaupt was the professor of canon law at the Jesuit-operated university at Ingolstadt. A number of researchers believe Weishaupt was not the one who originated the idea of the Illuminati; rather, he was hired by the house of Rothschild to unite various esoteric ideas into a perfected formula. Weishaupt drew from the deep wells of occult esotericism embodied within the bloodlines and blended it with the precepts that were honed to perfection within the Jesuit order.

Weishaupt's perfected concept became known as the "Law of Fives," in which he took the concept of fives to a whole new level. It appears that he was obsessed with a universal application of this number.

He started with only five members in his inner circle of the Illuminati—which formed a pentagram. He either borrowed the concept of the "star chamber" from the Elite or he may have formed the very first one.

He had five goals for the Illuminati:

1. Abolition of monarchies and all ordered governments
2. Abolition of private property and inheritances
3. Abolition of patriotism and nationalism
4. Abolition of family life and the institution of marriage, and the establishment of communal education of children
5. Abolition of all religion[142]

He blended five esoteric concepts:

1. Islamic mysticism
2. Jesuit mind-control techniques
3. Luciferianism
4. Freemasonry concepts of eternal life
5. Mind expansion through hallucinogenic drugs

He believed that history repeated itself in a cycle of five stages. If you could take control of those stages, you could redirect the outcome. These stages are:

Stage 1—Chaos
Stage 2—Discord
Stage 3—Confusion
Stage 4—Bureaucracy
Stage 5—Aftermath [143]

I have wondered, during my research regarding Weishaupt's obsession with the Law of Fives, if it was not an advanced occult principle at work to create a more stable conduit that would tap into the false grace Lucifer created when he fell. Every aspect of occult endeavors in the world functions through some aspect of that perverted anointing. When you examine the historical movements of the mystery religions, their advancement appears to have accelerated in strength, depth, and global power since Weishaupt formulated the amalgamation of the various branches into one focused plan.

 With these principles in hand, Adam established the Illuminati on May 1, 1776. By 1777, he joined the Masonic Lodge Theodor zum guten Rath in Munich. [144] From there, his principles were embedded into Masonic philosophy and were the main force behind the French Revolution.

Our peace sign today is an eighteenth-century Illuminati symbol that represents the fulfillment of Adam Weishaupt's satanic Law of Fives. [145]

Another individual in human history who made the hand sign for the

Law of Fives popular was Winston Churchill. Here's a statement he made between the two world wars:

> From the days of Sparticus, Wieskhopf, Karl Marx, Trotsky, Rosa Luxemberg, and Emma Goldman, this world conspiracy has been steadily growing. This conspiracy played a definite recognizable role in the tragedy of the French revolution. It has been the mainspring of every subversive movement during the 19th century. And now at last this band of extraordinary personalities from the underworld of the great cities of Europe and America have gripped the Russian people by the hair of their head and have become the undisputed masters of that enormous empire.[146]
> [Note: Churchill is referring to how the Elite toppled the czars in Russia and worked to establish a communistic nation.]

However, in 1929, Churchill's attitude changed dramatically regarding the Elite. It was not by accident that he was standing inside the New York Stock Exchange on Black Thursday, October 29, 1929, when the US Stock Market crashed. There are historical researchers who believe he was led there by the elite to be shown the power they possessed over the finances of the world. (The Elite were not hurt by the crash of 1929; in fact, many expanded their wealth greatly during the Great Depression.) The evening of the crash, Churchill was guest of honor at a bizarre "celebration" attended to by more than forty "bankers and master plungers" of Wall Street at the Fifth Avenue mansion of Bernard Baruch.[147] With this show of raw power, Churchill's attitude began to change. With all this in mind, it is little wonder that Churchill chose the hand sign of the Law of Fives as the sign of victory during World War II. It was his public signal indicating that he understood their plans and would submit to them.

The Law of Fives was later embedded into pop culture through a cult known as "Discordianism." An article from the Virginia Commonwealth University tells how this cult began:

Kerry Thornley and Greg Hill met at high school in East Whittier, California in 1956. They, and their friends Bob Newport and Bill Stephens were enthusiastic fans of *Mad* magazine, science fiction, radical politics, and philosophy. In 1957, the friends were drinking in a twenty-four hour bowling alley where they allegedly had a vision of a chimpanzee that showed them the Sacred Chao, a symbol similar to the *yin-yang*, with pentagon in one half, and an apple captioned *Kallisti* ("most beautiful") in the other half. The Sacred Chao is a symbol of Eris, the Goddess of Chaos (Discordia in Latin). Five nights later Eris herself appeared to Thornley and Hill. She told them:

I have come to tell you that you are free. Many ages ago, My consciousness left man, that he might develop himself. I return to find this development approaching completion, but hindered by fear and by misunderstanding. You have built for yourselves psychic suits of armor and clad in them, your vision is restricted, your movements are clumsy and painful, your skin is bruised, and your spirit is broiled in the sun. I am chaos. I am the substance from which your artists and scientists build rhythms. I am the spirit with which your children and clowns laugh in happy anarchy. I am chaos. I am alive and I tell you that you are free (Malaclypse the Younger 1994:2–3).[148]

Originally, the men presented Discordianism as a joke, a parody of religion that exposed the deficiencies of mainstream Christianity, and the materialist and conformist culture of post-war America. However, after the publication of the book, *Principa Discordia*, it began to take on a life of its own. The movement began to lean toward a type of paganism. Robert Anton Wilson was a major player in intensifying this movement toward complete Paganisation.[149]

Therefore, within the movement, the goddess of chaos (Eris) provided mankind with the "apple of discord" to begin the process of the Law of Fives being played out in human history. Discordianism represented an amalgamation of the biblical story of the Fall of man in the garden with Weishaupt's Law of Fives.

You might ask, "Is this Law of Fives working in our country today?" Just look at what has happened in America over the past few decades. Bureaucracy (Stage 4) has gotten out of control. In an article, Representative Ron Paul details how, on the first day of January 2012, forty thousand new laws were officially placed on the books.[150] It would seem that our current leaders have a god complex. With Washington micromanaging every aspect of our lives, they have us dancing on the precipice of a total collapse—morally, financially, and spiritually.

The only wild card that can derail the current luciferian cycle of organized chaos toward a New World Order is the body of Christ:

If my people, which are called by my name, shall humble themselves, and pray, and seek my face, and turn from their wicked ways; then will I hear from heaven, and will forgive their sin, and will heal their land. (2 Chronicles 7:14)

The Word does not tell us that the Elite conspirators must repent and pray. God instructs the body of Christ to do so. If we can wake up from the Babylonian spell of slumber that the Elite have cast upon us and return to true spiritual/biblical disciplines, we can prevent their plans from coming to pass. I was surprised at the testimony of Chaplain Lindsay Williams, in which he conveys how the Elite confessed to him that if Americans (especially Christians) would just wake up, it would either delay or stop their plans. It is time that we do just that! (More on this in the "Preparing the Remnant" chapters.)

The Hegelian Dialectic

An article in *Real News Australia* provides a good working definition and example of the Hegelian Dialectic:

What exactly is the Hegelian Dialectic? Georg Wilhelm Friedrich Hegel was a 19th century German philosopher who devised a particular dialectic, or, method of argument for resolving disagreements. His method of arriving at the truth by the exchange of logical arguments is a system of thought process is still use to this day.

To put it simply, the basis of Hegelianism dictates that the human mind can't understand anything unless it can be split into two polar opposites. Good/Evil, Right/Wrong, Left/Right.

For example when people are talking about 2 political parties, Labor or Liberal, what they're actually referring to, without realising it, is the **thesis** and the **antithesis** based off the Hegelian Dialectic. The only real debate that occurs is just the minor differences between those two parties. Nothing is said or done about the issues that neither left or right is discussing. This in particular will become more apparent as the election draws near.

Another form of the Hegelian Dialectic is **Problem—Reaction—Solution**. Most of us unwittingly fall victim to it all too often and sadly if we don't stop, we will continue to lose our free will and liberties. It has been widely used by our governments and corporations around the world. You could say that in terms of controlling the masses, and society in general, its deployment has been an effective tool in keeping humanity in check.

Almost all major events in history employ the Hegelian Dialectic of:

Problem—manufacture a crisis or take advantage of one already in place in order to get the desired **Reaction** of public outcry whereby the public demands a **Solution** which has been predetermined from the beginning.

A classic example is 9/11.

Only when you break the left/right paradigm and come to the realisation that the invasion of Iraq and Afghanistan and the whole fake, and not to mention contradictory, **war on terror** was the desired outcome for the neo-conservatives within the Bush administration and the whole military industrial complex. They in fact stated in their own white papers the need for another catastrophic and catalysing event like a "new Pearl Harbour."[151]

When you understand the hypothesis of the Hegelian Dialectic, you begin seeing it in virtually everything:

- Liberal vs. conservative
- Communism vs. capitalism
- Us vs. them (whites vs. blacks, nationals vs. foreigners, the list can go on and on)
- Crisis vs. solution by Washington (Remember when Chief of Staff Rahm Emanuel suggested that they should never let a good crisis go to waste?[152] Secretary of State Hillary Clinton also made the same statement later on as well.[153])

In each situation, we see the Hegelian Dialectic at work: Simply create (or wait for) a problem (thesis), offer a solution (antithesis), and move society where you really wanted it in the first place, where it normally would have refused to go (synthesis).

It seems Shakespeare was correct when he penned: "All the world's a stage, and all the men and women merely players."[154]

If you have viewed the outstanding documentary DVD, *Secret Mysteries of America's Beginnings—Volume 1: The New Atlantis,* you would know that William Shakespeare was a pen name for Sir Francis Bacon and a guild of esoteric writers who transformed the English language in their day. Within the works of Shakespeare, they embedded many occult practices and beliefs. It seems Mystery Babylon hides many of its workings in plain sight.

Now, when I watch the evening news, I no longer view it through the mental lens of information and events. I see the world as a stage and events as pieces upon the global chessboard. This allows me to look past the events to see the possible strategies of the Elite and enables me to become more effective as a watchman within the ministry to which God has called me.

I have found that the only way to step outside the wake of the continual tsunami of agendas inflicted upon society today is to stop, pray, and follow God's leading. You may end up looking like the odd duck in society, but they are the ones being herded to the slaughter. Paul's admonishment not to conform to the world is more powerful today than when he first penned it in the book of Romans.

> I beseech you therefore, brethren, by the mercies of God, that ye present your bodies a living sacrifice, holy, acceptable unto God, which is your reasonable service.
>
> And be not conformed to this world: but be ye transformed by the renewing of your mind, that ye may prove what is that good, and acceptable, and perfect, will of God. (Romans 12:1–2)

Congressman Verifies the Hegelian Dialectic as a Global Work

If you will recall in the last chapter, I shared how the Rockefeller and Rothschild dynasties combined to work toward a New World Order. Congressman Larry P. McDonald observed the Hegelian Dialectic in motion between communism and capitalism.

> The drive of the Rockefellers and their allies is **to create a one-world government combining super-capitalism and Communism under the same tent**, all under their control.... Do I mean conspiracy? Yes I do. I am convinced there is such a plot, international in scope, generations old in planning, and incredibly evil in intent. (Emphasis added)

McDonald made this statement in 1976. He was later killed by the Soviets when they shot down the Korean Airlines 747 on which he was a passenger.[155]

We have now examined the basic philosophical mechanisms the Elite are using to herd us toward a One World Order. Now let us examine their troops on the ground.

Freemasonry

The origin of Freemasonry, according to Masonic scholars, seems to focus on two theories:

1. Nimrod was the first Mason and established the order.
2. The Knights Templar and their secrets evolved into modern-day Freemasonry.

I have been asked over the years which theory is correct. I have come to believe that both are correct. The seeds of Freemasonry were planted in Babylon, watered by Egypt, and nurtured over the millennia by the mystery religions. The progression of its infection upon mankind went from Babylon to Egypt to Greece to Rome. Constantine's brilliant political and occult move was to encase the mystery religions in a veneer of pseudo Christianity. (This same concept was adopted by Freemasons in America, who clothed their esoteric work in a cloak of Protestant Christianity.) Prophecy researcher Walter J. Veith has hypothesized in his video on *The Secret behind Secret Societies*[156] that with the Reformation came a moving away from the mystery religions established within the Catholic Church and a move toward a pure biblical faith. The Jesuit Order's countermove was to establish Freemasonry to reestablish the mystery religions in the Protestant Movement. If this is the case, Jesuit Professor Adam Weishaupt was either a course correction or the second phase of the plan. It would seem to even the casual observer that they were very successful. I have been amazed at how many fundamental, evangelical ministers are Masons today. As a minister of the gospel, I would have a problem with any organization that uses primarily Egyptian symbols for its organization.

I do not believe I need to convince those who would read my book that Freemasonry is esoteric and part of the mystery religions. The cursory readings of Albert Pike or Manly P. Hall (or even just the names of their works) would convince any open-minded believer. However, I will say this for any member of the Blue Lodge that might stumble upon this work: The oath and ceremony you went through to enter the Lodge is word for word and step for step the same ritual used to become a witch within any coven.[157] (So which came first, the coven or the Lodge?) Again, the words of the apostle Paul are more relevant today than when he wrote them long ago:

> Be ye not unequally yoked together with unbelievers: for what fellowship hath righteousness with unrighteousness? and what communion hath light with darkness?
>
> And what concord hath Christ with Belial? or what part hath he that believeth with an infidel?
>
> And what agreement hath the temple of God with idols? for ye are the temple of the living God; as God hath said, I will dwell in them, and walk in them; and I will be their God, and they shall be my people.
>
> Wherefore come out from among them, and be ye separate, saith the Lord, and touch not the unclean *thing*; and I will receive you,
>
> And will be a Father unto you, and ye shall be my sons and daughters, saith the Lord Almighty. (2 Corinthians 6:14–18, emphasis added)

The Scope of Freemasonry

We need to understand that Freemasonry literally covers the globe. As the influence of America began to swell internationally, Freemasonry spread throughout the world in its wake. It is interesting to note that Skull and Bones (an elite Masonic organization) member George W. Bush went to war against 33rd-degree Freemason and Central Intelligence Agency (CIA)-trained operative Osama bin Laden.[158] This has led many to believe that America was behind the attack on 9/11/01. I believe their scope of vision is too small. Every bit of information I have uncovered, to include the reoccurrence of the number eleven (which is very significant in both Masonic and esoteric workings) points to the fact that it was the work of the Luciferian Elite. The tragedy of 9/11 was simply one piece to a much larger puzzle to facilitate a New World Order (and not, as many have postulated, to move America toward neoconservatism).

Masonic Lodges worldwide are the recruiting grounds for the Elite in search of new ground troops. Freemasons who have the temperament and belief system for the luciferian work are shuffled off to the side and then brought into separate circles of influence within the Masonic system. The average members of the Lodge labor within their communities and become the outer layer of protection for the occult core. Those members become part of local churches, civic organizations, businesses, and political parties. Whether or not they realize it, they are indeed connected to those within the darker circles of Freemasonry, with a stronger cord than the tow that was originally placed around their necks. I have mentored aspirants of the gospel ministry now for more than thirty years, and I have counseled students regarding the stifling of revival in their ministries by certain members of the board or congregation: Most of the time, those individuals were Freemasons. I remember a particular case in the early 1990s: God began moving in the ministry of one of our students. During a vacation Bible school, he saw nearly seventy children accept Jesus as their Lord and Savior within a two-week period. Any Christian would have been overjoyed by such an event. Within less than a week after this event, he was fired from his position as pastor. He later discovered that most of board members were Masons and active members of the local Lodge. Needless to say, he was dismayed and devastated by the actions against him.

Skull and Bones

The definitive work on the Skull and Bones is the book *America's Secret Establishment: An Introduction to the Order of Skull and Bones* by Anthony C. Sutton. I would also like to mention that my colleagues at Defender

Publishing, Terry Cook and Dr. Thomas Horn, provided a noteworthy summary of the Order in their book, *Beast Tech*. It is not my desire to replicate their fine work. I would prefer to examine the Order through the lens of a Christian educator and focus on the unfinished work of Nimrod.

The Order was founded in 1833 at Yale University by General William Huntington Russell and Alphonso Taft.[159] The Order is known by several names: Brotherhood of Death, Skull and Bones, Bones, the Order, and Chapter 322. The Order is a chapter of a German secret society that is linked directly to the Illuminati. This secret society is dominated by several old-line American Elite families as well as new wealth that has existed from 1833 to the present day.

- Whitney Family
- Stimson Family
- Perkins Family
- Taft Family
- Wadsworth Family
- Gilman Family
- Payne Family
- Davison Family
- Pillsbury Family
- Sloane Family
- Weyerhaeuser Family
- Harriman Family
- Rockefeller Family
- Lord Family
- Bundy Family
- Phelps Family [160]

Each year, fifteen new members are accepted into the Order from the group of junior-year students at Yale University. I believe the number of candidates is important, and it shows a philosophical link to the Illuminati: There are three groups of five candidates. Weishaupt's Law of Fives seems to govern the activities of the Order. Members of Elite families seem to be guaranteed membership. Other exceptional students at Yale can be offered membership if their particular skill set and education would prove beneficial to the plans of the Order.

The power and reach of the Order is tremendous. Sutton writes:

> Above all, the Order is powerful, unbelievably powerful. If the reader will persist and examine the evidence to be presented—which is overwhelming—there is no doubt his view of the world will suddenly come sharply into focus, with almost frightening clarity.[161]

After researching the Order, I have concluded that it is a more powerful and extremely exclusive Masonic Lodge reserved for the American Elite. If the local Masonic Lodges are for the gathering and indoctrination of the ground troops, then the Order is the Illuminati's war college here in the United States. (Its sister institution is Oxford University, which we will look at shortly.) It is in the Order that the high-ranking officers of the Elite's army are prepared for various assignments worldwide. At the beginning of his book, Sutton places a quote from a Yale student in 1873:

> We offer no objections to their existing clan. No one disputes with them this right, we question but the plan on which they act, —that only he who wears upon his breast their emblem, he for every post shall be considered best.[162]

Even in 1873, a degree from Yale was not enough for the most powerful posts in the United States. Skull and Bones members were given strategic positions in every field: government, financing, foreign affairs, religion, and the corporate world. Their members became chiefs who established policies in literally every aspect of American life. Sutton declares that "the Order has penetrated or been the dominant influence in sufficient policy, research, and opinion making organizations **that it determines** the basic direction of American society" (emphasis added).[163]

One of the ways the Order gains control over various groups or movements is to ensure that the FIRST president, chairman, or main leader is a member.[164] It is the first leader of any organization who sets the foundational agenda and philosophy maintained throughout its lifecycle. Having the highest level of leadership in these organizations also allows freedom to embed other members into key positions. Since this networking and embedding of members have been going on since the 1830s, it is easy to see how the Order controls nearly every aspect of our society.

This penetration of the Order includes all Protestant denominations. Sutton writes:

> About 2 percent of the Order is in the Church (all Protestant denominations), although this percentage has declined in recent years. A key penetration is the Union Theological Seminary, affiliated with Columbia University in New York. This Seminary, a past subject of investigation for Communist infiltration, has close links to the Order.[165]

Is it any wonder why Protestant denominations have been slowly moving away from true biblical standards in both beliefs and moral standards over the past hundred years? The Order has actively been working in the background to produce this backslidden state!

The Order's Involvement in Education

Sutton goes into great detail about how the Order perverted education in America. Although not an Order member, American psychologist G.

Stanley Hall was the agent of choice for the Order to use to infect the education of our children.

Hall was a student at Union Theological Seminary and was highly influenced by Henry B. Smith. This is where his indoctrination and training appears to have begun. After graduation, Smith was financially broke, but was encouraged by Smith to go to Europe to study experimental psychology under Wilhelm Wundt. Another member of the Order contributed one thousand dollars to help finance his trip. (In those days, this was a very large sum of money.)

While in Europe, Hall studied under Wilhelm Wundt at the University of Leipzig. At the time, he was also highly influenced by the philosophies of Hegel (think Hegelian Dialectic). His training in Europe lasted about twelve years.

Upon returning home, Smith was again flat broke. This financial setback did not last long, as the Order had plans for him. One day, the president of Harvard showed up, out of the blue, at his home and invited him to lecture at Harvard on education. Then, in 1881, to his surprise, Johns Hopkins University offered him the Chair of Professor of Psychology and Pedagogy (Education). We also find that Smith was not the only one being groomed by the Order. Sutton provides the following chart of where students of Wundt were placed and the number of doctoral graduates their efforts generated.

American Students of Wundt Teaching at U.S. Universities[25]	Career At	Number of Doctorates They Awarded up to 1948
G. Stanley Hall	Johns Hopkins and Clark University	149 doctorates
J. McKeen Cattell	Columbia University	344 doctorates
E.W. Scripture	Yale University	138 doctorates
E.D. Titchener	Cornell University	112 doctorates
H. Gale	Minnesota University	123 doctorates
G.T.W. Patrick	Iowa University	269 doctorates
C.H. Judd	University of Chicago	196 doctorates

Just imagine the impact that 1,331 experts at the doctoral level with training specifically tailored to the agenda of the Elite can have upon the American educational system.

All were trained with concepts that originated at the University of Leipzig. Why is this so important? Wilhelm Wundt was a pioneer in psychological conditioning. We are all familiar with Ivan Pavlov and his experimental conditioning of a dog to salivate when a bell rang. **Pavlov was a student of Wundt**. These men and their doctoral graduates brought conditional training into the elementary and secondary educational systems in the United States. Our children are no longer taught; they are trained and conditioned to respond to the stimuli provided by the Order. In the eyes of the Order, there is little difference in the average American citizen and the dogs Pavlov trained to respond to his cues. Thanks to the Order, education in America today pales in comparison to that of the 1890s! Now we are conditioned to vote their candidates into office, work in their corporations, and purchase their goods. Don't think, don't connect the dots; just respond to the stimuli they provide in the media. It would appear that all of the testing advertising does in marketing research groups is merely to find the right "trigger" to gain the planned, conditioned response they want.

Perhaps one of the reasons that home schooling is frowned upon today is not because home-schooled children are academically inferior (in fact, the opposite is true), but because they lack the psychological conditioning provided within the structured educational system the Elite built in the early twentieth century. (We must also remember that one of the goals of Weishaupt was the communal education of children.) Is it possible that the home-schooled children present a threat to the system of psychological conditioning in education and, thus, to the overall plans for our nation? If one would take time to listen to the Progressive rants against home schoolers, one would think they were an actual plague upon society! Yet colleges and universities are beginning to realize that home-schooled children are far better prepared for the rigors of postsecondary learning. The Elite's response was Common Core, which: (1) changes the educational structure so that home-schooled children will not meet the academic requirements of postsecondary education unless Common Core programming is added to their curriculum; and (2) further enhances the psychological conditioning of the next generation to become even more compliant to the stimuli provided by the Elite.

The Order's Work Does Not Stop There

In additional chapters of Sutton's book, we find documentation that the Soviet Union was the creation of the Order. That's right: Communism with a capital "C." The Order is also linked to the financing of the Nazis—the National Socialist Party in Germany. If you do your homework, Karl Marx's *Communist Manifesto* is nothing more than a reworded version of Weishaupt's work and the Illuminati document, *Protocols of the Learned Elders of Zion!*[166] The Order is not involved in building up America or even in hedging up American interests. The Order is about moving the world into the New World Order that Weishaupt envisioned for the Illuminati!

With World War I, the Order removed the czars of Russia and replaced them with communism. With World War II, they weakened Europe (and the Church in Europe), and moved it toward socialism. (Now you know why our leaders in the US continually compare what we should be doing to Europe, from health/medicine to law. They are using Europe as a justification for converting America into a socialistic state.) World War III has been planned to be between Israel and Islam; the synthesis will cause the world to abandon all other religions and embrace luciferianism.[167]

So, is America moving toward communism? Nikita Khrushchev, the former general secretary of the Communist Party of the Soviet Union during the Cold War, bragged that we would.

> We can't expect the American People to jump from Capitalism to Communism, **but we can assist their elected leaders in giving them small doses of Socialism**, until they awaken one day to find that they have Communism.
> —Nikita Khrushchev[168] (Emphasis added)

I am amazed at what is going on in the political left today. Just this week, an article in the *Washington Examiner* detailed the conflict between the chairman of the Federal Exchange Commission and Democrats who desire to violate the First Amendment and either censor or ban certain conservative books:

> The Chairman of the Federal Election Commission today blasted Democratic colleagues opposed to his effort to protect conservative media after they imposed rules on the publisher of Rep. Paul Ryan's new book, opening the door to future book regulations—or even a ban.
>
> "By failing to affirm this publisher's constitutional right, statutory right, to disseminate a political book free from FEC conditions and regulations, we have effectively asserted regulatory jurisdiction over a book publisher," warned Chairman Lee E. Goodman, one of three Republicans on the six-person FEC.
>
> "That failure reveals a festering legal uncertainty and chill for the free press rights of books and book publishers to publish and disseminate political books free from government regulation," he added.[169]

Is it just me, or do political speeches and news headlines seem to be more appropriate in Russia than America lately? Unless Americans (and especially Christians) wake up and take action, the Elite will have America spelled as "Amerika!"

With all of that said, I don't think communism is the end goal of the Illuminati or of the Order. Communism creates dependence upon the state, enables the state to own everything (to include its citizens), and removes God from the collective consciousness of that society. These three things must be accomplished in order to create a luciferian New World Order. So, communism is just step B to get us to step C—luciferianism!

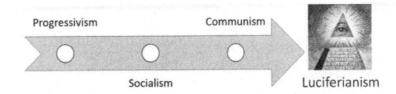

Progressivism   Communism

Socialism   Luciferianism

The Elite's Global Round Tables and Connection with Oxford

The Elite leave nothing to chance in the completion of Nimrod's work. Various Round Tables needed to be built to create a prison planet. This was the vision of Cecil Rhodes. We find quite a bit of information on Rhodes and his Round Tables on Wikipedia:

> The **Round Table movement**, founded in 1909, was an association of organisations promoting closer union between Britain and its self-governing colonies. The movement began at a conference at Plas Newydd, Lord Anglesey's estate in Wales, over the weekend of 4–6 September. The framework of the organisation was devised by Lionel Curtis, but the overall idea was due to Lord Milner. Former South Africa administrator Philip Kerr became secretary to the organisation.
>
> **Society of the Elect**
> Historian Carroll Quigley claimed that the Round Table Groups were connected to a secret society, which South African diamond baron Cecil Rhodes is believed to have set up with similar goals. Rhodes was believed by some to have formed this secret society in his lifetime. This secret society is supposed to have been named the *Society of the Elect.*
>
> Rhodes first formalised his idea with William T. Stead, editor of the *Pall Mall Gazette*, when he and Stead agreed on the structure of the secret society. This proposed secret society had an elaborate hierarchical structure, based on that of the Jesuits, which comprised: at the top, the position of "General of the Society"—a position mod-

elled on the General of the Jesuits—to be occupied by Rhodes, with Stead and Lord Rothschild as his designated successors; an executive committee called the "Junta of Three," comprising Stead, Milner and Reginald Baliol Brett (Lord Esher); then a "Circle of Initiates," consisting of a number of notables including Cardinal Manning, Lord Arthur Balfour, Lord Albert Grey and Sir Harry Johnston; and outside of this was the "Association of Helpers," the broad mass of the Society. One of the puzzles surrounding this meeting is whether the "Society of the Elect" actually came into being. Carroll Quigley claims in *Tragedy and Hope* (1966) that Rhodes's "Society of the Elect" was not only "formally established" in 1891, although its first inception existed several years prior (1889), but that its "outer circle" known as the "Association of Helpers" was "later organised by Milner as the Round Table."

In several of his wills, Rhodes left money for the continuation of the project. However, in his later wills, Rhodes abandoned the idea and instead concentrated on what became the Rhodes scholarships, which enabled American, German and English scholars to study for free at Oxford University.

Similar Organisations

Lionel Curtis founded the Royal Institute of International Affairs in June 1920. A year later its sister organisation, the Council on Foreign Relations, was formed in America. One of the founders of the sister organisation was another member of the Round Table groups, Walter Lippmann.[170]

Cecil Rhodes belonged to one of the thirteen bloodlines and was a Luciferian Elite. He was also a graduate of Oxford University. Oxford is the European university of choice for the Elite families in preparing the next generation for their work. Rhodes developed his fortune through raping the resources of Southern Africa, in particular, diamonds. He created the De Beers Diamond consortium (or perhaps a better word would be "cartel") and used his wealth to advance the plans of the Elite.

What the information in Wikipedia gets wrong is that Rhodes did not abandon his concept of creating Round Table/think tank groups for the development of the Scholarship Program. Rather, the work on the prototype for the think tanks was completed. Lionel Curtis and others within the Elite would go to work replicating his Round Table/think tank concept worldwide. Now, Rhodes' task was to create a scholarship fund that would bring the best and the brightest into the Elite's fold by initiating them at Oxford University through the prestigious Rhodes Scholarship Program. He required well-educated postgraduate initiates to fill the ranks of the newly developing Round Tables worldwide.

Today, his Round-Table effort spans the entire globe.

These think tanks now develop policies that virtually control every segment of the globe. One of the primary purposes of the United Nations was to become the enforcement agency for the new policies. Most Americans would be surprised to learn that treaties can usurp the Constitution in the United States. UN treaties are being used to bring the agenda of the Elite to nations, whose own constitutions or charters would normally prevent the implementation of their plans. (This means the Second Amendment does not necessarily need to be overturned by our government. All they will need to do is ratify a treaty from the United Nations to bring complete gun control to our nation.)

Evidence of More Round Tables

While listening to a newly released briefing by Chaplain Lindsay Williams, some of the information he provided proved very enlightening.

There are now Asians among the Elite, and the Asian Round Tables seem to be at odds with the European/American ones.

The plan of the Elite for the past two hundred years was to eventually collapse America, after which the occult core would jettison its Protestant Christian outer cloak. Then America would become the phoenix rising from the ashes as a gleaming pagan super society. The delays in their plans over the past decade are because the Asian Elite are no longer in love with that plan.[171] They would prefer a permanent transfer of power and wealth to Asia, thus stifling the overall plan. If it were not for this conflict, the United States dollar would have been worthless after 2009.

I believe this conflict was caused by the grace of God. In America, we need more time to wake up the slumbering saints, equip them for the spiritual battle, and prepare them for the struggle ahead. If the body of Christ would awaken from slumber and move into maturity, instead of Christianity being jettisoned, we could see the occult core banished from our shores and lodged in Europe, where they prophetically belong!

The Controlled Media

In the colonies that originally formed our great nation, the freedom of the press was a revolutionary idea. The press accepted a unique task within the formation of America to become the watchdog over the newly discovered freedom from the Elite in Europe that had oppressed humanity for so long. It was almost, in a sense, a social sacred trust with the people of our nation. It served to keep a balance within our democracy. In fact, at the founding of our nation, freedom of the press only existed here. This free press became the model for other nations that desired to form republics similar to ours.

What course of action would the Elite need to take to control information within a nation that had embraced the concept of freedom of the press? The answer is: Buy and control the press. In 1917, Congressman Oscar Callaway entered into the congressional record the fact that JP Morgan had hired twelve top news managers to first determine the most influential news agencies in America and then to calculate how many of them would need to be purchased to control the general policy of the daily news. The men informed JP Morgan that only twenty-five agencies would be required to basically control the flow of information that was reported to the American people. An agreement was reached; the policy of the papers was bought, and an editor was placed at each paper to ensure that all published information was in keeping with the new policy. Shortly after the purchase, a front group was formed by Morgan, Warburg, and Rockefeller to define the new policy and, thus, control the news in the United States.[172] From that time on, the control of our news information was entwined with the Rhodes think tank known as the **Council on Foreign Relations**. Here are the top twenty media corporations in the US according to mediaowners.com. All but two of the following are members of the Council on Foreign Relations (numbers 18 and 19 are not).

1. Time Warner Inc.
2. Walt Disney Co. (ABC)
3. Viacom Inc.
4. News Corp.
5. CBS Corp.
6. Cox Enterprises
7. NBC Universal
8. Gannett Co., Inc.
9. Clear Channel Communications Inc.
10. Advance Publications Inc.
11. Tribune Co.
12. McGraw-Hill Cos.
13. Hearst Corp.
14. Washington Post Co.
15. The New York Times Co.
16. E. W. Scripps Co.
17. McClatchy Co.
18. Thomson Corp.
19. Freedom Communications Inc.
20. A&E Television Networks [173]

These news agencies control the flow of information in this country. Each answers to the Elite regarding news policy, what news items are covered, the correct agenda slant to embed within the reports, what information should be suppressed, which candidates for political office should be given air time, and even what items are to be added as distractions to keep the American people away from what is really going on.

When I travel outside the United States, the main complaint I hear about America is how controlled our news media is. Citizens in Europe and Canada have expressed to me in detail their amazement about just how controlled our news is and how the media works so hard to keep Americans in the dark.

From the turn of the twentieth century to the age of the Internet, freedom of the press was an illusion. Fringe newspapers across the country did try to publish the truth, but they were actively marginalized by the mainstream media. To show how ridiculous this situation has become, there have been several major stories in the past two decades that a national tabloid, *The Star*, broke! Just imagine a story that would torpedo an Elite-endorsed political hopeful running for office right between articles such as "Aliens Are among Us" and "Elvis Lives!" Then came the Internet, which began to change the dynamics of the flow of information in our country. Internet news services and news bloggers have become a real problem for the Elite and their controlled news media. Congress has attempted to define who the members of the press are (i.e., only those of the Elite media) through new legislation, as well as resurrecting the "Fairness Doctrine," which is not fair at all. So far, the Fairness Doctrine has not been successfully reintroduced, and Congress has failed to redefine who can receive protection as "the press." Let's pray they never succeed!

The Elite's Control: Beyond the News

Did you know that a small, select group of writers controls everything from the scripts in movies and your favorite TV shows...all the way to the dialogues by your favorite late-night television show host? A few years ago, the Writers Guild of America went on strike. The only program with fresh scripts was the evening news. Production of movies, TV shows, and, yes, even late-night TV stopped. That year, several new TV shows died—not because they were flops, but because no one wanted to watch the same four or five shows over and over again. By the time the strike was over, several shows were cancelled and even a few movies in production died in its wake.

I am not complaining because the new shows that I really liked were cancelled (although two were); I am pointing out the power of one small group of writers. These writers have the ability to incorporate concepts into the storylines that the original authors did not include. The Elite have turned entertainment in America into a tool used by social engineers. They have slowly taken us from believing that *Leave it to Beaver* depicted the typical American family to accepting *Roseanne* as portraying the norm. Those in Hollywood have become social alchemists who have transmuted the very foundational collective consciousness of our society. Just like the hand-picked news editors of JP Morgan and associates, they set the policy of what we will watch and where we will go ethically, emotionally, and spiritually as a nation. We will examine in more detail in the upcoming chapter on mind control just how TV is used to transform society and our very belief systems.

Mankind Caught in the Net

Between Freemasonry, Skull and Bones, the Round Tables, the centralized banking cartel, and the news media/entertainment industry, just about everything on this planet is controlled. Analogously speaking, we have come to the scene in the movie, *The Matrix*, in which Morpheus is giving Neo the choice between the "red pill" or the "blue pill." I can envision the scene, except the one offering the choice is Almighty God, and He uses somewhat different terminology in His offer:

And after these things I saw another angel come down from heaven, having great power; and the earth was lightened with his glory.

And he cried mightily with a strong voice, saying, Babylon the great is fallen, is fallen, and is become the habitation of devils, and the hold of every foul spirit, and a cage of every unclean and hateful bird.

For all nations have drunk of the wine of the wrath of her fornication, and the kings of the earth have committed fornication with her, and the merchants of the earth are waxed rich through the abundance of her delicacies.

And I heard another voice from heaven, saying, Come out of her, my people, that ye be not partakers of her sins, and that ye receive not of her plagues.

For her sins have reached unto heaven, and God hath remembered her iniquities.

Reward her even as she rewarded you, and double unto her double according to her works: in the cup which she hath filled fill to her double. (Revelation 18:1–6, emphasis added)

God is calling every believer to unplug from the **Illuminati's matrix of control** so that He can judge it. Regardless of your eschatological position on the returning of Christ (pre-Tribulation, mid-Tribulation, or post-Tribulation), being completely disconnected from Babylon is the only way to be ready for His return. Jesus is not coming back for a bride, wearing Babylonian garments, that is in service to Baal. He is coming back for a victorious bride that has overcome the influence and control of the Luciferian Elite and is wearing garments of true biblical holiness. May the process of waking up, cleaning up, and growing up begin this very hour!

chapter eight

The Unfinished Work of Nimrod

Part 4: Mind Control

And the kings of the earth, who have committed fornication and lived deliciously with her, shall bewail her, and lament for her, when they shall see the smoke of her burning,

Standing afar off for the fear of her torment, saying, Alas, alas, that great city Babylon, that mighty city! for in one hour is thy judgment come.

And the merchants of the earth shall weep and mourn over her; *for no man buyeth their merchandise any more*:

The merchandise of gold, and silver, and precious stones, and of pearls, and fine linen, and purple, and silk, and scarlet, and all thyine wood, and all manner vessels of ivory, and all manner vessels of most precious wood, and of brass, and iron, and marble,

And cinnamon, and odours, and ointments, and frankincense, and wine, and oil, and fine flour, and wheat, and beasts, and sheep, and horses, and chariots, and slaves, and *souls of men*.

—Revelation 18:9–13, emphasis added

Babylon has always sought to control and own the souls of men. In ancient times, Nimrod used giants, fear, intimidation, and governmental power to enslave the populations of the world. Through the millennia, the only one of Nimrod's original weapons of control that was lost was the giants (although transhumanism may soon restore this key tool). Today, government oppression, fear, and intimidation are not enough. Mankind has tasted freedom occasionally in its history. That desire for freedom has caused a multitude to press through their fears to demand more and to fight against such draconian societies.

What we will discover in this chapter is that a multitude of new weapons of control has been devised since the turn of the twentieth century, coinciding with the return of the Watchers. Most researchers of the Tower of Babel estimate that less than one million individuals were alive when God confused the languages. The truth is, with nearly seven and a half billion people living on the planet today, the Elite require a whole new arsenal to bring the level of control needed for the return of Nimrod.

Of course, the Elite leave nothing to chance. They will not trust fulfilling the unfinished work of Nimrod to a single strategy. Why use one strong rope when ten thousand smaller ones would prove more effective in both capturing the souls of men and keeping them captive?

After the turn of the twentieth century and two world wars, we saw the development of the military-industrial complex. This new amalgamation of private industrial and governmental interests provided new weapons to overcome Nazi Germany's threats to liberty worldwide. The complex continued to grow through the conflicts in Korea and Vietnam—as well as the threat of the Soviet Union. The Elite saw to the exponential growth of this newly formed complex. Today, it is the military-industrial-agricultural-chemical-pharmaceutical-medical complex. It has grown to the place that it has become like a stage-four cancer within humanity. The very mechanism that was used to ensure liberty is now being used by the Elite to exterminate it!

The corporations that genetically modify our foods and fill them with chemicals (that slowly poison our bodies) are the same corporations that rake in billions to produce medicines and operate medical facilities to treat our diseases. Members of their boards serve and control the governmental agencies that were established to protect us from them! While they create future generations of new customers for their medical centers, there is much more at work.

The organic food movement began to really pick up steam with the personal involvement of the royal family of England. While they dine on only the best organic foods and are treated by skillful naturopaths, the Elite sell us on the need for genetically modified organism (GMO) foods and create new illnesses that require more advanced pharmaceutical compounds.

The truth is that the same witch's brew they use—both to make us ill and to treat our illnesses—is dumbing us down and making us more susceptible to forms of mind control. However, mind control extends far beyond the foods we eat, the fluoridated water we drink, and the never-ending supply of pills (*pharmakeia*—Revelation 9:21) we swallow every day.

MKUltra and the Fracturing of the Human Mind

As I broach the subjects of mind control, the reality of MPD (Multiple Personality Disorder[174]), and the perfecting of the ultimate spy/weapon, I want to preface this subject with a confession. I originally thought these topics were fantasy and the result of urban legend. However, beginning around 1995, my family and I had our world (and our worldview) turned upside down.

My wonderful wife, Mary, had suffered quietly from depression most of her life. She would experience pressure on the back of her head any time she tried to read the Word of God. This was perplexing for her, because she loved God and knew that depression should not be a part of a Christian's life. She had prayed every prayer she could think of, but the depression remained. Then, one day, she cried out to God in desperation and declared that He was Almighty, begging Him to change her because her children and husband deserved better. At first, nothing happened. Then, in early 1994, she woke up, and everything had changed. The depression was gone; even the colors around her had more depth and appeared to be brighter. She began an eight-month journey of devouring the Word of God and getting lost in His awesome presence.

During this time, Mary grew in the Lord, and her understanding of the Word deepened every day. During that time, someone we respected with a prophetic gift told Mary, "God has changed your bloodline." We later realized just how right this man of God was.

After eight months of getting deep into the Word and enjoying God's presence and His voice, the depression returned. Mary was dismayed. After a time of deep personal struggle, she determined that she was going to hear from God and get an answer. She wrapped herself up in a blanket, sat out on the back patio on our picnic bench, and refused to move until she heard from God. Here is her testimony of what happened next:

> I once more cried out to God, "Well, God, I have to know what happened to me—please show me!" I was determined to stay out in the cold until I broke through and heard from Heaven. God spoke very clearly to me. He said that I had demons oppressing me. He told me to bind the demons and that He would show me how to make them leave. My first thought was, "Christians can't have demons, so this can't be God talking to me." I pressed in harder and heard the same thing. God told me that He had taught me His Word, and I now had the faith to fight. I did exactly what God told me. I said, "I bind you in the name of Jesus." The minute I said that, I felt like I was hit in the back of the head with a hammer. I ran inside and told my husband, so he could pray for me. My journey to freedom had begun.[175]

This event, when Mary struggled with the demonic forces that flowed upon her bloodline, proved to be pivotal for our ministry; God wanted to open our eyes to the reality of the world around us. Someone said that Mary's great grandmother had been involved in witchcraft. Mary asked God to forgive the sin of witchcraft in her family line. When God temporarily changed her bloodline, it separated her from the demonic forces that sought to stifle her growth and freedom as a believer. After those eight months of training by the Holy Spirit, Mary was ready to clean house spiritually.

The prayers of my wife were not only bringing her healing and restoration, but they were, no doubt, affecting the occult community. Through a long analytical process, we concluded that my wife, along with other citizens in the area surrounding Fort Leonard Wood, Missouri, was a victim of mind-control programming. It also became apparent that some individuals were very concerned about her restoration and emerging memories. Needless to say, I went to bed one night believing I lived in Mayberry and woke up the next morning in Amityville!

It did not take me long to realize that I was dealing with situations I could never have imagined. My position with Biblical Life College and Seminary allowed me access to noted experts in both psychology and deprogramming. I cannot tell you how many hours I spent on the phone describing events or sharing strange phrases that came out of the victims' mouths. What shocked me most were not the strange utterances from those we were praying with, but the fact that the experts could stop me in the middle of a sentence and finish the statement for me. The individuals I was consulting were always kind enough to provide lists of books I needed to research. I certainly kept Amazon busy during those months when I was ordering all the books I needed. I would usually research after we saw or heard something unusual in the town or in our church services. Every time, I would find what we saw or heard confirmed in one of the books. I concluded that either these testimonies of occult activity were true or these individuals had read all of these books and formulated some elaborate plan to take advantage of our ministry and waste our time. It had to be one or the other. The torment I witnessed in the people we were praying with, the changes in physical characteristics, and the attempts to kill our family finally convinced me it was real.

It became obvious that victims were being sent in on assignment. We could see the struggle within each victim, as he or she would feel the safety everyone has always felt around my wife (even before she was healed). But we could also see the overwhelming fear that these victims had of their oppressors if their assignment against us was not completed. Once Mary understood the horrible position the victims were in and the threats against their families, she told them that we forgave them for coming against our family, and she assured them that Almighty God would protect us and provide a way of escape for them. If you ever want to see my wife go on the warpath, just let her hear of someone threatening a child. Unfortunately, some of the individuals who came in had hidden personalities that weren't concerned about their children at all; they just wanted another notch on their occult belt for taking down another ministry. My wife stated that this was just the preparation phase of her learning how to properly assess those who come for help and, more specifically, how to determine whether they had a sincere desire to follow God.

We were told that we lived in an area of Missouri the occult community called the "Crystal Cauldron." A geographic cauldron is unique, and there are only a few that we know of across the United States. There are many occult groups whose basic philosophies cause them to be at odds with one another. An example would be how the Ku Klux Klan (KKK)/neo-Nazi groups are at odds with the Wiccans. (The KKK's philosophy includes hatred for gays/bisexuals, while bisexuality is part of the Wiccan practice.) Yet within a cauldron, all work together to complete certain assignments provided by an overseeing council. All the various factions, controlled by a council, create the "witch's brew" within the cauldron. From various reports concerning occult activity, we were able to determine that the council is in St. Louis, Missouri. When describing the cauldron in an email to noted researcher Cris Putnam, the first thing he asked was, "Is there a military base within the cauldron?" Fort Leonard Wood is positioned in the center of it. This confirmed my belief that official government mind-control experiments were conducted at the fort, under the leadership of the CIA. Part of the protocol of the projects was to use local occult members for the work of recruiting subjects from the area. After the revelations of MKUltra (one of the many CIA mind-control experiments) were made public by a congregational investigation, the official experiments stopped. However, these technologies were still in the hands of the occult community, which continued to use them to build their own power base and create the cauldron. Although some of this is speculation on my part, it does fall in line with the facts we discovered and seems to be the most plausible hypothesis.

It is not my desire to recount all the situations we walked through, but

I feel burdened by the Holy Spirit to share some of the important facts I discovered in my research.

1. Mind-control techniques have been around for a long time. The Elite used the Nazis during World War II to advance the techniques. After WWII, the United States, the Soviet Union, and Great Britain were used to perfect the control.

Mind-control researcher Ken Adachi shares this basic introduction to the subject:

> The topic of mind control is elaborate, multifaceted, and multi layered. For the casual reader, it can quickly become numbing, overwhelming the senses and creating a desire to exit the topic, but avoiding this subject is the most foolish thing you could possibly do since your only chance of surviving this hideous and insidious enslavement agenda, which today threatens virtually all of humanity, is to understand how it functions and take steps to reduce your vulnerability.
>
> The plans to create a mind controlled workers society have been in place for a long time. The current technology grew out of experiments that the Nazis started before World War II and intensified during the time of the Nazi concentration camps when an unlimited supply of children and adults were available for experimentation. We've heard about the inhumane medical experiments performed on concentration camp prisoners, but no word was ever mentioned by the media and the TV documentaries of the mind control experiments. That was not to be divulged to the American public. Mind control technologies can be broadly divided into two subsets: trauma-based or electronic-based.
>
> The first phase of government mind control development grew out of the old occult techniques which required the victim to be exposed to massive psychological and physical trauma, usually beginning in infancy, in order to cause the psyche to shatter into a thousand alter personalities which can then be separately programmed to perform any function (or job) that the program-

mer wishes to "install." Each alter personality created is separate and distinct from the front personality. The "front personality" is unaware of the existence or activities of the alter personalities. Alter personalities can be brought to the surface by programmers or handlers using special codes, usually stored in a laptop computer. The victim of mind control can also be affected by specific sounds, words, or actions known as triggers.

The second phase of mind control development was refined at an underground base below Fort Hero on Montauk, Long Island (New York) and is referred to as the Montauk Project. The earliest adolescent victims of Montauk style programming, so called Montauk Boys, were programmed using trauma-based techniques, but that method was eventually abandoned in favor of an all-electronic induction process which could be "installed" in a matter of days (or even hours) instead of the many years that it took to complete trauma-based methods.

Dr. Joseph Mengele of Auschwitz notoriety was the principle developer of the trauma-based Monarch Project and the CIA's MKUltra mind control programs. Mengele and approximately 5,000 other high-ranking Nazis were secretly moved into the United States and South America in the aftermath of World War II in an Operation designated Paperclip. The Nazis continued their work in developing mind control and rocketry technologies in secret underground military bases. The only thing we were told about was the rocketry work with former Nazi star celebrities like Warner Von Braun. The killers, torturers, and mutilators of innocent human beings were kept discretely out of sight, but busy in U.S. underground military facilities which gradually became home to thousands upon thousands of kidnapped American children snatched off the streets (about one million per year) and placed into iron bar cages stacked from floor to ceiling as part of the "training." These children would be used to further refine and perfect Mengele's mind control technologies. Certain selected children (at least the ones who survived the "training") would become future mind controlled slaves who could be used for thousands of different jobs ranging anywhere from sexual slavery to assassinations. A substantial portion of these children, who were considered expendable, were intentionally slaughtered in front of (and by) the other children in order to traumatize the selected trainee into total compliance and submission.

Mind Control "Programmed" Individuals

The lone gunman that we hear about in assassinations, assassination attempts, school shootings, etc., are mind controlled individuals who had been "programmed" to carry out those missions. Ted Bundy, the "Son of Sam" serial killer David Berkowitz, Oswald, Timothy McVeigh, the Columbine shooters, Chapman, Sirhan Sirhan, etc. were mind controlled individuals who were programmed to perform these killings. Tens of thousands of young teenage boys were kidnapped and forced into the mind control training program called The Montauk Project starting around 1976. Al Bielek, under mind control, was involved in many areas of the secret Montauk Project. After slowly recovering his memories beginning in the late 1980s, he came to realize that there were at least 250,000 mind controlled "Montauk Boys" produced at 25 different facilities similar to the underground base at Montauk, Long Island. Many of these boys were to become "sleepers" who are individuals who were programmed to go into action at a later date when properly "triggered" to engage in some sort of destructive or disruptive conduct. Other Montauk Boys were woven into the fabric of mainstream American life as journalists, radio & TV personalities, businessmen, lawyers, medical professionals, judges, prosecutors, law enforcement, military men, etc.[176]

Adachi's research is similar to that of Alex Constantine, Colin A. Ross, MD, Jim Keith, and many others.

Researcher and author Jim Keith shares on the involvement of the Tavistock Institute with mind control:

At its core, Tavistock consists of Freemasonic British intelligence agents collaborating with the hydra heads of world psychiatry to achieve two goals:

(1) A one world order where the nation state has been abolished and a single totalitarian control center established.

(2) The simultaneous psychological control of the world or, using their term, *"society."* Even the official literature of Tavistock is candid in admitting its broad world mind control orientation.

In 1932 German psychologist Kurt Lewin, one of the creators of the American OSS intelligence network, precursor to the CIA—took over the steering of Tavistock from Reese. Lewin was an early proponent of the use of trauma for reprograming both individuals and societies, his ***modus operandi*** possibly more than merely an analog of the Freemasonic dictum ***"Ordo Ab Chaos,"*** meaning, "order out of chaos."[177]

Before I go on, let me share something with you. When Ken Adachi spoke of scores of children stacked in steel cages, it was hard for my mind to believe such a thing. Yet we have spoken with survivors who have described these cages to us. In my attempt to research for the purpose of dismissing their memories as distorted, I found verification of the information from the reports of other survivors as well as from government contractors who shared these truths as they approached death. We need to remember that the same people who brought us the concentration camps in Nazi Germany were used in America to develop this technology during the Cold War. Adachi also said that trauma-based programming was "abandoned in favor of an all-electronic induction." I have suspected this for some time. Evidence coming from other researchers has confirmed my fear: Welcome to the electronic age of mind control. This also explains why some victims of mind control have all the programming markers, but none of the memories. The trauma-based methodology has been replaced with an all-electronic induction method.

This arms race, of sorts, to perfect mind control really launched into high gear after the Korean War (although it had existed since the end of

WWII). Many of our men who were prisoners of war (POWs) returned with completely altered personalities. The Chinese had conducted mind-control experiments on American POWs. These experiments were known as the **Chinese Manchurian Candidate Program.**

BRIEFING NOTE

The Manchurian Candidate

The fact that our soldiers were returning from the war in Korea with altered personalities inspired the 1962 movie, *The Manchurian Candidate,* with Frank Sinatra. In this movie, a victim of mind control was used in an attempt to assassinate a candidate for public office. Interestingly, after the assassination of John F. Kennedy, the film was banned in the US for several decades. Now we have the remake of *The Manchurian Candidate* with Denzel Washington, *Conspiracy Theory* with Mel Gibson, and Joss Whedon's *Dollhouse* TV series. Today, if someone brings up mind control, he is told, "You saw that on TV. It's all in your head!"

In 1954, there was an exchange of POWs between the United States and China dubbed "Big Switch." Mind-control researcher Colin A. Ross, MD, shares some interesting facts about the Manchurian Candidate Program:

> It appears that American psychiatrists including or known to Robert Lifton, Louis Jolyon West and Margaret Singer must have been knowledgeable about the Chinese Manchurian Candidate program by 1953.
>
> According to my definition, the Manchurian Candidate is an experimentally created dissociative identify disorder that meets the following four criteria:

Created deliberately
A new identity is implanted
Amnesia barriers are created
Used in simulated or actual operations[178]

The Elite used the Chinese program to ignite research by the US and
Russia in a cold-war arms race for the perfect superspy: a spy who did not
know he was a spy! Therefore, the military-industrial complex went to
work (and activated their Nazi scientists) under the direction of the CIA
to create the ultimate human weapon for the ongoing cold war.

**2. Psychologists/psychiatrists and university departments of psy-
chology/psychiatry were used by the CIA in the development of mind
control.** The following is Wikipedia's information on **MKUltra:**

> **Project MKUltra**—sometimes referred to as the **CIA's mind con-
> trol program**—is the code name of a U.S. government human
> research operation experimenting in the behavioral engineer-
> ing of humans. Organized through the Scientific Intelligence
> Division of the Central Intelligence Agency (CIA), the project
> coordinated with the Special Operations Division of the U.S.
> Army's Chemical Corps. The program began in the early 1950s,
> was officially sanctioned in 1953, was reduced in scope in 1964,
> further curtailed in 1967 and officially halted in 1973. The pro-
> gram engaged in many illegal activities; in particular it used
> unwitting U.S. and Canadian citizens as its test subjects, which
> led to controversy regarding its legitimacy. MKUltra used numer-
> ous methodologies to manipulate people's mental states and alter
> brain functions, including the surreptitious administration of
> drugs (especially LSD) and other chemicals, hypnosis, sensory
> deprivation, isolation, verbal and sexual abuse, as well as various
> forms of torture.
>
> The scope of Project MKUltra was broad, with research
> undertaken at 80 institutions, including 44 colleges and universi-
> ties, as well as hospitals, prisons and pharmaceutical companies.

The CIA operated through these institutions using front organizations, although sometimes top officials at these institutions
were aware of the CIA's involvement. As the Supreme Court later
noted, MKULTRA was:

"concerned with 'the research and development of chemical,
biological, and radiological materials capable of employment in
clandestine operations to control human behavior.' The program
consisted of some 149 subprojects which the Agency contracted
out to various universities, research foundations, and similar institutions. At least 80 institutions and 185 private researchers par-
ticipated. Because the Agency funded MKUltra indirectly, many
of the participating individuals were unaware that they were dealing with the Agency."

Project MKUltra was first brought to public attention in 1975
by the Church Committee of the U.S. Congress, and a Gerald
Ford commission to investigate CIA activities within the United
States. Investigative efforts were hampered by the fact that CIA
Director Richard Helms ordered all MKUltra files destroyed
in 1973; the Church Committee and Rockefeller Commission
investigations relied on the sworn testimony of direct participants
and on the relatively small number of documents that survived
Helms' destruction order.

In 1977, a Freedom of Information Act request uncovered a
cache of 20,000 documents relating to project MKUltra, which led
to Senate hearings later that same year. In July 2001 some surviv-
ing information regarding MKUltra was officially declassified.[179]

Notice that, in public records, forty-four colleges and universities were
used just in this one program. The departments of psychology and psychiatry worked with the CIA in the development of mind control. MKUltra
was not the only program. Here are a few others:

- Bluebird
- Artichoke

- MKSearch
- MKNaomi
- Project Often
- MKDelta
- Monarch

Not all used trauma. Some used drugs and hypnosis. In fact, LSD was created by the CIA for use in these programs.

As with many of the experiments of that era, military bases with surrounding rural areas were used. The CIA employed psychologists who served as the leaders in the research, but others were needed for the groundwork and the selection of candidates for the programs. Therefore, the CIA sought out perpetrators of incest and pedophilia to assist in the selection of participants (victims) as well as members of the occult. The

BRIEFING NOTE

CIA and the False Memory Foundation

Many of the founding members from the academic community of the False Memory Foundation were formerly experts hired by the CIA for the MKUltra and the Monarch Projects.[180] What a brilliant move; these experts would be highly motivated to actively cover their own official activities in these projects. Although there may be cases of false memories implanted by overzealous counselors/ministers, I suspect these cases are rarer than we want to admit. In fact, some cases could have been a planned setup to entrap unwitting counselors and provide a mechanism for denial of the abuse in the programs. The majority of the cases I have reviewed appear to be genuine.

purpose of this was twofold: (1) Their victims were already predisposed for purposeful splitting of their minds and would be more compliant to receive programming; and (2) The perpetrators would be more apt to keep their mouths shut about the ongoing black (covert) projects.

3. Most of these projects have been "officially" mothballed. Once projects such as MKUltra and others were brought to light in America, a congressional investigation was launched. As with any intelligence agency, protocols were in place to destroy the records if the programs were compromised. Sadly, less than 10 percent of the real documentation made it to Congress, but it was enough to officially shut them down.

There have been reports in the intelligence community that, since 1975, the CIA has used independent contractors for the development of new technologies. This allows it to have plausible deniability regarding ongoing projects.

This perfected science is now used by the Elite to create the super-soldier army discovered by Russ Dizdar and outlined in his book, *The Black Awakening.* We had witnessed the mind-controlled soldiers in their black uniforms in my wife's hometown, but we were unaware of the significance of the uniforms until we read *The Black Awakening.*

How many are affected by this kind of programming? Dizdar presents some older numbers from 1992:

> By 1992, Dr. Holly Hector who worked in the psych ward at Centennial Hospital in Denver stated that there is an estimated 2.4 million victims of "multiple personality disorder." Going beyond that Dr. Collin Ross in his original first edition "PROJECT BLUEBIRD: the purposeful creation of multiple personalities" agrees with an assessment that there may be 10 million victims of this form of mind and life control.[181]

How Does the Program Work?

To be most effective, the splitting of the mind and the programming must start at a young age. Within occult families, the primary caregiver is the one who abuses the child to create a fragment within his or her personality. This can be repeated many times to create as many subpersonalities as needed to meet their objectives. Some personalities are used to govern the internal system (gatekeepers); others are used for specific tasks. Code words, specific tones or sounds, and gestures are used to trigger the switching of the personality to the desired one or to kick in a specific program with a preset mission or action encoded into it. Certain personalities will be highly trained witches, while others are programmed to be anything from a sexual slave (or seducer) to an assassin. I have found that the front personality most of the world sees can be nothing more than a shell to hide what lies behind. The farther back you go into their subpersonalities, the more intelligent and powerful they become. It has been reported that those ministering to them can suffer from nosebleeds, instant migraine headaches, and worse; while the front personality is crying out for help, the trained witch in the back is actively attacking the minister. My wife and I can testify to the almost-instant migraines, and my wife experienced many nosebleeds. We eventually learned to pray and guard ourselves from such attacks. We also discovered something interesting: While Russ Dizdar saw members of the Black Awakening receive supernatural power to run away (even through walls) when too much "real" progress was made, several of the individuals we were praying with would instantly fall into a deep sleep the moment we began getting too close to the truth. This could happen standing up or sitting down; the position really didn't matter.

Many of the trigger phrases used within the Monarch Project were taken from movies such as *The Wizard of Oz, Alice in Wonderland, Peter Pan,* and many others. When we see scenes or phrases being used repeatedly in national advertising or the evening news, we recognize that a nationwide trigger is being implemented, possibly calling victims to action or for reprogramming.

Through the years, Mary was able to gain an understanding of the mind-control programming through her own personal healing and by watching and praying for other victims. She has always believed that Almighty God will prepare a place of safety and restoration, and we are prayerfully making plans for the future.

Where Are We Now With All of This?

We need to realize that this type of mind control is at least fifty years old. In technological terms, it is downright ancient! I believe the official government testing has been over for years. For those within the Black Awakening and other segments, the process is self-replicating; it is repeated within the families with each new generation. This was part of the premise of the Monarch Project—that the basic encoding could be embedded within DNA and passed on to the next generation. I am not sure just how much can be passed on genetically, as far as programming is concerned. However, the propensity for the personality to split is passed on. Then the process begins anew with the next generation. Additional technology or techniques can up upgraded within the family system.

Outside of official government or Elite-sanctioned circles, it continues on as well. As I have already shared, I believe that is what we ran across here in Missouri. If those involved in incest, pedophilia, and the occult were used as facilitators for the experiments, they carried the information with them after the official programs ceased operations. Now some of that technology is being used by covens and drug cartels and within white slavery. Although they may not have official ties to government organizations, they can receive cover support from them…to keep the secrets hidden.

I also have a personal hypothesis regarding another aspect (or side benefit) of the Elite in the splitting of the mind to create separate personalities. When man fell in the garden, God capped off many of the abilities Adam had. Although neuroscientists would tell us that we use 100 percent of our brain throughout the average day (i.e., no sections of the brain are permanently dormant),[182] we do not use its full potential. Within your brain, there is enough power and potential for several hundred lifetimes. The human brain is still the reigning champion as the most advanced computer known to man. (We are still waiting for those working within quantum computing to develop a system that surpasses mankind. When that happens, even the Elite's own experts predict it could be detrimental to the human race.) It has been reported that with increased capacity comes increased power. There has been an overlapping theme of increased psychic abilities among advanced subjects within these experiments: Astral projection, telepathy, telekinesis, and other abilities have been reported. Many Christian researchers have considered this a part of the occult personalities simply filled with demonic power, and this may be true to a certain extent. However, I have come to believe the Elite are actively working to overcome everything God did as a part of His judgment against mankind—from the lost psychic abilities to gaining eternal life without God.

Control for the Masses

It has been estimated that there are one hundred million or more active programmed individuals worldwide. These individuals are vital in the intelligence network of the Elite, as well as being super soldiers for the Black Awakening. What about the remaining estimated 7.2 billion people on planet earth? How do you control the rest of them? We will look at some of the technologies being used today. You will be surprised to find that some of them are in your own home!

Television—More Than Just Entertainment!

It is an interesting coincidence that, at the same time we had covert agencies working on mind control, America went from a nation that listened to radio to watching hours of TV. We need to understand that watching TV affects how our minds operate. According to the Applied Neuro Technologies website, TV profoundly affects the state of consciousness:

> Studies have shown that watching television induces low alpha waves in the human brain. Alpha waves are brainwaves between 8 to 12 HZ. and are commonly associated with relaxed meditative states as **well as brain states associated with suggestibility**.
> While Alpha waves achieved through meditation are benefi-

cial (they promote relaxation and insight), too much time spent in the low Alpha wave state caused by TV can cause unfocussed daydreaming and inability to concentrate. Researchers have said that watching television is similar to staring at a blank wall for several hours.

We all like to watch TV from time to time, and this is not meant to suggest that people should never watch TV again. However, it is only fair that people understand what happens to the brain each time it is exposed to television.

In an experiment in 1969, Herbert Krugman monitored a person through many trials and found that in less than one minute of television viewing, the person's brainwaves switched from Beta waves—brainwaves associated with active, logical thought—to primarily Alpha waves. When the subject stopped watching television and began reading a magazine, the brainwaves reverted to Beta waves.

Research indicates that most parts of the brain, including parts responsible for logical thought, tune out during television viewing. The impact of television viewing on one person's brain state is obviously not enough to conclude that the same consequences apply to everyone, but research has repeatedly shown that watching television produces brainwaves in the low Alpha range.

Advertisers have known about this for a long time and they know how to take advantage of this passive, suggestible, brain state of the TV viewer. There is no need for an advertiser to use subliminal messages. The brain is already in a receptive state, ready to absorb suggestions, within just a few seconds of the television being turned on. All advertisers have to do is flash a brand across the screen, and then attempt to make the viewer associate the product with something positive.[183] (Emphasis added)

There are a couple of points I want you to notice in this quote from Applied Neuro Technologies:

- You are placed in an "alpha" state—so you are more susceptible to suggestion.
- The logical/analytical side of your brain is switched off.

In other words, you are susceptible to suggestion on an emotional level that bypasses the analytical side of your mind. WOW!

In the TV programs and movies that only a select group of writers develop, they have the ability to introduce new information that bypasses your ability to analyze or think through. The Writers Guild of America is serving as the modern-day, esoteric guild of Sir Francis Bacon. Their guiding hand continually works to embed new concepts through the medium of television and movies directly into the emotional side of your mind. This is how they have reengineered society to include much of the body of Christ. They are programming us emotionally to violate God's Word and to leave godliness behind. This is why so many Christians are questioning what the Word of God has to say about marriage, sexuality, and a host of other topics, based on their emotions. I have found that you cannot talk logically through these issues with them either. Bible-believing Christians will respond to logical questioning of their unbiblical beliefs with emotions of anger, mistrust, outrage, and even hatred. These unsuspecting Christians had no idea that their favorite shows and movies were reprogramming them to reject what the Bible clearly says is true.

Noted health expert Dr. Joseph Mercola has stated that "TV is one of the most powerful brainwashing devices there is."[184] Instead of our minds being washed with the water of the Word, the Elite have psychotronically washed our minds with the sewer water of Babylon.

With this understanding of how TV and movies can affect us comes the question: What can we do?

First, limit what you watch. The TV does not have to be on all the time. Watch a show or two, turn it off, and read the Bible or a book. Reading switches you back into the analytical portion of your brain. When you do watch TV, you should do two things:

- Plead the blood of Jesus between you and the TV screen.
- Keep the mindset of analyzing what you are watching; don't allow yourself to go into "I'm being entertained" mode.

These simple steps will change your TV and movie watching forever. You would be surprised at how many lies and half-truths you will begin to catch that you never noticed before. A few times, I have startled my wife when, all of a sudden, I would yell out, "That's wrong!" at the TV. By speaking my objection aloud, I was embedding in my unconscious mind the idea that the information I just heard was wrong and that I needed to reject it.

The apostle Paul warns us to "prove all things; hold fast that which is good" (1 Thessalonians 5:21). The Greek word used for "prove" is *dokimazo* (dok-im-ad'-zo), which means "to test, examine, prove, scrutinize— to see whether a thing is genuine or not."[185] When we allow our minds to descend into entertainment mode, we bypass our ability to carry out Paul's admonishment.

By the way, entertainment is defined as "amusement or diversion provided especially by performers."[186] When you dig a little deeper, you find that the archaic (or original) definition of amuse is "to divert the attention of so as to deceive."[187] In a culture addicted to entertainment, we realize we're actually addicted to the Elite diverting our attention so that they can continually deceive us!

Programming Beyond the TV and Movie Screen

The Soviet Union's Woodpecker Grid

During the Cold War, both the United States and the Soviet Union were experimenting with both the use of extremely low-frequency (ELF) radio waves and microwaves to affect the human mind. Scientist and researcher Dr. Nick Begich shares about a leap forward in 1975 by the Soviet Union:

The Soviets took their technologies a huge jump forward by 1975. It was that year they began using seven giant radio transmitters to pulse ELF waves in the 3.26 to 17.54 megaHertz range. These waves were pulsed at 6 and 11 Hertz—key brain wave rhythms—and became known to ham radio operators as the "woodpecker" signal. The Soviet story, like the HAARP story, indicated that these were used for communication with submarines, but many believe that the negative side effects were intentional. These "side effects" have been speculated to have caused communications interference; power failures; mood alterations over significant areas, affecting a large percentage of the population; and weather modifications which have had a devastating effect on food production since the 1970's.[188]

ELF: Just the Tip of the Iceberg

This was just one of the many technologies being developed by both countries. Dr. Begich continues:

By the early 1970's, within certain military and academic circles, it became clear that human behavior could be modified by the use of subtle energetic manipulations. By 2006, the state of the technology had been perfected to the point where emotions, thoughts, memory and thinking could be manipulated by external means.

Stop for a moment and consider the impact of what this means—the idea that human thinking can be disrupted or manipulated in a way that can't be resisted. The ability to impact thinking in this way comes through, according to a leading Russian scientist, Dr. Igor Smirnov, "as if it were a commandment from God, it cannot be resisted." Think about this for a moment. What else could be a greater violation of our own personhood? These new systems do not pierce the tissue—they violate the very essence of who we are—they violate the internal and private aspects of who we are as individuals. The idea that some external force can now disrupt not only our emotional states, but our health as well, should not come as such a great surprise. What is surprising is the volume of evidence now available to use that documents that these technologies are here now.[189]

Our government confirmed Dr. Begich's statements. In an article released by the United States War College, "The Mind Has No Firewalls," we find:

A recent Russian military article offered a slightly different slant to the problem, declaring that "humanity stands on the brink of a psychotronic war" with mind and body as the focus. That article discussed Russian and international attempts to control the pschyo-physical condition of man and his decision-making processes by the use of VHF-generators, "noiseless cassettes" and other technologies.[190]

The Russian Computer Virus 666

Dr. Begich shares several other technologies in his research. One of the more interesting is a Russian designed computer virus known as "Russian Virus 666."

According to Solntsev, at least one computer virus has been created which will affect a person's psyche—"Russian Virus 666." This virus appears in every 25th frame of a computer's visual display where a mix of color, pulse and patterns are reported to put the computer operators into a trance. The subconscious perception of the display can be used to induce a heart attack or to subtly manage or change a computer operator's perception. The same system could be used in any television or visual broadcast.[191]

What is frightening is when we realize just how far such a technology could have evolved since that time. From the televisions in nearly every room of our homes to the computers and tablets we use every day to the smart phones we carry with us everywhere with a near addiction, the implications of the Russian Virus 666 is indeed alarming! **An interesting note:** During the season of my wife's healing as a victim of mind control, she watched very little TV; what little she did watch was teaching on the Word of God and the evening news.

The Use of Infrasound

I want to revisit, for a moment, the information I shared in the bestselling collaborative book by Dr. Tom Horn, *Blood on the Altar*. On pages 99 and 100, I share:

> In the video entitled, "Weapons of the New World Order," Dr. Nick Begich (also author of "Angels Don't Play This HAARP; Advances in Tesla Technology") shares the fact that there are already European Parliament regulations banning the use of non-lethal weapons that would use ELF (extremely low frequency) similar to 7.83 hertz to project thoughts into the minds of an approaching army. He demonstrated this technology before a sub-committee of the European Parliament investigating non-lethal ELF weapons with a few simple pieces of equipment he picked up at Radio Shack. In his demonstration before the subcommittee, Dr. Begich's voice transmitted through the homemade infrasound device that he had constructed and resonated in the body of a volunteer. The volunteer was able to clearly hear his voice without the use of his auditory senses.[192]

Advancements in infrasound have come a long way since Dr. Begich's demonstration to the European Parliament. In a 1999 BBC TV Canada show called, *Undercurrents*, Dr. Begich was discussing infrasound and how it could produce the irresistible "voice of God." One of the other researchers shared how the technology has been developed to the place that it could be broadcast over television and radio![193] I believe we could add notebook computers, tablets, and smart phones to the researcher's statement as well.

ADHD, Hyperstimulation of the Mind, and Sound Bites

ADHD (Attention Deficit Hyperactivity Disorder) and ADD (Attention Deficit Disorder) have become almost epidemic in Western society. According to the CDC (Centers for Disease Control), in 2011, around 11 percent of all children in the United States suffered from ADHD. It is now considered one of the most common neurobehavioral disorders of childhood.[194] There is still a great deal of speculation as to the cause of this disorder; some believe it is genetics while others hypothesize that it may be caused by ingredients in childhood immunizations or the overuse of electronics, such as TV.

Beyond childhood disorders, ADD has now become a part of our collective consciousness. We have been programmed by our television shows to believe that most problems are solved in thirty to sixty minutes, while earth-threatening events can take up to three hours in the average action movie. The vital news of the day has been reduced to a carefully crafted summary that can be covered in two minutes or less. Truths are no longer truths, and lies are no longer lies; what matters is how you spin your truth or lie to create the perfect sound bite to move the masses.

The hyperstimulation of the mind through TV, movies, and video games that is delivered through a host of mediums (from flat-panel, high-definition TVs to the latest smart phones) has reduced our attention span to merely eight seconds.[195] The very electronic marvels that promised to make our lives better have preconditioned our minds for deception.

Contemplation and reflection have always been considered essential not only in our overall well being, but in our ability to think critically through the major issues of life and as a society. Yet, in a recent series of experiments at the University of Virginia and Harvard University, the researchers had both men and women sit quietly in a room for fifteen to twenty minutes. They were also given a device that could administer a low-level electric shock. The studies provided an amazing discovery. Here is an excerpt from the report:

In the most dramatic finding from the research, participants were left alone in the room with a button, which administered a mild electric shock to them.

Of the 18 men in the study, 12 gave themselves at least one shock over a 15-minute "thinking period."

One unusually bored man pressed the button 190 times, although this was not typical.

Of the 24 women in the study, 6 gave themselves at least one shock.

The much higher rate amongst men is likely down to greater sensation-seeking amongst males.

The authors note that:

What is striking is that simply being alone with their own thoughts for 15 minutes was apparently so aversive that it drove many participants to self-administer an electric shock that they had earlier said they would pay to avoid.[196]

In Western society, we have been so conditioned by the Elite that we cannot even spend fifteen minutes alone with our own thoughts. If that is the case, how can we examine the critical issues before us or even spend the time in quiet prayer long enough to still our minds to hear the voice of God? In fact, the Bible tells us that stillness is a prerequisite to getting to know God:

Be still, and know that I am God: I will be exalted among the heathen, I will be exalted in the earth. (Psalms 46:10)

"Be still" in Hebrew is the word *rapheh* (raw-faw'), which means to "relax, refrain, withdraw, and to be quiet."[197] It is in the quiet times of meditation on the Word and in prayer that we tune our minds to God's kingdom, His purposes, and His voice.

Part of the unfinished work of Nimrod was to precondition the masses not to think, but only to respond to stimuli. In the twenty-first century, extensive or lengthy propaganda is no longer necessary to deceive most of our population. All that is needed is the correctly phrased sound bite that elicits the proper, preprogrammed, emotional response. It would seem that Hitler understood the process the Elite would use. Just read several of Hitler's better-known quotes:

- "By the skillful and sustained use of propaganda, one can make a people see even heaven as hell or an extremely wretched life as paradise."
- "If you tell a big enough lie and tell it frequently enough, it will be believed."
- "It is not truth that matters, but victory."
- "Great liars are also great magicians."
- "He alone, who owns the youth, gains the future."[198]

It would seem that Hitler was reading from the political and social engineering playbooks being used today by the Elite. Maybe he was not just reading their playbooks; Nazi Germany was an experimental laboratory for the Elite to refine their methodology for mass control. Today, knowledge gained from every corner of Nazi science is utilized to its fullest extent to bring humanity under luciferian control.

Now you know why there are not extended discussions of key political positions or detailed analysis of proposed laws. Such activities would reveal hidden agendas. Today, we are simply bombarded with the proper sound bites countless times a day. In the end, it is the one with the best sound bite and the most money to saturate the airwaves who wins. This is Orwellian mind control at its finest!

This Chapter Could Easily Become a Book in Itself

As I write this chapter, I am sitting by my main desk with a side desk covered in books I have researched on mind control and the technologies being used. Honestly, I find myself standing between two places: providing the information that will convince you that this is real and the burden of the Holy Spirit to move on to solutions the body of Christ needs now. This burden by the Holy Spirit has never weighed so heavily upon me as it does today.

To be truthful, you can go to Amazon.com and quickly build an entire library on the reality of mind control written by scholars whose expertise in and knowledge of these technologies far surpass mine. What we have learned (and what I want to share so badly) is how to overcome them!

It was just a few days ago when I had emailed Dr. Horn at Defender Publishing to inform him that this chapter could easily be a hundred pages or more in length. Since then, the Holy Spirit has changed my mind. If I am going to write a chapter that long, I want it to be about how to overcome what the Elite have accomplished! Heaven is not finished with the body of Christ; we have much to undo and much to relearn. Heaven is waiting to empower us for the challenges ahead! At this very moment, the fire of the Holy Spirit is burning within me to get to some kingdom solutions, but we will have to endure one more chapter before we begin empowering the Remnant for the unfolding of end-time prophecy!

chapter nine

The Unfinished Work of Nimrod

Part 5: Dimensional Portals, Transhumanism, and Armageddon

We do not want another committee, we have too many already.
What we want is a man of sufficient stature to hold the allegiance
of all the people and to lift us up out of the economic morass into
which we are sinking. Send us such a man, and whether he be
God or devil, we will receive him.

—Paul-Henri Spaak, first president of the United Nations[199]

No one will enter the New World Order unless he or she will
make a pledge to worship Lucifer. No one will enter the New Age
unless he will take a Luciferian Initiation.

—David Spangler, director of Planetary Initiative,
United Nations[200]

Over the past century, the Elite have been influencing key world leaders and initiating them into luciferianism. From the United Nations
to the Bohemian Grove, the signature of paganism and luciferianism can be clearly seen.

The UN Meditation Room

There is a special meditation room at the United Nations into which its leaders can go to meditate and pray. It is a starkly bare room—no symbols are there to identify the faith it represents. In the middle of the room is a jet-black altar made of iron. To the uninitiated, it would appear to be a peaceful place where all faiths can come to pray for world peace.

Here is the dedication that Dag Hammarskjöld, UN Secretary-General (1953–1961), wrote regarding this special room:

> We all have within us a center of stillness surrounded by silence.
>
> This house, dedicated to work and debate in the service of peace, should have one room dedicated to silence in the outward sense and stillness in the inner sense.
>
> It has been the aim to create in this small room a place where the doors may be open to the infinite lands of thought and prayer.
>
> People of many faiths will meet here, and for that reason none of the symbols to which we are accustomed in our meditation could be used.
>
> However, there are simple things which speak to us all with the same language. We have sought for such things and we believe that we have found them in the shaft of light striking the shimmering surface of solid rock.

So, in the middle of the room we see a symbol of how, daily, the light of the skies gives life to the earth on which we stand, a symbol to many of us of how the light of the spirit gives life to matter.

But the stone in the middle of the room has more to tell us. We may see it as an altar, empty not because there is no God, not because it is an altar to an unknown god, but because it is dedicated to the God whom man worships under many names and in many forms.

The stone in the middle of the room reminds us also of the firm and permanent in a world of movement and change. The block of iron ore has the weight and solidity of the everlasting. It is a reminder of that cornerstone of endurance and faith on which all human endeavour must be based.

The material of the stone leads our thoughts to the necessity for choice between destruction and construction, between war and peace. Of iron man has forged his swords, of iron he has also made his ploughshares. Of iron he has constructed tanks, but of iron he has likewise built homes for man. The block of iron ore is part of the wealth we have inherited on this earth of ours. How are we to use it?

The shaft of light strikes the stone in a room of utter simplicity. There are no other symbols, there is nothing to distract our attention or to break in on the stillness within ourselves. When our eyes travel from these symbols to the front wall, they meet a simple pattern opening up the room to the harmony, freedom and balance of space.

There is an ancient saying that the sense of a vessel is not in its shell but in the void. So it is with this room. It is for those who come here to fill the void with what they find in their center of stillness.[201]

Notice that the United Nations' desire is to fulfill a Messianic promise of turning swords into plowshares—only without Jesus! However, there is a clue to the origin and purpose of this room that any Freemason (or member of any esoteric society) would recognize. The symbol is the room itself; it is trapezoid in shape. The room serves as a Masonic altar and represents the unfinished work of Nimrod. World leaders go there to meditate on how they can serve in the ongoing Masonic work of completing Nimrod's plan on the earth.

Pieces to the Occult Puzzle Still Needed

I have already written many chapters outlining the unfinished work of Nimrod; in this chapter, we will put together the final pieces of the occult puzzle. These final pieces are necessary to complete the work, and the Elite are pouring billions of dollars into research through the various nations they control around the world.

We may have a significant clue as to what Nimrod had in mind, when he constructed the Tower of Babel, and why the Elite have pooled the resources of the planet to continue his work. That clue is found in a book in the Apocrypha, the *Book of Jasher*:

> And they all went before the king, and they told the king these words, and the king agreed with them in this affair, and he did so.
>
> And all the families assembled consisting of about six hundred thousand men, and they went to seek an extensive piece of ground to build the city and the tower, and they sought in the whole earth and they found none like one valley at the east of the land of Shinar, about two days' walk, and they journeyed there and they dwelt there.
>
> And they began to make bricks and burn fires to build the city and the tower that they had imagined to complete.
>
> And the building of the tower was unto them a transgression and a sin, and they began to build it, and whilst they were building against the Lord God of heaven, **they imagined in their hearts to war against him and to ascend into heaven.**

And all these people and all the families divided themselves in three parts; the first said We will ascend into heaven and fight against him; the second said, We will ascend to heaven and place our own gods there and serve them; and the third part said, We will ascend to heaven and smite him with bows and spears; and God knew all their works and all their evil thoughts, and he saw the city and the tower which they were building.

And when they were building they built themselves a great city and a very high and strong tower; and on account of its height the mortar and bricks did not reach the builders in their ascent to it, until those who went up had completed a full year, and after that, they reached to the builders and gave them the mortar and the bricks; thus was it done daily.

And behold these ascended and others descended the whole day; and if a brick should fall from their hands and get broken, they would all weep over it, and if a man fell and died, none of them would look at him. (Jasher 9:22–28, emphasis added)[202]

For those involved in hermeneutical or exegetical studies, it is common to examine extrabiblical texts, whether to gain a better understanding of word usage within similar historical periods or to gain insight into how biblical stories were mythologized within those cultures. The *Book of Jasher* has significant weight in the minds of many researchers, since it is referred to twice in the Word of God—in Joshua 10:13 and 1 Samuel 1:18. This is not to say the writings of the *Book of Jasher* (or any of the books of the Apocrypha) are inspired. I am simply pointing out that our inspired Scriptures recognize the validity of the history contained within the book and, therefore, should be considered in our research.

The *Book of Jasher* seems to indicate that Nimrod aspired to become much more than just a hunter "before the Lord." Nimrod aspired to become a hunter *of the Lord!* This concept can be seen in both the *Book of Jasher* and in the esoteric concepts of *apotheosis* and *ascension*. The mystery religions seek to transcend into godhood; they seek to displace Almighty God with themselves. No wonder God intervened!

The *Book of Jasher* also shows God's contempt for the tower itself:

And they ceased building the city and the tower; therefore he called that place Babel, for there the Lord confounded the Language of the whole earth; behold it was at the east of the land of Shinar.

And as to the tower which the sons of men built, the earth opened its mouth and swallowed up one third part thereof, and a fire also descended from heaven and burned another third, and the other third is left to this day, and it is of that part which was aloft, and its circumference is three days' walk.

And many of the sons of men died in that tower, a people without number. (Jasher 9:37–39)[203]

Could the Elite's final attempt lead to even a greater response from Almighty God—the final battle in Armageddon?

More than Height at Work

The story of the Tower of Babel is not God's judgment against the first man-made skyscraper. There are now towers on the earth so tall that one can see the curvature of the earth from their top floors. The tallest tower in the world, which has 163 floors and stands 2,717 feet tall, is the Burj Khalifa in Dubai.

View from top of Dubai Tower

One could also ask, "If Nimrod wanted more height, why did he build his tower in the middle of a plain, rather than on the top of a great mountain?" The answer may be found in the theory that many physicists have regarding the multiverse and the reality of dimensional portals.

Welcome to the Multiverse

When science fiction writer H. G. Wells proclaimed in 1895 in his story, "The Door in the Wall," that there were portals or doors to others worlds, universes, or dimensions, was he revealing a secret the mystery religions have known since Nimrod? Some researchers believe that Wells was both an Illuminatist and a Freemason. Although we can possibility connect his involvement with the Illuminati through his work entitled *The New World Order* (as well as how the Elite have followed many of his suggestions in the book), there is little evidence that he was a Freemason.[204] However, like many of the science fiction writers of his era, he possibly received inspiration for many of his stories through the esoteric teachings of one of the many mystery religion groups throughout Europe. (Freemasonry is just one of many such groups.)

Today, with the concepts of Superstring Theory, M Theory, and many others, physicists are beginning to realize that our universe many be one of many, each contained within in its own dimensional bubble.

In an article entitled, "Multiverse Controversy Heats Up over Gravitational Waves," Clara Moskowitz shares in March of 2014:

> The multiverse is one of the most divisive topics in physics, and it just became more so. The major announcement last week of evidence for primordial ripples in spacetime has bolstered a cosmological theory called inflation, and with it, some say, the idea that our universe is one of many universes floating like bubbles in a glass of champagne. Critics of the multiverse hypothesis claim that the idea is untestable—barely even science. But with evidence for inflation theory building up, the multiverse debate is coming to a head.

The big news last week came from the Background Imaging of Cosmic Extragalactic Polarization 2 (BICEP2) experiment at the South Pole, which saw imprints in the cosmic microwave background—the oldest light in the universe, dating from shortly after the big bang—that appear to have been caused by gravitational waves rippling through the fabric of spacetime in the early universe. The finding was heralded as a huge breakthrough, although physicists say confirmation from other experiments will be needed to corroborate the results.

If verified, these gravitational waves would be direct evidence for the theory of inflation, which suggests the universe expanded exponentially in the first fraction of a nanosecond after it was born. If inflation occurred, it would explain many features of our universe, such as the fact that it appears to be fairly smooth, with matter spread evenly in all directions (early inflation would have stretched out any irregularities in the universe).

Inflation might also mean that what we consider the universe—the expanse of everything we could see with the most perfect telescopes—is just one small corner of space, a pocket where inflation stopped and allowed matter to condense, galaxies and stars to form, and life to evolve. Elsewhere, beyond the observable universe, spacetime may still be inflating, with other "bubble" universes forming whenever inflation stops in one location.

This picture is called eternal inflation. "Most inflationary models, almost all, predict that inflation should become eternal," says Alan Guth, a theoretical physicist at the Massachusetts Institute of Technology (MIT), who first predicted inflation in 1980.[205]

The concept of other dimensional realities or other bubble universes has been known to the occult for millennia.

1. Noted occultist Dr. John Dee was able to open a portal to another dimension and commune with what he believed was an angel. This communion resulted is his formation of Enochian Magic. This form of magic is now studied by any serious occultist today.

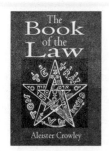

2. **Satanist supreme, Aleister Crowley, opened a portal in which he released a being from another dimension known as Aiwass, which claimed to be a messenger of Horus.** Aiwass then dictated the work that became known as *The Book of Law*.[206] This book is extremely anti-Christian, and this spirit announced to Crowley that the end of Christianity was near and that mankind would be entering into a new age called "The Age of the Fascinating Child." This new age would release an age-old secret held by Freemasonry and many other mystery religions—a system to gain eternal life through sexual vampirism of children…in other words, an age of homosexual pedophilia to extend one's life and to enhance one's occult powers.

3. **Between January and March of 1946, occultists Jack Parsons, L. Ron Hubbard, and Marjorie Cameron conducted the Babylonian Working.** This ritual was essentially designed to manifest an individual incarnation of the archetypal divine feminine called Babalon.[207] Parsons and Hubbard were not as adept in opening dimensional portals as their mentor, Aleister Crowley, was. They accidently ripped the portal wide open. The men never shared what they saw, but it terrified them. Hubbard abandoned such occult workings after that event and went on to create Scientology. Parsons continued with his research as a rocket scientist, but later died in a horrific accident at Jack Parsons Laboratories in June of 1952. It is an interesting fact that the Roswell incident happened the following year, 1947. UFO sightings in the US and around the world have become much more commonplace since then. It leaves many researchers to speculate the connection of Roswell with the Babylonian Working of Hubbard and Parsons.

The Ten Vile Vortices

In researching dimensional portals, I came across a reference by Perry Stone in his book, *Secrets from Beyond the Grave:*

The Bermuda Triangle is one of two places on the earth where a magnetic compass does point toward true north. Normally it points toward magnetic north. The difference between the two is known as compass variation. The amount of variation changes by as much as twenty degrees as one circumnavigates the earth. If this compass variation or error is not compensated for, a navigator could find himself far off course and in deep trouble. Strange, glowing white water and green fog have been spotted there from satellites. The Bermuda Triangle has a deep trench near San Juan measuring twenty-seven thousand feet deep.

Another area where the same strange phenomena occur is the Devil's Sea. The sea is located on the other side of the world, opposite the Bermuda Triangle. The area is located east of Japan between Iwo Jima and Marcus Island. The Japanese government labeled this area as a danger zone. Near Guam is the world's largest underwater trench, measuring thirty-six thousand feet deep. It is unknown why these areas have such strange magnetic fields, and this book will not detail research related to these incidents. However, there are numerous places in the world where there is odd magnetic activity that occurs on a consistent basis, including areas where the compass actually goes in the opposite direction.

A man named Ivan Sanderson, a professional biologist who founded the Society for the Investigation of the Unexplained in Columbia, New Jersey, claims to have discovered twelve electromagnetic vibrations around the world, called by some the "Ten Vile [Strong] Vortices." In 1972, Sanderson wrote an article in *Saga Magazine* calling his discovery "The Twelve Devil's Graveyards Around the World." Sanderson had researched the areas around the world where ships and planes had allegedly disappeared and discovered ten regions of the world, spaced equally apart, that experienced these strange phenomena.[208]

Perry's brief description regarding the Vile (Strong) Vortices piqued my interest, and I began conducting my own research. Although Sanderson originally believed there were twelve of these vortices around the world, other researchers have concluded that there are only ten. The vortices appear to come in pairs and are similar to magnetic poles in that the corresponding vortices will appear on the exact opposite side of the planet. A well-known example would be the Bermuda Triangle. Few realize that the Bermuda Triangle has a twin portal known as the Devil's Triangle on the opposite side of the planet, near Japan.

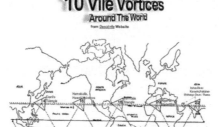

I was also surprised to discover that every single portal is in the shape of a triangle or pyramid. These triangles appear to be constructed with ley lines.

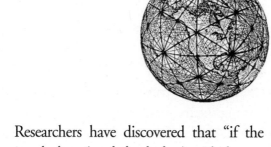

Researchers have discovered that "if the earth is mapped out as an *icosahedrons* (or *dodecahedron*) grid, these are all equidistant geometric points (vortices) of intersecting (ley) lines."[209] Ley lines have always been important to the occult. They are defined by Wikipedia as "hypothetical alignments of a number of places of geographical interest, such as ancient monuments and megaliths. Their existence was suggested in 1921 by the amateur archaeologist Alfred Watkins, whose book *The Old Straight Track* brought the alignments to the attention of the wider public."[210]

In the mystery religions, such ley lines are considered sources of power and are very important to their work. In the documentary entitled *Riddles in Stone*, Chris Pinto points out that the original thirteen colonies in the United States and Washington, DC, are constructed on a ley line that leads directly to Stonehenge in Great Britain.[211]

Could the intersecting of certain ley lines, along with variances in the magnetic fields on our planet, provide a catalyst for the opening of dimensional portals, whether into Heaven or to the lower dimensions of *Sheol*—or worse?

Science Beginning to Catch Up With Mystery Religions

Science is beginning to wrestle with many new concepts:

- There is a possible reality of a multiverse.
- Evidence suggests that our universe may be a holographic project.
- Our universe has self-correcting software running in the background.
- The darkness of space is not empty; it is filled with dark matter.
- There are dimensions within our reality beyond the four that Einstein hypothesized. (M Theory states that there are ten.)

Discover magazine announced in June of 2011 that "physicist Brian Greene explains how properties at the black hole's surface—its event horizon—suggest the unsettling theory that our world is a mere representation of another universe, a shadow of the realm where real events take place."[212]

While physicists argue about whether there are parallel universes with an untold number of earths with many versions of you, the Bible clarifies the matter. There are many realities, but each is unique and is a subset of the parent reality—we call that parent reality "Heaven," or "eternity."

God's Concept of a Multiverse

As I shared earlier, the Word of God speaks of three Heavens. However, we find within Holy Writ details about so much more:

1. **Hell.** What is commonly translated in the English language as "Hell" is the Hebrew word, *Sheol* (sheh-ole'). *Sheol* contains more than just a place of torment. In fact, it has two compartments, according to Jesus, with an impassible gulf between them. Jesus tells of *Sheol* in his teaching on Lazarus and the rich man.

There was a certain rich man, which was clothed in purple and fine linen, and fared sumptuously every day:

And there was a certain beggar named Lazarus, which was laid at his gate, full of sores,

And desiring to be fed with the crumbs which fell from the rich man's table: moreover the dogs came and licked his sores.

And it came to pass, that the beggar died, and was carried by the angels into Abraham's bosom: the rich man also died, and was buried;

And in hell he lift up his eyes, being in torments, and seeth Abraham afar off, and Lazarus in his bosom.

And he cried and said, Father Abraham, have mercy on me, and send Lazarus, that he may dip the tip of his finger in water, and cool my tongue; for I am tormented in this flame.

But Abraham said, Son, remember that thou in thy lifetime receivedst thy good things, and likewise Lazarus evil things: but now he is comforted, and thou art tormented.

And beside all this, between us and you there is a great gulf fixed: so that they which would pass from hence to you cannot; neither can they pass to us, that would come from thence.

Then he said, I pray thee therefore, father, that thou wouldest send him to my father's house:

For I have five brethren; that he may testify unto them, lest they also come into this place of torment.

Abraham saith unto him, They have Moses and the prophets; let them hear them.

And he said, Nay, father Abraham: but if one went unto them from the dead, they will repent.

And he said unto him, If they hear not Moses and the prophets, neither will they be persuaded, though one rose from the dead. (Luke 16:19–31)

Notice that these Scriptures don't say this teaching was a parable. Since Jesus included the name of Lazarus, He was sharing an event rather than a parable. One side of *Sheol* was a place of torment and the other was the "Bosom of Abraham." In the Bosom of Abraham, those who died before Jesus' redemptive work on the cross were waiting in that paradise for its fulfillment. When Jesus resurrected, He emptied Abraham's Bosom and took that great cloud of witnesses with Him to Heaven as the first-fruits offering.

There are still more realities the Word speaks of.

2. **Outer Darkness.** The term "outer darkness" is only used three times in the Word of God; all are in the Gospel of Matthew—Matthew 8:12; 22:13; and 25:30. Finis Dake, in his *Annotated Reference Bible*, connects outer darkness with Hell in Matthew 13:42:

> [**Furnace of fire: there shall be wailing and gnashing of teeth**] Another description of eternal hell, not the grave (Mt. 13:42,50; Rev. 9:2). Wailing, here and in Mt. 13:50; weeping in Mt. 8:12; 22:13; 24:51; 25:30; Lk. 13:28; and gnashing of teeth in all these passages picture bitter remorse and pain.[213]

It seems Dake connects the "gnashing of teeth" in Hell with outer darkness. The *Preacher's Sermon and Outline Bible* provides additional information regarding this outer darkness:

> There will be *outer darkness*: a region, a place, a habitation, a home of pitch black that forbids any sight whatsoever. A place without light, without gleam or hope of any light whatsoever. It is a place

of utter darkness in which one lives completely incapacitated, help-less, and hopeless. It is far away from the splendor and glory and brightness of God's presence. It is being cast into the gloom and blackness of the outer world. It is misery, the misery of a lost soul.[214]

It seems to me that the rich man in Jesus' story was not in outer dark-ness, since no sight was available there at all. The rich man could see Laza-rus clearly in Abraham's Bosom. Therefore, it could be an additional place of punishment.

3. **Tartarus.** The most common word used in the Greek New Testa-ment for "Hell" is "Hades." Yet, Peter chose to use another word in his second epistle.

> For if God spared not the angels that sinned, but cast them down
> to hell, and delivered them into chains of darkness, to be reserved
> unto judgment. (2 Peter 2:4)

The Greek word Peter uses is *tartaroo* (tar-tar-o'-o), which refers to the subterranean region known as Tartarus.[215] In Greek mythology, Tartarus was the abysmal region **below Hades**, where the Titans were confined.[216]

Since Peter was referring to the angels who sinned, he most likely was referring to the Watchers who had sinned with human women to produce the original giants (or Titans) of Genesis 6. The *Book of Enoch* tells us they were chained or imprisoned under the earth.

If we could diagram this, it would look something like this:

Third Heaven
Eternity
Second Heaven
Principalities and Powers
First Heaven
Our Universe
Sheol
Place of Torment/Abraham's Bosom
Outer Darkness
Tartarus

I diagrammed it in layers to demonstrate a point. Each reality is contained with a barrier (or in a bubble) to keep them separate. Instinctively, man has always known that Heaven was "up" and Hell was "down." Since the Third Heaven is the parent reality, all subset realities are in subjection to it. I have also come to believe that these separate realities can reside in the same physical space. This is why traveling to distant places is not necessary to access these realities; it only requires a dimensional portal.

This may explain why UFO researcher Jacques Vallée has come to a similar conclusion regarding UFOs; he believes they are actually interdimensional incursions:

> The **interdimensional hypothesis (IDH or IH)**, is an idea advanced by Ufologists such as Jacques Vallée that says unidentified flying objects (UFOs) and related events involve visitations from other "realities" or "dimensions" that coexist separately alongside our own. It is an alternative to the extraterrestrial hypothesis (ETH). IDH also holds that UFOs are a modern manifestation of a phenomenon that has occurred throughout recorded human history, which in prior ages were ascribed to mythological or supernatural creatures.[217]

In the following excerpt, Dr. Tom Horn discusses the possible connection of pilots of UFOs and demons:

> Later in Operation Trojan Horse, Keel spoke of the intangible nature of the aliens and their craft as "transmogrifications tailoring themselves to our ability to understand." Dr. John Mack not only made the same conclusion—that the UFOnauts illustrate behavior resembling historical demons—but that the intangible nature of such is illustrated in how ETs traverse dimensional gateways, portals, and stargates, such as we have focused on in this study.[218]

The Theory of the Multiverse/Life after Death

Notice what an article entitled "Quantum Theory Proves Consciousness Moves to Another Universe at Death" reveals concerning the multiverse and human consciousness.

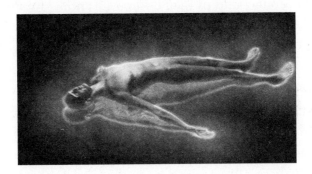

Biocentrism: How Life and Consciousness Are the Keys to Understanding the Nature of the Universe is a book written by the scientist Dr. Robert Lanza. The book has stirred up the Internet, because it contained a notion that life does not end when the body dies, and it can last forever. Lanza who was voted the 3rd most important scientist alive by the NY Times, has no doubts that this is possible.

Beyond time and space

Lanza is an expert in regenerative medicine and scientific director of Advanced Cell Technology Company. Before he has been known for his extensive research which dealt with stem cells, he was also famous for several successful experiments on cloning endangered animal species.

But not so long ago, the scientist became involved with physics, quantum mechanics and astrophysics. This explosive mixture has given birth to the new theory of biocentrism, which the professor has been preaching ever since. Biocentrism teaches that life and consciousness are fundamental to the universe. It is consciousness that creates the material universe, not the other way around.

Lanza points to the structure of the universe itself, and that the laws, forces, and constants of the universe appear to be fine-tuned for life, implying intelligence existed prior to matter. He also claims that space and time are not objects or things, but rather tools of our animal understanding. Lanza says that we carry space and time around with us "like turtles with shells." meaning that when the shell comes off (space and time), we still exist.

The theory implies that death of consciousness simply does not exist. It only exists as a thought because people identify themselves with their body. They believe that the body is going to perish, sooner or later, thinking their consciousness will disappear too. If the body generates consciousness, then consciousness dies when the body dies. But if the body receives consciousness in the same way that a cable box receives satellite signals, then of course consciousness does not end at the death of the physical vehicle. In fact, consciousness exists outside of constraints of time and space. It is able to be anywhere: in the human body and outside of it. In other words, it is non-local in the same sense that quantum objects are non-local.

Lanza also believes that multiple universes can exist simultaneously. In one universe, the body can be dead. And in another it continues to exist, absorbing consciousness which migrated into this universe. This means that a dead person while traveling through the same tunnel ends up not in hell or in heaven, but in a similar world he or she once inhabited, but this time alive. And so on, infinitely. It's almost like a cosmic Russian doll afterlife effect.[219]

Lanza unknowingly validated what the Bible has said all along: The real you is your spirit/soul. Our physical body is nothing more than an "earth suit" to allow us to function in the First Heaven (our universe). At death, we either ascend to a greater reality (Heaven) or a lower reality (Hell). Lanza's secular mindset has restricted him from acknowledging (or recognizing) this truth and has our consciousness traveling to alternate realities.

Back to Nimrod

Is it possible that the Tower of Babel was more than just a tower? Was the tower built in a place where there was a dimensional portal to allow "the gods" to land on earth? Dr. Tom Horn shares this possibility in his book, *Nephilim Stargates:*

> Scientist Stan Deyo has done analysis of a Tower of Babel Stele with speculation about whether the original Tower of Babel was actually designed to facilitate reaching "the heavens" as indicated in the comments above. Was it a building whose top was high enough to allow higher-dimensional beings to descend slowly while discharging voltage directly into the lower energy density universe? Deyo notes the uppermost portion of the stele may show a 'bright' or burning circular area, while the edges of the tower layers themselves are smooth like a high voltage insulator, as if for dissipating electricity. Stan emphasizes the analysis is inconclusive at this time, but it is interesting, given that beings who descended from heaven were typically accompanied by fire or lightning (electrical discharge ?), while beings that ASCEND from lower energy densities (regions) tend to cool the atmosphere, such as in the classic 'ghost' entering a room. Ancient artwork that may support this theory is widespread throughout ancient times including depictions of gods accompanied by fire.[220]

Perhaps Nimrod was diligently laboring to create more than just an interdimensional landing pad; it is quite possible that he was building an ancient interdimensional portal generator. It is quite possible that the wrath of God fell upon the tower because mankind was "of one mind" to create a mechanism to storm Heaven itself! Now, mind you, they had no better chance of winning than did Lucifer with one-third of the angels. However, their very audacity required an answer from Heaven.

Enter the Large Hadron Collider at CERN

There has been both excitement and dread among the scientific community regarding the experiments at the CERN Hadron Collider in Switzerland. While parts of the scientific community are wanting to find the "god particle," others are fearful of either creating a tear in the very fabric of space-time or a black hole that could destroy the planet.[221]

Since then, CERN has powered up its collider several times and has conducted experiments. The scientific community has been both fascinated with the data gathered and has collectively exhaled with a sigh of relief. However, there is more to the story. These experiments were conducted with only a small fraction of the power the collider can generate. Were the past experiments merely a "knocking on the door" of creating a dimensional portal? Perhaps we have several clues at CERN itself. The first is its logo.

The CERN Hadron Collider has encoded within it the Illuminati signature of "666." In the minds of many biblical researchers, the logo itself connects the collider with the coming Beast system. Some have speculated that the logo was only meant to resemble *synchrotron particle accelerators.*[222] Yet it is concerning to me that *synchrotron particle accelerators* create a 666 pattern. It is a common practice within esoteric societies to hide the truth in plain sight and to misinform the uninitiated as to the symbolism's true meaning.

Then, there is the idol of Shiva outside of CERN. Here is a description of Shiva from Wikipedia:

> The main iconographical attributes of Shiva are the third eye on his forehead, the snake Vasuki around his neck, the crescent moon adorning, the holy river Ganga flowing from his matted hair, the trishula as his weapon and the damaru as his instrument.[223]

Here is a basic definition of who Shiva is:

Shiva is the god of the yogis, self-controlled and celibate, while at the same time a lover of his spouse (shakti). Lord **Shiva is the destroyer of the world**, following Brahma the creator and Vishnu the preserver, after which Brahma again creates the world and so on. Shiva is responsible for change both in the form of death and destruction and in the positive sense of destroying the ego, the false identification with the form. This also includes the shedding of old habits and attachments.[224] (Emphasis added)

Isn't it a little unnerving that the scientists at CERN, who have essentially declared that they do not believe in the God of the Bible as Creator, chose to place an idol outside of their facility that represents a being that follows after Brahma the creator and destroy worlds? Shiva, according to Hindu belief, can dismantle all matter and reality itself.

I have come to believe that CERN is only one of many such colliders around the globe that the Elite are using in experiments to find a way of creating a stable portal into other dimensions. Such technology could assist in completing Nimrod's war on Heaven itself.

The Final Piece: Transhumanism

Wikipedia provides the following definition of "transhumanism":

Transhumanism (abbreviated as **H+** or **h+**) is an international cultural and intellectual movement with an eventual goal of fundamentally transforming the human condition by developing and making widely available technologies to greatly enhance human intellectual, physical, and psychological capacities. Transhumanist thinkers study the potential benefits and dangers of emerging technologies that could overcome fundamental human limitations, as well as the ethics of developing and using such technologies. They speculate that human beings may eventually be able to transform themselves into beings with such greatly expanded abilities as to merit the label "posthuman."[225]

The Lifeboat Foundation provides a quick overview of transhumanism:

Transhumanists advocate the improvement of human capacities through advanced technology. Not just technology as in gadgets you get from Best Buy, but technology in the grander sense of strategies for eliminating disease, providing cheap but high-quality products to the world's poorest, improving quality of life and social interconnectedness, and so on. Technology we don't notice because it's blended in with the fabric of the world, but would immediately take note of its absence if it became unavailable. (Ever tried to travel to another country on foot?) Technology needn't be expensive—indeed, if a technology is truly effective it will pay for itself many times over.

Transhumanists tend to take a longer-than-average view of technological progress, looking not just five or ten years into the future but twenty years, thirty years, and beyond. We realize that the longer you look forward, the more uncertain the predictions get, but one thing is quite certain: if a technology is physically possible and obviously useful, human (or transhuman!) ingenuity will see to it that it gets built eventually.

As we gain ever greater control over the atomic structure of matter, our technological goals become increasingly ambitious, and their payoffs more and more generous. Sometimes new technologies even make us happier in a long-lasting way: the Internet would be a prime example. In the following list, I take a look at what I consider the top ten transhumanist technologies.[226]

Transhumanists paint themselves as futurists and, possibly, the ultimate benefactors for all humankind. They seek to cure all diseases, greatly improve our intelligence, and prolong our lives. Yet, when you peel back the carefully crafted public relations hype, you discover so much more.

One of the terms circulating to accurately describe the work of transhumanism is GRINS. Here is what this acronym stands for:

G enetics

R obotic

Artificial **I** ntelligence

N ano Technology

S ynthetic Lifeforms

We need to realize that transhumanists are not satisfied with the creation of man from the hand of God. They use the luciferian deception of evolution as a foundation to build upon. The transhumanists seek to assist the evolutionary process by rewriting our genetic code, using computers to enhance our minds, using nanotech and synthetic DNA to modify our bodies, and even utilizing cyberspace to expand the reach of our spirits. Elaine Graham at the Oxford University Press writes in the abstract of her paper, "Nietzsche Gets a Modem: Transhumanism and the Technological Sublime," the following:

Transhumanism is a futuristic philosophy which celebrates the potential of advanced technologies to augment human functioning to unprecedented degrees, ushering in a new phase of "posthuman" evolution. Some trans-humanists even regard digital technologies as capable of "re-enchanting" the world. Such visions of "cyberspace as sacred space" conceal many value-judgments, however, not least in the universalisation of a metaphysics of technoscience founded on longings for invulnerability, incorporeality and omniscience. Such propensities cloak ideologies of technocratic consumerism that refuse to engage with the global implications of new technologies. A theologically-derived critique not only exposes the ideology of "transcendence" at the heart of transhumanism, but also challenges its claim to represent a latter-day Nietzschean sensibility.[227]

Graham reveals in her abstract that transhumanism is a technoscience religion. Notice that she addresses the belief that cyberspace is actually some type of sacred space. It is very possible that transhumanism will eventually become the one-world religion: man transcending the limitations placed on him by the Creator and becoming a god. Although transhumanists promise to provide the fulfillment of the serpent's promise in Genesis 3, they will eventually reconstruct the genetic mutation of Genesis 6!

I shared the dangers of tampering with the human genome in my chapter in *Blood on the Altar: The Coming War between Christian vs. Christian:*

The Image of God and the Human Conscience

By God's leading, I have embarked on an adventure in reading this year. As a Christian educator, I have attempted to read every systematic theology book ever written in English. As I recently viewed several videos by a seasoned man of God named R. T. Kendall on YouTube, I noticed that he had printed the lectures he conducted as pastor of Westminster Chapel. I was so blessed by the videos that I decided to read through them for a refresher. These lectures are called "Understanding Theology." As I read, I came upon this quote: "The conscience is what is left of *the image of God* in us, incapable of saving us and yet leaving us without excuse"[228] (emphasis added).

Even in sinful man, the image of God remains (though marred) and is manifested as his conscience. I read the sentence through about ten times and leaned back in my chair as it impacted my spirit and mind.

- DNA holds incredible volumes of information that we can only begin to understand.
- DNA has an antenna array to pick up planetary or cosmic vibrations.
- The 7.83-hertz frequency resonance is essential for life. If the resonance changed, it would affect how man thinks and acts.
- The conscience is the image of God within (although marred by the Fall). This image is alive and speaks—our conscience tells us when we have done something wrong.
- The image of God within is restored through the new birth. The conscience of man becomes revitalized, and we slowly learn to hear God's voice with clarity.

What If?

And he had power to give life unto the image of the beast, that the image of the beast should both speak, and cause that as many as would not worship the image of the beast should be killed.

And he causeth all, both small and great, rich and poor, free and bond, to receive a mark in their right hand, or in their foreheads:

And that no man might buy or sell, save he that had the mark, or the name of the beast, or the number of his name.

Here is wisdom. Let him that hath understanding count the number of the beast: for it is the number of a man; and his number is Six hundred threescore and six. (Revelation 13:15–18)

Notice the sequence in which Revelation reveals Lucifer's plan.

The False Prophet has power to give life to the image of the Beast. Is he able to mimic the Holy Spirit and erase the image of God within man and replace it with the image of the Beast (possibly a resequencing of man's DNA to form a new and superior species)? Man would have no more conscience. It would be impossible to respond to the gospel and repent. These men and women would be unredeemable.

Worship of the image of the Beast. How do we worship God? We pray to Him. We respond to the leading of His Spirit. We give reverence to His Word. Maybe the worship of the Beast here is that those who receive the mark only listen to the Beast. They are hardwired to only respond to his word and his voice. Worship used in Revelation 13:15 in the Greek is προσκυνέω (*proskuneo*), which means "to give reverence, to bow the head down to the ground in homage."[229] In other words, it denotes complete submission to the newly created image of the Beast within: spirit, soul, and body.

Those who do not worship the image are killed. Darwin would be proud. We are taught in his book, *On the Origin of Species by Means of Natural Selection, or the Preservation of Favoured Races in the Struggle for Life,* that as mankind evolved into homo sapiens, the new species rose up and killed out the old. This has been drilled into the minds of our children in our school systems for several generations. According to Darwin's rationale, the new, improved *homo perfectus* would rise up to wipe out the old, inferior race (similar to the logic the Nazis used during World War II). This slaughter would be fueled by the image of the Beast within.

Mark of the Beast. If you change the basic genetic coding of mankind, it would most likely change the appearance of man. I have heard from several sources that the members of the Illuminati maintain control of script writers for TV programs and movies. These powerful individuals boast that they continually foretell their plans via the scripts. The CW broadcasts a show that has aired for two seasons now, *Beauty and the Beast.* Vincent, the main character, is a victim of genetic alterations to produce a super soldier in a secret program fashioned for the government. (It is very interesting to note that the genetic coding came from a beast that was on the earth thousands of years ago—i.e., Nephilim.) When Vincent goes into "beast mode," there are distinct changes in his body—particularly in his forehead and hands. The writers of this show have thought through how changing the genetic code would alter one's appearance—except in our case in the future, there would be no on-and-off switch. The appearance (and the soul) would be forever changed.

Number of the Beast—666. Lucifer has now completed the promise he made to Adam and Eve in the garden…with a twist. They are now recreated in the image of Lucifer rather than in the image of God. Six is biblically the number of man. Man is now complete spirit, soul, and body without God and appears to be the next evolutionary step for mankind. This superman is now only tuned into the resonance of Lucifer himself.[230]

As transhumanists seek to rewrite the human genome to assist or accelerate evolution so that man can enter into a techno-godhood, they may very well erase the image of God that resides within mankind. I believe their work to overcome death will be directly connected to the eradication of God's image within man's DNA.

Wikipedia's post regarding transhumanism provides the following history:

> According to Nick Bostrom, transcendentalist impulses have been expressed at least as far back as in the quest for immortality in the Epic of Gilgamesh, as well as historical quests for the Fountain of Youth, Elixir of Life, and other efforts to stave off aging and death.
>
> There is debate about whether the philosophy of Friedrich Nietzsche can be considered an influence on transhumanism despite its exaltation of the "Übermensch" (overman or superman), due to its emphasis on self-actualization rather than technological transformation.[231]

The ultimate goal of transhumanism can be expressed (I believe) in this two premises:

1. To become immortal.
2. To become Nietzshe's Übermensch that has moved beyond good and evil.

The Elite would seem to be using the Transhumanist Movement to overcome death, so they would never be answerable to God. To be honest, that is a very dangerous combination: no sense of right and wrong and no fear of death. Imagine for a moment having a Hitler, Mussolini, or some other despot who could never be killed! Welcome to the last days.

Therefore, posthumanity or "Human 2.0" will be augmented with greater intelligence in immortal and super-powered bodies and will be linked directly into their sacred space (cyberspace). The Elite's intent is not to make all of humanity into pseudo gods; they are building a new breed of mind-controlled Nephilim to become Nimrod's ultimate army.

I am not saying this is the goal of the transhumanists themselves, no more than it is the ultimate goal of many of the scientists at the CERN Hadron Collider to create multidimensional portals. Similar to the many black science projects that our own government has conducted in the past, various aspects can be compartmentalized to maintain secrecy. Only a select few have all of the information and the power to put it all together, when the time is right.

Plato, Transhumanism, and the Antichrist's Strange Army

In the book of Revelation, we have several glimpses of various groups that follow the Antichrist. To understand all that we are seeing in the book of Revelation, we need to understand how the Elite plans to divide up the inhabitants of the earth. I believe the document they are using as a blueprint is Plato's *Republic*.

In this book, Plato postulates his version of the perfect society. Here is my synopsis of his book. This society is comprised of three groups of people:

1. **The benevolent Elite,** who are filled with great wisdom on how to govern this ultimate republic
2. **The citizens/worker drones,** who labor to produce what the Elite decree is necessary for this republic

3. **The military/police force,** which keeps the citizens in line and under the control of the Elite

Here is my hypothesis on how Plato's *Republic* ties into what is being accomplished in transhumanism and how it works into the book of Revelation. (Remember, we are all still seeing "through a glass darkly.")

The Elite: The Elite will enhance their minds and bodies to include achieving immortality. They will become like demigods (or posthumans).

The workers: The Elite will provide some of these benefits to regular members of society to overcome the cost of illness and, therefore, overcome periodic reduction in production of what they need. There will be sufficient modification to the DNA of the workers to remove the image of God within (i.e., mark of the Beast), thereby removing all concepts of right and wrong. The standard worker will not be able to afford the gift of immorality, but will have to settle for an extended life span, which will be extremely disease resistant. Some form of mind control or hive mind will most likely be included in the enhancements.

The military force: The Elite's enforcers will be given more powerful bodies with greater life spans than the worker class and will have a perfected version of unbreakable mind control/hive mind installed. These military forces will be nearly impossible to kill, but will meet their end at the Valley of Armageddon.

When I place this understanding with the book of Revelation, it all makes sense. All three classes have received the mark of the Beast and have had their DNA changed. All of the human race (except for the Remnant) will have the image of God removed and are beyond salvation. With elements of mind control installed within both the worker class and the military class, the world becomes "of one mind," just like in the story of the Tower of Babel. The Elite will finally overcome God's intervention at the Tower of Babel and can unify the entire planet toward completing the unfinished work of Nimrod.

It also answers some problematic situations I see in Revelation:

One class of citizens is tormented in Revelation 9 by a transgenic horde. Death seems to flee from them, and they cannot die. They may also be the same segment of society that is thrown alive into the Lake of Fire (Revelation 19:20). In a sense, this is poetic justice. The Elite have worked for centuries to recreate the Genesis 6 experiment. It is fitting that they are hunted down and tormented by similar creatures that may have been the product of the original experiment!

Not all who receive the mark are immortal. Later, in Revelation 9, four angels are loosed (most likely Watchers) who either bring their own two-hundred-million-member army with them, or they take command of the transgenic army that was released earlier in the chapter. This army slays one-third of the population on the planet.

Then we find in Revelation 17:8:

> The beast that thou sawest was, and is not; and shall ascend out of the bottomless pit, and go into perdition: and they that dwell on the earth shall wonder, whose names were not written in the book of life from the foundation of the world, when they behold the beast that was, and is not, and yet is.

It is clear from this Scripture that the one who ascended out of the pit is the Antichrist/Nimrod. Then you have a class of citizens whose names were never written in the Book of Life from the foundation of the world. Let us first examine what Dake says about the Book of Life in his *Annotated Reference Bible:*

> This is the first mention of the book of God in which the names of the righteous are written. It is referred to in Scripture under various terms: "Thy book" and "My book" (Ex. 32:32–33); "the book of the living" (Ps. 69:28); "the book" (Dan. 12:1); "the book of life" (Php. 4:3; Rev. 3:5; 13:8; 17:8; 20:11–15; 22:18–19); and "the Lamb's book of life" (Rev. 21:27). Just because "book of life" does not appear in all of these passages does not mean the reference in any one instance is to something else. Just as we have several names for the Bible—"the holy scriptures" (Rom. 1:2; 2Tim. 3:15); "the oracles of God" (Rom. 3:2; Heb. 5:12; 1 Pet. 4:11);

"the law and the prophets" (Lk. 24:25–44); "the word of God" (Mk. 7:13; Rom. 10:17; Heb. 4:12); "the sword of the Spirit" (Eph. 6:17); and others—so we have several names for the book of life.

Here God confirmed Moses' belief that names can and will be blotted out of the book of life when men incur the eternal death penalty (Ex. 32:33). The psalmist predicted it in the case of Judas (Ps. 69:20–28). Christ warned of it regarding all who would not overcome sin (Rev. 3:5; 22:18–19). This—God's word, not man's—is definite, not doubtful; it is universal and eternal in application, not local and limited.[232]

Every human ever born on this planet has his or her name written in the Book of Life. It was always the desire of the Father that everyone would be saved (1 Timothy 2:4). When a human being dies without Christ, God is forced to blot that person's name out of the book. For me, the only logical position is that these individuals were never human. It is very possible that part of the Antichrist's army will be created as some type of transgenic chimera, similar to what happened in Genesis 6 after the Titans were destroyed in a civil war. The *Book of Jasher* shares how the second incursion of Nephilim were created:

> And their judges and rulers went to the daughters of men and took their wives by force from their husbands according to their choice, and the sons of men in those days took from the cattle of the earth, the beasts of the field and the fowls of the air, and **taught the mixture of animals of one species with the other**, in order therewith to provoke the Lord; and God saw the whole earth and it was corrupt, for all flesh had corrupted its ways upon earth, all men and all animals. (Jasher 4:18, emphasis added)[233]

Stephen Quayle, in his book *Xenogenesis: Changing Men into Monsters*, details how DARPA (Defense Advanced Research Projects Agency) and many other agencies are working on the creation of artificial wombs.

Such artificial wombs are perfect for creating transgenic beings. Quayle
writes:

> Yet today there are those who seem intent on erasing this connec-
> tion between mother and child, severing a part of what it is to be
> human.
>
> Worse, one can only speculate on how the lack of a real mother
> and instead being raised in a vat somewhere alongside similar sib-
> lings with no human contact before birth would affect a baby.
>
> Would it be unfair to suggest such a person might lack some
> of the innate nurturing and desire for human contact that we take
> for granted?
>
> Might this even create an individual who suffers from some
> sort of disconnect between himself and other human beings?
>
> No one knows the answers, and unfortunately there's no way
> to find out short of experimenting on human beings, raising them
> in "hatcheries," and perhaps doing untold harm in the process.[234]

These artificial wombs would be perfect to develop a transgenic super
soldier for the Antichrist. You may think this is far-fetched, but those
within the academic community are already discussing the ability to create chimeras and the effects it could have on society. Notice the wording
in the Online Stanford Encyclopedia of Philosophy discussion of created
human/nonhuman chimeras (posted May 2008):

> A chimera is an individual composed of cells with different embry-
> onic origins. The successful isolation of five human embryonic
> stem cell (hESC) lines in 1998 increased scientists' ability to create
> human/non-human chimeras and prompted extensive bioethics
> discussion, resulting in what has been dubbed "the other stem
> cell debate." The debate about chimeras has focused on five main
> arguments. The Unnaturalness Argument explores the ethics of
> violating natural species boundaries. The Moral Confusion Argu-
> ment alleges that the existence of entities that cannot be defini-

tively classified as either human or non-human will cause moral confusion that will undermine valuable social and cultural practices. The Borderline-Personhood Argument focuses on great apes and concludes that their borderline-personhood confers a high enough degree of moral status to make most, if not all, chimeric research on them impermissible. The Human Dignity Argument claims that it is an affront to human dignity to give an individual "trapped" in the body of a non-human animal the capacities associated with human dignity. Finally, the Moral Status Framework maintains that research in which a non-human animal's moral status is enhanced to that of a normal adult human is impermissible unless reasonable assurances are in place that its new moral status will be respected, which is unlikely given the motivations for chimeric research and the oversight likely to be provided. These arguments provide different rationales for evaluating chimeric research and consequently differ in their implications both for the range of chimeric research that is unethical as well as the way chimeric research should be addressed in public policy.[235]

Scientifically, it is not a matter of "if" human/nonhuman chimeras can be created in a laboratory, but whether it is ethical to create them. If the truth were known (we have testimonies from those coming out of the occult and contractors from secret government projects sharing about these experiments before they died), human/nonhuman chimeras are no longer just a theory. The newest members of Nimrod's final army could very well be waiting in the wings.

Armageddon—Ultimate Battleground on Earth

I have pondered over what the Battle of Armageddon will look like many times throughout my years of study as an educator and minister. To be honest, the more I learn, the more incredible my picture becomes regarding it. I do not think either Steven Spielberg or George Lucas has the imagination to accurately portray this event. I don't think the sci-fi mind is big enough to wrap itself around it.

In the lead is Nimrod returned from the dead, and he is surrounded by his generals—man-made, immortal demigods wielding untold power.

His army is first made up of genetically modified, mind-controlled super soldiers that move with unprecedented precision by a perfected hive mind. They are supported by the return of the Nephilim spirits in genetically altered bodies that resemble what they had before the Flood—powerful and terrifying.

We might even be able to include the released Watchers, every fallen angel, and their minions. This scenario might include these angels standing as giants with flaming swords, backed up by UFOs providing air support.

Now Let's Bring It All Together

This time, Nimrod has a far superior army than he did at the Tower of Babel. God cannot confuse the language, because this army no longer uses language; its members are literally of one mind. Their desire is not only to wipe Israel off the planet, but they also intend to open a dimensional portal into the Third Heaven to confront Almighty God. Such an army has never been gathered since the beginning of time! God's darling human race, the only class of beings to whom He ever offered a way of redemption, has now been completely corrupted and stands against Him. Every fallen angel (principalities, powers, and rulers of darkness) is there, along with their children, the Nephilim. Every technological breakthrough humanity has ever developed is at the army's disposal in this ultimate showdown. This force believes this will be the mother of all wars and it could even affect eternity.

However, we find that this is one of the shortest wars in all of human history. Lucifer's shock and awe is nothing more than a firecracker!

And I saw heaven opened, and behold a white horse; and he that sat upon him was called Faithful and True, and in righteousness he doth judge and make war.

His eyes were as a flame of fire, and on his head were many crowns; and he had a name written, that no man knew, but he himself.

And he was clothed with a vesture dipped in blood: and his name is called The Word of God.

And the armies which were in heaven followed him upon white horses, clothed in fine linen, white and clean.

And out of his mouth goeth a sharp sword, that with it he should smite the nations: and he shall rule them with a rod of iron: and he treadeth the winepress of the fierceness and wrath of Almighty God.

And he hath on his vesture and on his thigh a name written, KING OF KINGS, AND LORD of LORDS.

And I saw an angel standing in the sun; and he cried with a loud voice, saying to all the fowls that fly in the midst of heaven, Come and gather yourselves together unto the supper of the great God;

That ye may eat the flesh of kings, and the flesh of captains, and the flesh of mighty men, and the flesh of horses, and of them that sit on them, and the flesh of all men, both free and bond, both small and great.

And I saw the beast, and the kings of the earth, and their armies, gathered together to make war against him that sat on the horse, and against his army.

And the beast was taken, and with him the false prophet that wrought miracles before him, with which he deceived them that had received the mark of the beast, and them that worshipped his image. These both were cast alive into a lake of fire burning with brimstone.

And the remnant were slain with the sword of him that sat upon the horse, which sword proceeded out of his mouth: and all the fowls were filled with their flesh. (Revelation 19:11–21, emphasis added)

Lucifer, in his arrogance, forgets whom he is warring against. Almighty God created all things in every dimensional reality with a word. The Bible tells us:

> Who being the brightness of his glory, and the express image of his person, and upholding all things by the word of his power, when he had by himself purged our sins, sat down on the right hand of the Majesty on high. (Hebrews 1:3)

The God who upholds all things by the word of His power does not require His army to fight for Him—neither angels nor saints. He rides into battle as Messiah ben David, the Conquering King. In the time it takes for a word to be spoken from His lips, the entire luciferian army is destroyed. The transgenic blood of that army flows four and a half feet deep over the entire two hundred miles of that valley.

The truth is: In all of those thousands of years when the Elite had labored to complete the unfinished work of Nimrod, they never stopped for a moment to consider that Jesus had some unfinished business of His own. The One and Only, True Messiah has been waiting more than two thousand years for the moment He will roll up His sleeves to begin the business of restoring the kingdom. The Battle of Armageddon (with the casting of the Antichrist and the False Prophet—alive—into the Lake of Fire) is nothing more than His taking out the trash. Now, He can establish the unending kingdom as prophesied by Daniel so many millennia ago. Finally, the earth knows peace—for one thousand years.

HOPE

My hope is built on nothing less
Than Jesus' blood and righteousness;
I dare not trust the sweetest frame,
But wholly lean on Jesus' name.
On Christ, the solid Rock, I stand;
All other ground is sinking sand.

—*My Hope Is Built on Nothing Less,*
    Edward Mote (1797–1874)

chapter ten

Preparing the Remnant

Part 1: Ancient Hebraic Wisdom, the Apostle John, and the Last Days

For the ships of Chittim shall come against him: therefore he shall be grieved, and return, and have indignation against the holy covenant: so shall he do; he shall even return, and have intelligence with them that forsake the holy covenant.

And arms shall stand on his part, and they shall pollute the sanctuary of strength, and shall take away the daily sacrifice, and they shall place the abomination that maketh desolate.

And such as do wickedly against the covenant shall he corrupt by flatteries: *but the people that do know their God shall be strong, and do exploits.*

—Daniel 11:30–33, emphasis added

In the previous nine chapters, I have provided a basic "Kingdom Intelligence Briefing." In those pages, I painted in broad strokes the agenda and tactics the enemy is using to bring about the war against God Nimrod envisioned at the Tower of Babel. Any of the many topics I touched upon could have been expanded into an entire book. However, the purpose of an intelligence briefing is to assist you in connecting the dots to see the overall plan of the enemy. God may lead you to study some of these topics in greater detail. You may be used by God to connect more of the dots and help prepare your family and the body of Christ for what the future holds as end-time prophecy unfolds before our very eyes.

So many books today seem to point at what the enemy is doing without providing kingdom solutions and empowerment for these trying times. In the following chapters, I want to empower you to both widen and deepen your walk with God. The verse I quoted above says, "**BUT** the people that do know their God shall be strong, and do exploits" (emphasis added). In my own personal Bible study, I have found that two of the most powerful words in the Word of God are "but" and "therefore." In the midst of the rise of the Antichrist, the prophet Daniel throws in a "but" that provides hope for the Remnant. The Hebrew word used by Daniel for "know" is *yada* (yaw-dah'), which means "to know, to learn to know, to perceive, to discern, discriminate, distinguish, to have knowledge, and be skillful in."[236] The second important word Daniel uses is "strong," which is the Hebrew word *chazaq* (khaw-zak'). *Chazaq* means "to strengthen, prevail, harden, be strong, become strong, be courageous, be firm, grow firm, and to be resolute."[237] Within these two Hebrew words we see exactly what God wants us to become!

The days of casual or weekend Christianity are over. All of the authors in the book, *Blood on the Altar: The Coming War Between Christian vs. Christian*, provided a multiple witness to the body of Christ to get serious about their relationship with Jesus and their daily walk! The only thing that casual Christianity will produce in your life is absolute deception. The same is true for those following a religious spirit rather than the Spirit of the Living God. BUT, God has promised us that those who become skillful in the knowledge of God, and who can perceive and discern God's voice and actions, will become strong and accomplish great exploits! As the tide of the Antichrist rises around the world, the Remnant is going to be strengthened, become courageous and bold, grow firm and resolute, and will prevail! There is hope!

Returning to the Book of Acts Church

As we read the book of Acts, we discover that the early Church (even in its infancy) was able to grow dynamically and thrive while living under the oppressive heel of the pagan Roman government. It was able to separate itself from the spirit of Babylon that surrounded it. The early Church faced persecution with the power of God and a boldness that ministers, throughout the ages, have longed for.

Historically, there have been many seeking revival who have issued a call to return to the book of Acts Church. Unfortunately, they issued the call from within the paradigms of their own particular denominational settings while failing to set the Church in the book of Acts back within its Hebraic setting. I believe that as God reawakens the Church to its Hebraic heritage in a balanced manner, we will find the missing pieces to our biblical puzzle that have frustrated us for so long.

God Has It All Under Control

Remember the former things of old: for I am God, and there is none else; I am God, and there is none like me,

Declaring the end from the beginning, and from ancient times the things that are not yet done, saying, My counsel shall stand, and I will do all my pleasure. (Isaiah 46:9–10)

We need to understand that there is nothing the Elite or Lucifer can do to catch God off guard. We serve the God who knows the end from the very beginning—even the ancient things that have not yet come to fruition. We need to become a people of "the entire Word of God" once again. Using just 30 percent of your Bible in your walk and in spiritual warfare will prove ineffective when the enemy brings 100 percent of his plan to your doorstep. Remember, A. W. Tozer said, "The Word of God well understood and religiously obeyed is the shortest route to spiritual perfection. Nothing less than a whole Bible can make a whole Christian."

As we have already seen throughout this book, God encoded much of what the enemy was going to do in the last days in the first five books of the Bible. Five is the biblical number for **grace**, and God was giving us His **grace** in what He anointed Moses to write.

Returning to Biblicity

In chapter 2, I introduced you to many Hebraic concepts that are not widely known in today's churches. There is an untapped wealth of information in the Word of God; to be truthful, we need all of it to become Daniel's courageous and prevailing believers! I do not think that the *harpazo* (har-pad'-zo),[238] or being "caught up" in 1 Thessalonians 4:17, is a safety mechanism to extract the body of Christ before we are decimated by the Antichrist and his transgenic army! We will leave this world when our work is complete, and we will celebrate the Marriage Supper of the Lamb while the wrath of God is poured out upon a completely corrupted world.

Jesus is coming back for a victorious Bride who has prepared her garments. In biblical types and shadows, garments always represent one's walk with God. The Bride of Christ's garments will not be tattered, stained, or torn through abuse, sin, and false doctrine. The Remnant must labor to repair the damage Babylon has caused to our personal faith and our families, and we will once again understand how to "work out our own salvation with fear and trembling" (Philippians 2:12).

Speaking of Types and Shadows

A wonderful mystery is contained within the original pattern of the tabernacle in the wilderness. This pattern can serve as a universal pattern for many things in the kingdom of God. The writer of the book of Hebrews tells us:

Who serve unto the example and shadow of heavenly things, as Moses was admonished of God when he was about to make the tabernacle: for, See, saith he, that thou make all things **according to the pattern** shewed to thee in the mount. (Hebrews 8:5, emphasis added)

Years ago, I developed a course for Biblical Life College and Seminary entitled, "Priesthood of the Believer: The Order of Melchizedek." During my research for that course, God began to reveal secrets about the pattern of the tabernacle. I want to address some of the concepts that the Holy Spirit taught me as I was preparing to teach this subject to our students.

Tabernacle in the Wilderness: Shadow of Many Things

Before I begin, I want to make something very clear: Every item, every inch, of the tabernacle and its service is about Jesus! Volumes have been written on how He is so wonderfully revealed there. However, we need to understand something about types and shadows in the Word: Sometimes revelation is given to us based on how we approach them. Hebraically, part of the learning process is discovering how to ask the right questions. The question I asked as I approached the tabernacle was, "How does my Lord want to be served, since I am now His temple?" (1 Corinthians 3:17). With that question, a revelation about the tabernacle began to form within my spirit.

Tabernacle in the Wilderness

As I studied the tabernacle in the wilderness, the Holy Spirit unveiled truths regarding Almighty God, man, our service to God, and so much more.

Outer Court

Brazen Altar (blood sacrifice)

Laver (ministry of the Word)

Holy Place

Menorah (understanding given by the Holy Spirit)

Table of Shewbread (fellowship with Messiah and His suffering)

Altar of Incense (prayer)

Holy of Holies

Mercy Seat—God's throne upon the earth

The writer of Hebrews (post-Calvary) moves the Altar of Incense into the Holy of Holies (Hebrews 9:4).

Each of the items placed within the tabernacle speak volumes regarding our walk with God.

We all start in the Outer Court and must wrestle with our need for the sacrifice on the Brazen Altar. Bronze represents judgment. Jesus received our judgment for sin upon the cross. Until we accept this truth and His sacrifice, we cannot enter God's kingdom.

The Laver is used twice by the priests in their service in the Outer Court: once before offering the sacrifice and once after their work is completed at the Brazen Altar. The water in the Laver represents the Word of God. Before the sacrifice is made, we look into the Word and find that we are sinners in need of redemption. The sin in our lives requires judgment, and that judgment is poured out upon the sacrifice. After we receive the redemption made through the sacrifice, we return to the Laver to wash our hands and our feet. As we look back into the Word of God, we discover "who" we have become through the atoning work completed at the altar. We are recreated in Christ Jesus. From that moment on, the Word transforms what we do with our hands and where we go with our feet.

Now we can enter the Holy Place. We receive illumination from the anointing and fire of the Holy Spirit; we learn as we have fellowship at the Table of Shewbread; and we intercede at the Altar of Incense. And then…by the blood of the Lamb, our High Priest takes us into the Holy of Holies, and we become true worshippers. What splendor flows through us as we get lost in the manifested presence of the Holy One of Israel! If you have never pressed through the veil, I encourage you to. There is strength, wonder, and transformation waiting for you at the feet of God's throne! If you can ever get a believer there, he or she is never the same. Time can stand still, and the worries of this world melt away. At the same time, weary souls receive a supernatural strength that empowers them in the service to their King. We are going to need that renewing strength, for we are all called to be strong and to do great exploits in this world shrouded in darkness.

God Represented in the Tabernacle

> For through him we both have access by one Spirit unto the Father. (Ephesians 2:18)

The first ministry of the Holy Spirit is to convict us of sin and draw us to Jesus. Once we are "in Christ," Jesus makes the way available to us to fellowship with the Father. The goal is to draw us into the Holy of Holies to commune with our Heavenly Father.

The tabernacle is a perfect representation of the God-head and His ministry to bring us before His throne.

We Discover Ourselves in the Tabernacle

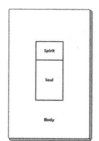

When we accept Messiah, our spirit is born again and Jesus places His throne within our spirit.

As we fellowship with Jesus and study His Word, the Holy Spirit brings understanding and begins the renewing of our minds. Our bodies are made clean and useful to God, through "DOING" His commandments.

We Discover the Practices of Our Faith in the Tabernacle

Our faith must move beyond where we are now. There is a progression to biblical sanctification.

Because I am now accepted "in the beloved" (Ephesians 1:6), I have access to the Father (Ephesians 2:18). As the relationship grows with God, the Holy Spirit makes the Word of God come alive in my life—from Genesis to Revelation. I bow my will to the Word of God and receive it with meekness, which begins the process of saving my soul (James 1:21). The Greek word for "save" in James 1:21 is *sozo*, which means to "save, keep safe and sound, to rescue from danger or destruction, to make well, heal, and restore to health."[239] If we are honest with ourselves, our old ways of thinking and doing are what get us into trouble after we enter the kingdom. As we learn of God's ways and make them our own, we become agents of change and restoration in our lives and in the lives of those around us.

Finally, we begin doing with our lives and bodies what God says to do. Biblically, those "doings" accomplished in our physical bodies are works of righteousness (or good works). The Bible is very clear that:

For we are his workmanship, created in Christ Jesus unto good works, which God hath before ordained that we should walk in them. (Ephesians 2:10)

We were born again to walk in these good works of the kingdom.

All scripture is given by inspiration of God, and is profitable for doctrine, for reproof, for correction, for instruction in righteousness:
That the man of God may be perfect, thoroughly furnished unto all good works. (2 Timothy 3:16–17)

In the life of the believer, the Word of God is here to correct us and to teach us how to walk in the new righteousness we have obtained through Jesus. The word used by Paul in 2 Timothy 3:17 for "perfect" is the Greek word *artios* (ar'-tee-os), which is defined as "fitted, complete, and perfect."[240] Therefore, the Word of God fits us with the tools we need to be about our Father's business and to accomplish His works on the earth—as defined by the Word itself.

Good works were never about gaining salvation, whether it was within Judaism or biblical Christianity. As I will examine a little later, the Pharisees from the School of Shammai basically invented a concept of "salvation through circumcision" and were teaching this new concept to Gentile believers. This was the reason the Jerusalem Council was convened in Acts 15 and the book of Galatians was written.

How We Live Out Our Faith

Contrary to modern Christianity, God has first called us as individuals to walk with Him. Abraham's call was to personally walk with God. Your call is to personally walk with God. Your pastor cannot do it for you. Your husband or wife cannot do it for you. Salvation is a personal relationship and must affect who you are at the very core of your being. It is time to go ahead and surrender everything to God, who laid down His life for you on the cross. We need to move from being weekend visitors to citizens of the kingdom of God who walk with Him 24/7, 365 days a year.

Once your individual walk is right, your family can begin walking with God as a microcommunity. Every husband is the priest and pastor of his home. Every wife is a nurturing dynamo, with kingdom power to love, encourage, and train her children. As a family, the home becomes a house of worship, a house of learning, and a house of fellowship. Without these three aspects of the home fully established in the kingdom, Babylon can creep in, and then the home becomes nothing more than a pit stop between events. God never intended for the home to be a pit stop; rather, His desire is for it to be a garden of blessing, love, and nurturing.

With the individual and the home in place, the local congregation can become a place of salvation, healing, restoration, learning, and worship. The modern Church can only be transformed from Greek theater to

Hebraic living in the kingdom by properly establishing both the personal and family walks!

The Book of Revelation—Fifth Gospel

The book of Revelation was written for several purposes. We see "who" it was written for in the very first verse:

> The Revelation of Jesus Christ, which God gave unto him, to shew **unto his servants** things which must shortly come to pass; and he sent and signified it by his angel unto his servant John:
>
> Who bare record of the word of God, and of the testimony of Jesus Christ, and of all things that he saw. (Revelation 1:1–2, emphasis added)

The Greek word John uses for "servants" is *doulos* (doo'-los), which means "servant or bondservant."[241] (This word also connects Acts 2 with Joel 3, which we will cover in the next chapter.) The book of Revelation was not written for those left behind or to a world full of sinners; it was written to the true servants of Messiah. I have called this book "the fifth Gospel" over the years. The primary purpose of the book of Revelation is to reintroduce Jesus to the Church! Let me explain.

The first time Jesus came, the Messianic expectation was at an all-time high among the Jewish people. They were expecting Messiah ben David, the Conquering King, to come and deliver them from Rome and to reestablish a United Kingdom of Israel. This expectation was so burned into their consciousness that His disciples even asked Him about it **after** the resurrection.

> When they therefore were come together, they asked of him, saying, Lord, wilt thou at this time restore again the kingdom to Israel? (Acts 1:6)

The overemphasis on Messiah's role as the Son of David blinded them to the reality that He came the first time to save—not to condemn, judge or conquer.

> For God sent not his Son into the world to condemn the world; but that the world through him might be saved. (John 3:17)

Their tunnel vision regarding Messiah ben David caused them to miss the coming of Messiah ben Joseph, the Suffering Servant. The absolute insistence upon Messiah coming as the Conquering King eventually caused **Rabbi Akiva** to declare **Simon bar Kokhba** the Messiah in AD 132. The results of the "would be" Messiah ben David were a complete failure in the second Jewish revolt, the total destruction of Jerusalem, and the separation of the true Messianic community from the Jewish people.

In the Church today, there is a great possibility that we have a similar tunnel vision of Jesus as Messiah ben Joseph, even to the point of distorting who He really is—through such teachings as "hyper-grace"—so that we, too, could miss the signs of His coming as the Conquering King.

Jesus is coming back—not to forgive, but to judge and to conquer. In His coming, He will reveal Himself as Elohim (God) of the Old Testament. I have already shown you how the Aleph-Tav/Elohim in Genesis 1 became the YHVH-Elohim of Genesis 2. The first time He came, He was YHVH in the flesh—the Mercy of God. The second time He comes, He will be Elohim—the Justice of God. If we are not careful, we could easily make the same mistake as the Jewish community of the first century and reject what Jesus is doing in His Second Coming!

We covered much of this in chapter 2, but it is important to review for the sake of clarity. Hyper-grace and misunderstanding of the proper purpose of the commandments of God can cause you to become completely deceived!

The first epistle of John was written about a year after he finished the book of Revelation. I believe the Apostle of Love spent many sleepless nights in prayer and study, desiring to prepare the people of God for the unfolding of the vision he had witnessed regarding the things to come. John's heart desired to prepare God's people, and I believe the first epistle of John was the answer to the cry of his heart. In his short epistle, he reconnects the Church to its Hebraic heritage.

The Main Writings of the Apostle John and Their
Respective Purposes

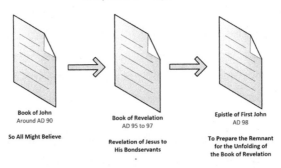

I have always found it amusing that the Apostle of Love wrote the bluntest book in the Bible. In his first epistle, he calls people "liars" five times! His epistles are the only books in the Bible that use the term "Antichrist": 1 John 2:18, 2:22, 4:3 and 2 John 1:7. He discusses the "commandments of God" in a positive light seven times: 1 John 2:3, 2:4, 3:22, 3:24, 5:2, 5:3, and 2 John 1:6. He also uses the word "commandment" ten times: 1 John 2:7 (3), 2:8, 3:23 (2), 4:21, and 2 John 1:4, 1:5, and 1:5. Needless to say, the apostle John was trying to make a point. His first letter is a powerful little book written with the end-time saints in mind. I would like to spend some time in this chapter examining the first epistle of John.

The Faithful Witness

> That which was from the beginning, which we have heard, which we have seen with our eyes, which we have looked upon, and our hands have handled, of the Word of life;
>
> (For the life was manifested, and we have seen it, and bear witness, and shew unto you that eternal life, which was with the Father, and was manifested unto us). (1 John 1:1–2)

John is the apostle who laid his head on the bosom of Messiah at the Last Supper and heard the very heartbeat of Almighty God. From that day forward, he was consumed with letting the world know who Jesus was. In his Gospel, the book of Revelation, and now in his first epistle, he declares that Jesus is the **Aleph-Tav** of Genesis 1:1. John is emphatic about the fact that Jesus is the incarnation of Almighty God, who came in the flesh and dwelt with man. This is an essential doctrine, and he stresses the fact that the spirit of error and the Antichrist will attack this truth.

What Is True Fellowship?

That which we have seen and heard declare we unto you, that ye also may have fellowship with us: and truly our fellowship is with the Father, and with his Son Jesus Christ.

And these things write we unto you, that your joy may be full. (1 John 1:3–4)

John moves from declaring "who" Jesus is to the subject of fellowship. He then stresses that the gospel was preached to them so they could enter fellowship with the Father and the Son. Once fellowship is established through the completed work of Christ at the cross, fellowship can then be established with other believers. Those who are born again can sense other believers in their spirits—they can sense kindred spirits.

In my years of ministry, I have been in countries where the people do not speak English. I remember a meeting in Germany that included Americans, Italians, and Germans. Few of those in attendance spoke more than their own native language. Yet in those meetings, we knew who were believers and who were not. It was not a matter of language; it was a matter of the kingdom of God residing in someone else—and our hearts could sense it.

This is even an important aspect of spiritual warfare. In the fourth century, Constantine announced to a world of weary saints that he had found the Messiah. At first, he offered all of the right sound bites to back

up his claims. However, it was not true. From that day forward, he began to amalgamate Christian terminology into the **mystery religions** and used the power of his office to enforce his agenda. The same tactic has been used by despotic leaders, including Hitler, in world history ever since. A recent article on Raiders News Network promoting the book, *Blood on the Altar,* featured the following photo and quote from Hitler:

ADOLF HITLER ON CHRISTIANITY
"We tolerate no one in our ranks who attacks the ideas of Christianity... in fact our movement is Christian."

We need to ask ourselves, "Are modern-day politicians following the example of Hitler to gain power?"

We need to stop being moved by sound bites and appearances. We need to learn to be led by the Spirit of God, and He will show us who belongs to the kingdom and who is just pretending.

The New American Standard Bible translation of 1 John 1:4 reads:

These things we write, so that our joy may be made complete.

The King James Version of the same verse reads:

And these things write we unto you, that your joy may be full.

Although there is debate among some academic circles as to which is correct, I would tend to be more Hebraic and say that BOTH are correct interpretations, in that it should be all inclusive. The apostolic witness is filled with joy when the lost are saved and brought into fellowship with both God and the community of faith. The community of faith is overjoyed at the new converts and can sense that each new member is a kindred spirit in the kingdom of God.

Later on in his epistle, John begins to point out the attitudes and teachings of those who pretend to be in the kingdom, but are not truly of the community of faith. These pretenders have no real fellowship with the gospel, the Father, or the kingdom. They move by the Spirit of error and are of the Antichrist.

Sin, Confession, Forgiveness, and the Power of the Blood of Christ

Einstein postulated that the only constant in the universe is the speed of light. We have since learned that the speed of light has changed throughout human history. However, there is a true constant, although physics has nothing to do with its reality. The absolute constant is the definition of sin. John tells us:

Whosoever committeth sin transgresseth also the law: for sin is the transgression of the law. (1 John 3:4)

All those years after Jesus' death and resurrection (and the writings of the apostle Paul), John states that sin is the transgression of the law. The eternal Word of God provides an important absolute: the definition of sin never changes. This is actually for our benefit. If the definition of sin continuously changed, how could man ever identify sin and seek to avoid it? Because of God's grace, the definition of sin is a kingdom absolute.

John also shares that those who have come to know Jesus will not live a lifestyle that violates God's law.

> And ye know that he was manifested to take away our sins; and in him is no sin.
>
> Whosoever abideth in him sinneth not: whosoever sinneth hath not seen him, neither known him. (1 John 3:5–6)

John is emphatic concerning how a true believer's lifestyle does **not** involve violating the law.

> And hereby we do know that we know him, if we keep his commandments.
>
> He that saith, I know him, and keepeth not his commandments, is a liar, and the truth is not in him. (1 John 2:3–4)

There will be occasions in which a believer falls into sin by being tempted by the enemy, but a true believer will seek a lifestyle of obedience to the Word of God. Praise be to the Father that the blood of Jesus is available and can restore fellowship!

> If we say that we have no sin, we deceive ourselves, and the truth is not in us.
>
> If we confess our sins, he is faithful and just to forgive us our sins, and to cleanse us from all unrighteousness.
>
> If we say that we have not sinned, we make him a liar, and his word is not in us. (1 John 1:8–10)

I love the way John penned this truth. Initially, when we sin, we are to run *toward* Jesus—not away from Him. Then, if we honestly confess our sins to Him, He is faithful to forgive us and cleanse us from ALL unrighteousness. John did not say, "You are forgiven when you feel like you are." Forgiveness is not based on feelings; feelings may take some time to catch up with spiritual reality. It is based solely upon HIS FAITHFULNESS.

Continuously Remaining Under the Blood of Jesus

> This then is the message which we have heard of him, and declare
> unto you, that God is light, and in him is no darkness at all.
>   If we say that we have fellowship with him, and walk in dark-
> ness, we lie, and do not the truth:
>   But if we walk in the light, as he is in the light, we have fel-
> lowship one with another, and the blood of Jesus Christ his Son
> cleanseth us from all sin. (1 John 1:5–7)

As we constantly seek to walk in fellowship with Jesus and in the light
of the kingdom, we can walk in a constant covering of His blood to sanc-
tify and empower us for service in His kingdom!

When we sin and do not immediately run to Jesus to confess and
be cleansed, it brings that part of our life out from under the sanctifying
cover of His blood. This area can then become the enemy's access point
into our lives. Dear saint of God, don't ever allow that to happen. When
you stumble, run immediately to Jesus and close the door to the enemy
of your soul!

The Spirit of Error/Antichrist Attacks Who Jesus Is

The Antichrist spirit will separate itself from the truth of the gospel:

> Little children, it is the last time: and as ye have heard that anti-
> christ shall come, even now are there many antichrists; whereby
> we know that it is the last time.
>   They went out from us, but they were not of us; for if they
> had been of us, they would no doubt have continued with us: but
> they went out, that they might be made manifest that they were
> not all of us. (1 John 2:18–19)

The more true believers press into God and begin walking in the
kingdom, the harder it is for the pretenders to remain in the fellowship.

This is one of the reasons that true revival both adds to and subtracts from the church: sinners are saved, and the pretenders usually cause a fuss and then leave.

The Antichrist spirit will cause many to refuse the truth of the gospel and align themselves with the world:

> They are of the world: therefore speak they of the world, and the world heareth them.
>
> We are of God: he that knoweth God heareth us; he that is not of God heareth not us. Hereby know we the spirit of truth, and the spirit of error. (1 John 4:5–6)

Many today claim to be Christians, yet deny the divinity of Jesus, His virgin birth, His atoning work on the cross, and His literal resurrection from the dead. These individuals flow with every wind of doctrine of the Antichrist that blows across our culture and can even fill the largest stadiums with like-minded crowds; we need to realize that these gatherings are comprised of those who will only hear error, because they have rejected the truth.

The Antichrist spirit will cause ministers to deny the divinity of Christ:

> Beloved, believe not every spirit, but try the spirits whether they are of God: because many false prophets are gone out into the world.
>
> Hereby know ye the Spirit of God: Every spirit that confesseth that Jesus Christ is come in the flesh is of God:
>
> And every spirit that confesseth not that Jesus Christ is come in the flesh is not of God: and this is that spirit of antichrist, whereof ye have heard that it should come; and even now already is it in the world. (1 John 4:1–3)

The primary subject in these verses is not the Spirit, but a false prophet (or teacher). To fully understand these verses, we must place them within their Hebraic context.

If there arise among you a prophet, or a dreamer of dreams, and giveth thee a sign or a wonder,

And the sign or the wonder come to pass, whereof he spake unto thee, saying, Let us go after other gods, which thou hast not known, and let us serve them;

Thou shalt not hearken unto the words of that prophet, or that dreamer of dreams: for the LORD your God proveth you, to know whether ye love the LORD your God with all your heart and with all your soul.

Ye shall walk after the LORD your God, and fear him, and keep his commandments, and obey his voice, and ye shall serve him, and cleave unto him. (Deuteronomy 13:1–4)

A false prophet cannot exist without a spirit speaking to him and through him. In the Old Testament, even if the prophet did miracles and accurately foretold the future, *if he led them away from God and His commandments, the people were not to listen.* God would even allow the false prophet within the Community of Faith to "prove" the people. The Hebrew word here for "prove" is *nacah* (naw-saw'), which means to "test, prove, try, and to assay."[242] There will be times in all of our lives when God will test us to see if we will stay true to His Word and cleave to Him or follow the next spiritual fad that comes along that draws a crowd. This testing comes to ministers and ministries just as much as it does to individual believers. How many ministers have we seen in the last several decades abandon sound doctrine for something that would build bigger ministries and larger crowds? How many believers have abandoned their small congregations that remained faithful to attend some new thing that caught the attention of their flesh? How many have failed God's proving?

John now attributes this same premise to who Jesus is. He has already shared in his Gospel that Jesus was the Creator of the world, and the world did not recognize him (John 1:10). He has stated in the book of Revelation that Jesus is the God who will judge the whole earth as Messiah ben David, the Conquering King. Finally, at the start of his epistle, he once again connects Jesus to the **Aleph-Tav** and Elohim in Genesis 1:1. Why am I saying all of this? Because Christians will use this verse to test spirits. They will ask a spirit manifesting, "Has Jesus Christ come in the flesh?" To be truthful, even Hitler would have answered, "Yes!" It is a historical fact that there was a man named Jesus, whom many called "the Messiah." Placing the question back into the context of these verses, it was a testing of the spirit behind the prophet. Was this man teaching that Jesus was Almighty God come in the flesh? If not, he was teaching by an Antichrist spirit.

It was so important for John to convey the concept of who Jesus really was that the apostle repeats himself in 2 John:

> For many deceivers are entered into the world, who confess not that Jesus Christ is come in the flesh. This is a deceiver and an antichrist.
>
> Look to yourselves, that we lose not those things which we have wrought, but that we receive a full reward.
>
> Whosoever transgresseth, and abideth not in the doctrine of Christ, hath not God. He that abideth in the doctrine of Christ, he hath both the Father and the Son. (2 John 1:7–9)

Going back to Deuteronomy 13, this leads us to another theological quandary: If we present a version of Jesus that has abandoned the ways of God and His commandments, have we not failed this test, too? (I will bring balance to this question later in this chapter.)

John's Teachings Concerning the Commandments

The Commandments Connected with Christian Conduct

> And hereby we do know that we know him, if we keep his commandments.
>
> He that saith, I know him, and keepeth not his commandments, is a liar, and the truth is not in him.

But whoso keepeth his word, in him verily is the love of God perfected: hereby know we that we are in him.

He that saith he abideth in him ought himself also so to walk, even as he walked. (1 John 2:3–6)

I really don't know how John could have been blunter. Some believers teach that the commandments have been done away with, which is contrary to what Jesus declared in Matthew:

Think not that I am come to destroy the law, or the prophets: I am not come to destroy, but to fulfil.

For verily I say unto you, Till heaven and earth pass, one jot or one tittle shall in no wise pass from the law, till all be fulfilled.

Whosoever therefore shall break one of these least commandments, and shall teach men so, he shall be called the least in the kingdom of heaven: but whosoever shall do and teach them, the same shall be called great in the kingdom of heaven.

For I say unto you, That except your righteousness shall exceed the righteousness of the scribes and Pharisees, ye shall in no case enter into the kingdom of heaven. (Matthew 5:17–20)

In properly interpreting Matthew 5, we need to realize that the terms "destroy" and "fulfill" in verse 17 are Jewish idioms. Therefore, these phrases have cultural meanings. Without an understanding of these meanings, we can miss what is being said completely. Noted scholars Dr. David Bivin and Dr. Roy Blizzard Jr. provide some clarity regarding these idioms in their book, *Understanding the Difficult Words of Jesus: New Insights from a Hebraic Perspective*:

Undoubtedly, in trying to understand this passage, everything hinges on the meaning of the words "destroy" and "fulfill" in verse 17. What does Jesus mean by "destroy the Law" and "fulfill the Law"?

"Destroy" and "fulfill" are technical terms used in rabbinic argumentation. When a rabbi felt that a colleague had misinterpreted a passage of Scripture, he would say, "You are destroying the Law!" Needless to say, in most cases his colleague strongly disagreed. What was "destroying the Law" for one rabbi, was "fulfilling the Law" (correctly interpreting Scripture) for another.

What we see in Matthew 5:17ff. is a rabbinic discussion. Someone has accused Jesus of "destroying" the Law. Of course, neither Jesus nor his accuser would ever think of literally destroying the Law. Furthermore, it would never enter the accuser's mind to charge Jesus with intent to abolish part or all of the Mosaic Law. What is being called into question is Jesus' system of interpretation, the way he interprets Scripture.

When accused, Jesus strongly denies that his method of interpreting Scripture "destroys" or weakens its meaning. He claims, on the contrary, to be more orthodox than his accuser. For Jesus, a "light" commandment ("Do not bear hatred in your heart") is as important as a "heavy" commandment ("Do not murder"). And a disciple who breaks even a "light" commandment will be considered "light" (have an inferior position) in Jesus' movement (Matthew 5:19).

"Never imagine for a moment," Jesus says, "that I intend to abrogate the Law by misinterpreting it. My intent is not to weaken or negate the Law, but by properly interpreting God's written Word I aim to establish it, that is, make it even more lasting. I would never invalidate the Law by effectively removing something from it through misinterpretation. Heaven and earth would sooner disappear than something from the Law. Not the smallest letter in the alphabet, the *yod*, nor even its decorative spur, will ever disappear from the Law."[243]

John shares that Jesus is the perfect interpretation of the Law. Jesus lived a perfect life, which means He kept the Law perfectly. **He is now our example.** John tells us in verse 6, "He that saith he abideth in him ought himself also so to walk, even as he walked." A "Jesus walk" properly interprets and applies God's commandments to daily living.

Another common explanation to avoid the commandments in the Old Testament is that Jesus provided new laws for us to live. There is no mandate issued by Jesus or given in the New Testament that would warrant that belief. It is true that there are more than a thousand commandments in the New Testament. Few realize that they are in perfect harmony with the commandments given in the Old Testament. They offer insights into how Jesus kept them and how His Spirit empowers us to live them.

Changing the definition of commandments for New Testament believers violates the hermeneutical principle of "first mention." Here is a summary of that principle:

THE LAW OF FIRST MENTION

The meaning of the Law of First Mention: The Law of First Mention may be said to be the principle that requires one to go to that portion of the Scriptures where a doctrine is mentioned for the first time and to study the first occurrence of the same in order to get the fundamental inherent meaning of that doctrine.

When this law is applied the simple precedes the complex.

A history of the development of anything will show that it sprang from something in the very simplest form (for example the steamship; airplane; automobile).

In the Scriptures the growth and development of ideas and doctrine might be illustrated by some simple word.

Throughout the history of a term it may have increased its meaning and undergone certain changes, yet the basic, original, fundamental thought is seldom lost.

The fundamental concept usually controls or is dominant in coloring every shade of idea expressed by a term in its current usage.[244]

The influence of the mystery religions upon our theology has caused such a jaundice toward the law of God. Without the law, we have no guiding principles to help us separate Babylon from the kingdom of God. The law teaches us what sin is, what pagan practices are, what sexually deviant behavior is, and what is clean and unclean. This is important for New Testament believers. The apostle Paul instructs the New Testament Church:

> Be ye not unequally yoked together with unbelievers: for what fellowship hath righteousness with unrighteousness? and what communion hath light with darkness?
>
> And what concord hath Christ with Belial? or what part hath he that believeth with an infidel?
>
> And what agreement hath the temple of God with idols? for ye are the temple of the living God; as God hath said, I will dwell in them, and walk in them; and I will be their God, and they shall be my people.
>
> Wherefore come out from among them, and be ye separate, saith the Lord, and touch not the unclean *thing*; and I will receive you,
>
> And will be a Father unto you, and ye shall be my sons and daughters, saith the Lord Almighty. (2 Corinthians 6:14–18)

Fellowship or communion can be achieved **through practices** as much as relationships. We have to know which practices, traditions, and beliefs are biblical and which ones originated in Babylon.

Notice the word "thing" in verse 17 is in italics. (I love the honesty of the KJV Bible.) This means the word was not in the original text. The word was added by the translators in their attempt to clarify Paul's statement. Anyone trained in Torah would have left the word "thing" out of the sentence. "Unclean" is an entire category of items, practices, and beliefs. All of these are defined clearly in the Torah.

The goal is not to become culturally Jewish—nor is it about running around in kippahs (skull caps) and prayer shawls. Our goal in Messiah is to become biblical—from Genesis to Revelation. What God said is unclean will always be unclean. What He said is sin will always be sin. How He said to walk with Him will always be the way of walking with Him. God is calling us to a level of maturity in which we follow Jesus' example of properly applying the commandments of God in everyday life. John, again, stresses:

> He that saith he abideth in him ought himself also so to walk, even as he walked. (1 John 2:6)

Commandments, Answered Prayer, and Dwelling in Him

> For if our heart condemn us, God is greater than our heart, and knoweth all things.
>
> Beloved, if our heart condemn us not, *then* have we confidence toward God.
>
> And whatsoever we ask, we receive of him, because we keep his commandments, and do those things that are pleasing in his sight.
>
> And this is his commandment, That we should believe on the name of his Son Jesus Christ, and love one another, as he gave us commandment.
>
> And he that keepeth his commandments dwelleth in him, and he in him. And hereby we know that he abideth in us, by the Spirit which he hath given us. (1 John 3:20–24)

Did you know that when you got saved, you obeyed a commandment? Verse 23 tells us, "And this is his commandment, That we should believe on the name of his Son Jesus Christ." We may have never thought about it that way; but God does. You might reply with the Scripture:

> [8]For by grace are ye saved through faith; and that not of yourselves: it is the gift of God:

⁹Not of works, lest any man should boast. ¹⁰For we are his work-manship, created in Christ Jesus unto good works, which God hath before ordained that we should walk in them. (Ephesians 2:8–10)

Notice, I left verse 9 connected to verse 10, so that we would understand that Paul was not doing away with works. Few have ever asked, "What does the phrase 'not of works' mean that Paul was referring to?" We find the answer in the very first verse of Acts 15.

And certain men which came down from Judaea taught the brethren, and said, Except ye be circumcised after the manner of Moses, ye cannot be saved. (Acts 15:1)

This is what caused the stir and triggered the council in Jerusalem to send for the apostle Paul, all of the other apostles, and the Pharisees in question.

As mentioned earlier in the book, there were two schools for the Pharisees during New Testament times. The first was the School of Hillel, of which the apostle Paul was a graduate. The motto of the School of Hillel was "the spirit of the law." The second was the School of Shammai, which the Pharisees that were causing all of the problems were from. The motto of the school of Shammai was "the letter of the law."

These graduates of the School of Shammai allowed their national history to circumvent what God was doing with the Gentiles coming into faith. These rabbis remembered the atrocities committed to their ancestors by **Antiochus IV Epiphanes,** when he annexed Judea during the Intertestamental Period. Thousands of Jewish men and children were slaughtered and "cooked alive" by this despot, simply because they were circumcised.

This horrid history caused them to miss what God was doing. They forgot that God called many times to them to circumcise their hearts:

Circumcise therefore the foreskin of your heart, and be no more stiffnecked.

For the LORD your God is God of gods, and Lord of lords, a

great God, a mighty, and a terrible, which regardeth not persons, nor taketh reward:

He doth execute the judgment of the fatherless and widow, and loveth the stranger, in giving him food and raiment. (Deuteronomy 10:16–18)

Jeremiah echoes the declaration of Moses:

Circumcise yourselves to the Lord, and take away the foreskins of your heart, ye men of Judah and inhabitants of Jerusalem: lest my fury come forth like fire, and burn that none can quench it, because of the evil of your doings. (Jeremiah 4:4)

Finally, Jeremiah not only saw a day in which God would circumcise the hearts of those that trusted in Him, but also a time when He would write His Law upon their hearts.

Behold, the days come, saith the LORD, that I will make a new covenant with the house of Israel, and with the house of Judah:

Not according to the covenant that I made with their fathers in the day that I took them by the hand to bring them out of the land of Egypt; which my covenant they brake, although I was an husband unto them, saith the LORD:

But this shall be the covenant that I will make with the house of Israel; After those days, saith the LORD, I will put my law in their inward parts, and write it in their hearts; and will be their God, and they shall be my people. (Jeremiah 31:31–33)

(Note: Jeremiah 31 is where the early Church adopted the concept of the *B'rit Hadasha* or "New Covenant.")

Now read Paul's rabbinical argument in the book of Romans:

For circumcision verily profiteth, if thou keep the law: but if thou be a breaker of the law, thy circumcision is made uncircumcision.

Therefore if the uncircumcision keep the righteousness of the law, shall not his uncircumcision be counted for circumcision?

And shall not uncircumcision which is by nature, if it fulfil the law, judge thee, who by the letter and circumcision dost transgress the law?

For he is not a Jew, which is one outwardly; neither is that circumcision, which is outward in the flesh:

But he is a Jew, which is one inwardly; and circumcision is that of the heart, in the spirit, and not in the letter; whose praise is not of men, but of God. (Romans 2:25–29, emphasis added)

Notice that keeping the law was not in question; the only practice in question was circumcision. If an uncircumcised Gentile believer was keeping the law by the power of the resurrected Messiah within his heart (Paul argues), should it not count for circumcision and him being accepted by the Jewish community?

God is calling us to biblical balance and the proper application of His Word to our lives.

Enough said—now back to 1 John 3:20–24.

The Heart, Spiritual Reality, and Answered Prayer

John has been dealing with Christians falling into sin and the need for repentance. Now, he comes to the concept of answered prayer. He comforts believers in that, after they confess their sins and their hearts still condemn them, God is greater than their feelings. The reality of our forgiveness in Christ is greater that the lingering effects of sin (and the enemy's attempts to keep us in condemnation after we have repented). Then, John adds something that should make our faith soar:

And whatsoever we ask, we receive of him, because we keep his commandments, and do those things that are pleasing in his sight. (1 John 3:22)

When we have been working to maintain our fellowship with the Father and to walk free of sin, we should have confidence that our prayers are being heard and answered. Obedience causes our hearts to soar in faith. Condemnation will cause our hearts to pull back from true faithful expectation.

God's Commandments for the Sake of the Community of Faith

Whosoever believeth that Jesus is the Christ is born of God: and every one that loveth him that begat loveth him also that is begotten of him.

By this we know that we love the children of God, when we love God, and keep his commandments.

For this is the love of God, that we keep his commandments: and his commandments are not grievous. (1 John 5:1–3)

John states that we should demonstrate both our love for God and for one another by keeping God's commandments. Over the years, I have seen so many situations arise within congregations that caused hurt or damage, which never would have happened if that congregation had been more commandment-conscious. The commandments of God teach us how to properly treat one another, how to handle business dealings, and so much more.

Connecting 1 John with Verses in Revelation

While I was researching the usage of the word, "commandments," in the New Testament for this chapter, I ran across some very interesting occurrences of this word and its concepts in the book of Revelation.

Here is the patience of the saints: here are they that keep the commandments of God, and the faith of Jesus. (Revelation 14:12)

The Greek word used for "patience" here is *hupomone* (hoop-om-on-ay'), which means "steadfastness, constancy, endurance. In the N[ew] T[estament] the characteristic of a man who is not swerved from his deliberate purpose and his loyalty to faith and piety by even the greatest trials and sufferings."[245]

In order for us to have steadfastness, constancy, and endurance in the face of persecution, God informs us that we must have faith in Jesus and keep His commandments.

> And I saw as it were a sea of glass mingled with fire: and them that had gotten the victory over the beast, and over his image, and over his mark, and over the number of his name, stand on the sea of glass, having the harps of God.
>
> And they sing the song of Moses the servant of God, and the song of the Lamb, saying, Great and marvellous are thy works, Lord God Almighty; just and true are thy ways, thou King of saints.
>
> Who shall not fear thee, O Lord, and glorify thy name? for thou only art holy: for all nations shall come and worship before thee; for thy judgments are made manifest. (Revelation 15:2–4)

Between our misunderstanding of the teachings of Paul and the influence of the mystery religions upon our theologies, we believe Moses and Jesus are opposed to one another. The truth is that they form a two-part harmony for the same song of the kingdom. Together, they will be the song of praise we will sing before the throne. Together, they are nitro and glycerin; they form an explosive spiritual power that fuels the kingdom of God. Together, they can become the Antichrist's worst nightmare!

> Blessed are they that do his commandments, that they may have right to the tree of life, and may enter in through the gates into the city. (Revelation 22:14)

This verse is referring to the New Jerusalem and those who can enter there. May this serve as an eye-opening verse for the saints of God in the last days.

A Final Word

I want to give a final word in this chapter to make myself crystal clear to the reader: The purpose of this chapter is not to serve as a call to make all Christians culturally Jewish. This chapter is to serve as a clarion call for the body of Christ to thoroughly examine its doctrines and practices to make sure they are based solely upon Scripture that flows from Genesis all the way to the book of Revelation. The mystery religions take their work of infiltration and gradual corruption within the body of Christ very seriously. They continually labored to pull Israel away from the One True God throughout the Old Testament. They did not stop their endeavors with the completed work of Christ. Today from pulpits, university lecterns, and even legislators' podiums in our nation's capital, the Elite's attack upon God's commandments (and definition of sin) is at an all-time historic high. Anyone who disagrees with their agenda is called a hatemonger.

Well, in a sense they are right. John tells us:

Love not the world, neither the things that are in the world. If any man love the world, the love of the Father is not in him.

For all that is in the world, the lust of the flesh, and the lust of the eyes, and the pride of life, is not of the Father, but is of the world.

And the world passeth away, and the lust thereof: but he that doeth the will of God abideth for ever. (1 John 2:15–17)

Somewhere along the line, we have forgotten that to love God means that we need to hate sin, unrighteousness, and the spirit of this world. Amos counsels us to:

Seek good, and not evil, that ye may live: and so the Lord, the God of hosts, shall be with you, as ye have spoken.

Hate the evil, and love the good, and establish judgment in the gate: it may be that the Lord God of hosts will be gracious unto the remnant of Joseph. (Amos 5:14–15)

Therefore, we must be diligent to rediscover and maintain the faith that was once delivered to the saints.

chapter eleven

Preparing the Remnant

Part 2: Joel, Acts, the Book of Revelation, and Spiritual Warfare

have been preaching the Word of God since I was thirteen years old. Over those forty-one years, I have both prepared and listened to myriad sermons. During the past few decades, I have noticed a perplexing phenomenon within the body of Christ: There are concepts (or even sound bites) that can be heralded from pulpits that will move the crowds to great excitement and releases of emotion that tap into some unrealized psychological need or carnal desire. However, when we examine many of the "truths" being proclaimed across the body of Christ, they lack any real scriptural legitimacy. In other words, conducting some basic biblical research will quickly reveal that there is no scriptural foundation for those beliefs. These unscriptural revelations may produce larger crowds and offerings, but they weaken the spiritual lives of those caught within their circles. One of two possible scenarios could have created this phenomenon:

- Somewhere along the line, we have unconsciously fallen into the same occupational trap as the Levites in the book of Malachi: We are preaching what the people WANT to hear instead of what Heaven says they NEED to hear.

- These unbiblical concepts were created as a part of the **Shinar Directive** to pull the body of Christ away from sound doctrine. In today's current climate within the Church world, the minister who gathers the largest crowds becomes the new prototype for Church growth. The end result is deception spreading like a cancer!

I remember a situation years ago that exemplifies this paradigm. I attended a church with a pastor I absolutely loved. You could see the love of God flowing from him as well as his contagious excitement about God's Word. He was teaching on the life of Abraham, and I couldn't tell which one of us was enjoying it more. This dear brother has served as the perfect example of a teaching pastor for me to this very day. I have to admit that, during his presentation, I mentally drew a circle around a few statements to examine later. However, this is typical for me; perhaps it is an occupational hazard of being a Christian educator. Whenever I listen to a message, my mind will categorize everything I am hearing and cross-index it with established truth I have already learned. Later, the resulting study will either allow me to expand my understanding of the Word or bring a realization that someone's own humanity has crept into his interpretation and preaching.

After the service, this pastor was having a long discussion with someone else in the congregation, and he called me in to assist him. A Berean within the fellowship had picked up on one of the concepts that I had earmarked within my mind to search out more fully. The pastor was hoping I could bring some clarity to the situation and assist him. He shared that one of the men he highly respected in ministry had taught those truths to him. The three of us opened the Word of God to examine the Scriptures in question, step by step. As we analyzed, the pastor began to realize that his teaching was slightly out of alignment with the Word. It was nothing major—just obvious. When he realized his mistake, he quickly apologized and then said, "That sure preached good though, didn't it?"

That situation has stuck with me over the years. I knew that wonderful pastor loved both God and His Word with a passion I had rarely seen. Yet, in his passion, he had picked up something in his preaching that was slightly off, because it just "preached better" that way. If this mature saint of God could fall prey to that, I was certain I also could have done so over the years. One of the sermons that just "preaches good" and gets the people excited, but does not line up with the Word, is the army described in Joel chapter 2.

Joel's Army

Blow ye the trumpet in Zion, and sound an alarm in my holy mountain: let all the inhabitants of the land tremble: for the day of the LORD cometh, for it is nigh at hand;

A day of darkness and of gloominess, a day of clouds and of thick darkness, as the morning spread upon the mountains: a great people and a strong; there hath not been ever the like, neither shall be any more after it, even to the years of many generations.

A fire devoureth before them; and behind them a flame burneth: the land is as the garden of Eden before them, and behind them a desolate wilderness; yea, and nothing shall escape them.

The appearance of them is as the appearance of horses; and as horsemen, so shall they run.

Like the noise of chariots on the tops of mountains shall they leap, like the noise of a flame of fire that devoureth the stubble, as a strong people set in battle array. (Joel 2:1–5)

Some ministers would say: "Come on, that just sounds good! The end-time saints are going to become the Joel chapter 2 army. The devil isn't going to know what hit him. This army is going to be so powerful that it is unstoppable. Look in verse 8: the healing power of God is there. They get wounded, pray for one another, are healed, and then they are right back in the battle. Oh, to be that army!"

BUT, when you place these verses back into the chapter in the book of Joel and follow the sequence of events, this army is not comprised of the people of God at all. We find the people of God later on in chapter 2 being called to fasting and prayer, **BECAUSE** the army earlier listed in chapter 2 is approaching! This approaching army is only God's army in the same sense that Nebuchadnezzar was the servant of God (Jeremiah 27:6) in enacting judgment on Israel.

The army in Joel 2 is most likely the transgenic army that will be released in Revelation 9. God's people cannot be the approaching army and the people who are praying and fasting because of the army's approach at the same time. This army in Joel 2 has many of the attributes the Elite have been laboring for so long to adapt from Genesis 6 in creating Nimrod's super-soldier army for his war against God.

- This army is unique throughout all time (2:2).
- Nothing escapes it (2:3).
- It has the appearance of horses (2:4).
- It is like a fire that devours everything before it—similar to locusts (2:5).
- Its soldiers will not break ranks, and they will not thrust one another—hive mind control (2:5, 6).
- Its soldiers fall upon the sword but are not wounded—transgenic, enhanced bodies (2:6).

What seems to be "good preaching" in today's churches is, in reality, calling all of us to become a part of the Antichrist's transgenic, unstoppable army. In my youth, I fell in line with whatever was going around in Christian circles that got results, and I preached it, too. Long ago, I abandoned such practices, and I now prefer to retreat to my prayer closet so God can instruct me about what to preach and teach. Just because a topic is popular and fiery does not mean that it is biblically correct. **It can just as easily be strange fire everyone is passing around and calling "revival."**

We do not see the body of Christ until verse 12:

¹² Therefore also now, saith the LORD, turn ye even to me with all your heart, and with fasting, and with weeping, and with mourning:

¹³ And rend your heart, and not your garments, and turn unto the LORD your God: for he is gracious and merciful, slow to anger, and of great kindness, and repenteth him of the evil.

¹⁴ Who knoweth if he will return and repent, and leave a blessing behind him; even a meat offering and a drink offering unto the LORD your God?

¹⁵ Blow the trumpet in Zion, sanctify a fast, call a solemn assembly:

¹⁶ Gather the people, sanctify the congregation, assemble the elders, gather the children, and those that suck the breasts: let the bridegroom go forth of his chamber, and the bride out of her closet.

¹⁷ Let the priests, the ministers of the LORD, weep between the porch and the altar, and let them say, Spare thy people, O LORD, and give not thine heritage to reproach, that the heathen should rule over them: wherefore should they say among the people, Where is their God? (Joel 2:12–17)

Notice that, in verse 17, the prophet says part of the prayer is, "give not thine heritage to reproach, that the heathen should rule over them." The word for "heathen" in the Hebrew is *gowy* (go'-ee). This word is usually translated as "Gentile" or "nation," but it is also used to refer to the descendants of Abraham on occasion. The interesting aspect of this word is that it can be used for "a swarm of locusts."[246] This word connects the Joel 2 a directly to Revelation 9 again!

Joel, Acts, and the Book of Revelation

This past week, as I was preparing to write chapter 10 of this book, I was researching the Greek word for "servant" in Revelation 1:1. I have already shared that this Greek word is *doulos* (doo'-los). This same Greek word used in the book of Revelation is also used in the books of Acts and Joel. This fact ties all three books together and provides great hope for the people of God.

In Peter's first sermon after the outpouring of the Holy Spirit in Acts 2, he proclaims:

> But this is that which was spoken by the prophet Joel;
> And it shall come to pass in the last days, saith God, I will pour out of my Spirit upon all flesh: and your sons and your daughters shall prophesy, and your young men shall see visions, and your old men shall dream dreams:
> And on my servants and on my handmaidens I will pour out in those days of my Spirit; and they shall prophesy:
> And I will shew wonders in heaven above, and signs in the earth beneath; blood, and fire, and vapour of smoke:
> The sun shall be turned into darkness, and the moon into blood, before that great and notable day of the Lord come:
> And it shall come to pass, that whosoever shall call on the name of the Lord shall be saved. (Acts 2:16–21)

Nowhere in the book of Acts do we see the wonders in Heaven or earth that Peter refers to in his sermon's foundational Scripture. There was no great smoke recorded in Acts. The sun was not darkened, nor was the moon turned to blood. What's going on here? Did Peter use the wrong proof text for his sermon, or are we missing something?

What we see in Acts 2 (and throughout the book of Acts) is an example of what God is going to do when this transgenic Antichrist army shows up in the midst of His people. **The Acts Church is a preview of the end-time Church!**

The smoke, fire, and darkening of the sun and moon are all a part of the events associated with the releasing of the hellish army in Revelation 9.

> And the fifth angel sounded, and I saw a star fall from heaven unto the earth: and to him was given the key of the bottomless pit.

And he opened the bottomless pit; and **there arose a smoke out of the pit, as the smoke of a great furnace; and the sun and the air were darkened by reason of the smoke of the pit.**

And there came out of the smoke locusts upon the earth: and unto them was given power, as the scorpions of the earth have power. (Revelation 9:1–3, emphasis added)

Because God's people respond to this scene with prayer, fasting, and repentance, the Holy Spirit is poured out upon them just like He was in Acts 2 (although I believe in a greater measure). Just as Joel stated that the people of God would pray that the locusts would not have dominion over them, we see the answer to this prayer in Revelation 9—this chimeric army does not touch those who are God's, but it turns to torment the Elite to the place where they long for the very thing they thought they had conquered—death. I call that poetic justice!

We see, when we properly combine Joel, Acts, and the book of Revelation, that the final outpouring of the Holy Spirit will result in revival (to bring all of God's people back into a proper state of functioning in the kingdom and for the salvation of those who have not received the mark of the Beast), with an elevated manifestation of spiritual gifts, divine protection, and divine judgment. Now that is what I call revival! This time, God is going to do more than save sinners and shut down taverns! Satan's supposed unstoppables meet God's redeemed untouchables.

We know that whosoever is born of God sinneth not; but he that is begotten of God keepeth himself, and that wicked one toucheth him not. (1 John 5:18)

As with so many aspects of biblical prophecy, we "see through a glass darkly" (1 Corinthians 13:12). The closer we get to a prophetic event, the clearer it can become. I believe that part of the reason it becomes clearer is so we can begin to understand the advanced technologies being developed by the Elite for the final showdown with God and His people in the **Shinar Directive** to complete the **unfinished work of Nimrod.**

When Will the Lord Return?

The more I study prophecy, the more I am convinced that the premillennial return of Christ is the correct eschatological position. Much of evangelical Christianity now holds to one of several positions regarding His premillennial return.

- Pre-Tribulation
- Mid-Tribulation
- Pre-Wrath
- Post-Tribulation

As a Christian educator, I have had students at Biblical Life College and Seminary come from a variety of evangelical backgrounds who have researched and defended all four of these positions with superb scholarship and convincing biblical arguments. The same can be said for the academic community (although there have been occasions when I have discovered misquotes and intellectual dishonesty to slant the information in the direction they were defending). The youngest of these theories is the Pre-Wrath Theory, which developed after evangelicals began rediscovering their Hebraic heritage (they used the Feasts of the LORD to assist in their investigations—Jesus fulfilled the Spring Feasts at His First Coming; we are now in Shavuot [Pentecost]; and Jesus will fulfill the Fall Feasts in His Second Coming). The second-youngest theory is the Pre-Tribulation Theory, which dates back to around the early 1800s and the development of dispensationalism. The most ancient seems to be the Post-Tribulation, premillennial return of the Lord.

In discussing the various positions with one of our professors, Dr. Bruce Booker related a story regarding a class he took years ago under the late Dr. Walter Martin. In this class were students from various positions on the premillennial return of Christ. (Note: At that time, the Pre-Wrath theory had not yet been developed.) All the students in the class were hoping Dr. Martin would make a ruling on the topic and settle the matter concerning which position was correct. Here is what Dr. Martin shared with them, according to Dr. Booker: "I have learned to pray for Pre, and prepare for Post."

I have always admired his honesty.

While we are fighting about things that are still, for the most part, relatively dark to us in end-time prophecy, we have unknowingly ceased from seeking the face of God with all of our hearts. We should be weeping and mourning over the state of the Church in America and the absolute lukewarmness of most Christians (the only thing that seems to get them excited is messages that appeal to their carnality). I have seen so many believers I thought were rock solid who are now allowing public opinion to sway them, and they have begun doubting what God has clearly said in His Word. I have listened to ministers, while they were sitting in my office or at conferences across the country, who have told me they do not believe that the Ten Commandments are for today. I have then watched as their families and ministries fell apart after making that confession. I have seen men who were once on fire for God fall into grievous doctrinal error and die early. I have seen Christian families slowly creep into darkness, until you could not tell them from the average sinner down the road. If there was ever a time to meet with God between the porch and the altar in weeping, fasting, and prayer, it is right now!

While I see in Scripture the reality of both revival and supernatural protection from God as the transgenic army of the Antichrist approaches, my heart longs to see an outpouring of revival now! We are not done yet! The body of Christ is in a mess, and the world is heading right into the arms of darkness at neck-breaking speeds. We have not realized that while we stopped to argue about where the finish line is, we stopped running the race. We must begin to prepare ourselves for both our kingdom assignments and the enemy's advancements in the days ahead.

Somehow, we have come to believe that having the correct timing of His return, within the framework of being premillennial, is part of biblical orthodoxy. The truth is, in this area, practical orthodoxy is both looking for His return and making sure that we are ready for it. When we realize that Jesus is coming back as Messiah ben David, and that He is coming back for a perfected (or mature) Bride, we begin the labor of putting away childish things; we start to get serious about our personal spiritual development and learn how to function in the kingdom of God. From what I have seen in the lives of most believers, we are more like children out on the playground during recess than mature believers in advanced training in our Lord's University of the Kingdom. Our paradigms must change, as well as our goals in every area of life.

The preparation process must encompass every aspect of our lives, and I believe it must follow a specific order. If we have survival food stored up in our homes but have forgotten to store up God's truth in our hearts, our long-term food supplies will do us little good. We need a spiritual awakening that fully engulfs our entire being—from lifestyle to our thoughts and every action.

- **Spiritual**—We must get serious about our spiritual walk with God and bring ourselves in line with our King and His kingdom. We all must invest the time and effort to develop ourselves spiritually. Without this part of our lives being strengthened, we can easily fall prey to the workings of both the Antichrist spirit and the Elite.

- **Mental**—We must get back into the Word of God and allow it to rule our thinking, emotions, and actions. We must also allow the Holy Spirit to do His work in us to make us courageous and resolute in our stand for God. My personal goal is to follow the leading of Daniel and to be resolute in my convictions and purposes in the kingdom.

- **Physical**—We must prepare for some tough times ahead. This includes both working on improving our health and storing supplies. Even if the Lord's return is Pre-Tribulation, it doesn't mean we will not go through some difficult situations as that day approaches; natural disasters can happen. The point is, do not be dependent upon the Babylonian system—be independent from it. We must only be dependent upon God.

Note: I also think part of the physical preparation is investing in your own library. One day, many of the books we have depended upon for strength, encouragement, or even research, may be restricted. Make sure you obtain a good supply of Bibles, while they can still be legally purchased.

I would also suggest using good Bible software to aid in your personal study now. Many great programs out there are cross-platform, meaning you can use them on computers running either the Windows PC operating system or the Mac operating system. Two programs that fit this category are WordSearch Bible and Logos Bible Software. For those on a budget, I would recommend the Windows program eSword (www.esword.net). This program is donation-based and has many great modules. You can also download an entire library into eSword from the website called Bible Support (www.biblesupport.com). Although the interface is antiquated in eSword, it is still quite usable. (You can also install eSword on Mac computers using the software, CrossOver.)

The point I am trying to make is that we all need to get serious about our knowledge of the Word and our spiritual development. Do not let the Babylonian haze of the Elite place you into an entertainment stupor. Wake up and get serious. God will lead and bless as you do!

I am not trying to promote fear, but I am promoting preparedness. When I served in the Army in my youth, they drilled in us that the best way to avoid a fight was to be fully prepared for one. General George S. Patton said shortly after World War II: "The more you sweat in peace, the less you bleed in war."

While I'm not speaking of a physical war, the same principle applies to spiritual growth and warfare. We must open our eyes to the truth of the Laodicean state of the church in America. We must also see that, as the political world aligns itself with darkness, it is first a spiritual reality and then a political one. The only way darkness is overcome in this world is through the light of God shining through His people as the fire of revival burns within their hearts! Things only get darker when the light is unable to shine through. That's why Jesus called us both the light of the world and the salt that preserves it.

Ye are the salt of the earth: but if the salt have lost his savour, wherewith shall it be salted? it is thenceforth good for nothing, but to be cast out, and to be trodden under foot of men.

Ye are the light of the world. A city that is set on an hill cannot be hid.

Neither do men light a candle, and put it under a bushel, but on a candlestick; and it giveth light unto all that are in the house.

Let your light so shine before men, that they may see your good works, and glorify your Father which is in heaven. (Matthew 5:13–16)

Other Concepts Regarding Spiritual Warfare

I have a couple of concepts that I promised to touch upon earlier in this book regarding spiritual warfare. Now seems to be the appropriate time to deal with them.

The Platform for Spiritual Warfare

The basic platform for spiritual warfare was four legs:

1. Salvation
2. The Blood of Jesus
3. The Name of Jesus
4. Obedience

1. Salvation: Of course, salvation is the prerequisite for spiritual warfare. There is a story in the book of Acts in which some brothers conspired to make a little money through establishing a deliverance ministry.

Then certain of the vagabond Jews, exorcists, took upon them to call over them which had evil spirits the name of the Lord Jesus, saying, We adjure you by Jesus whom Paul preacheth.

And there were seven sons of one Sceva, a Jew, and chief of the priests, which did so.

And the evil spirit answered and said, Jesus I know, and Paul I know; but who are ye?

And the man in whom the evil spirit was leaped on them, and overcame them, and prevailed against them, so that they fled out of that house naked and wounded. (Acts 19:13–16)

You cannot be a member of the kingdom of darkness and fight against it at the same time. Only those who are born again and members of the kingdom of God are in the proper position to fight against the kingdom of darkness.

2. The blood of Jesus: The blood of Jesus is the most powerful substance in the universe. You can have a life so filled with sin and shame that it is pitch black and so filthy that no one would believe it could be redeemed. Yet, through repentance, the blood of Jesus can free and cleanse that life and make it white as snow.

This probably seems basic to most believers. However, when things go south in warfare, a soldier is always told to return to the basics. As John instructed in his first epistle, stay in fellowship with God and with the blood that was shed for you. Do not participate in anything that takes you out from under the protection of the blood of Christ. Learn how to walk in the blood covenant Jesus has provided for you.

3. The Name of Jesus: Jesus was the One whose Name you called upon to be saved. It is His Name you use at the end of your prayers. It is His Name you use when you bind up the operations of the enemy in someone's life or even to cast out demons. It is the One whose Name you use when you pray for a sick friend to be healed. If we want Heaven and Hell to have respect for our use of that Name, we better have the deepest respect for it.

Ye have not chosen me, but I have chosen you, and ordained you, that ye should go and bring forth fruit, and that your fruit should remain: that whatsoever ye shall ask of the Father in my name, he may give it you. (John 15:16)

Since we have been disenfranchised from our Hebraic heritage, we cannot connect the cultural meaning to what Jesus said when He gave them His name to use in prayer in John 15:16. The name of Jesus is not something you just add to the end of your prayers so Heaven (or Hell) must respond. It is so much more.

> And whatsoever ye do in word or deed, do all in the name of the Lord Jesus, giving thanks to God and the Father by him. (Colossians 3:17)

Whenever you are given the use of someone's name, **you also accept the responsibility of representing him in all of your dealings**. Your conduct has to represent the one who sent you and whose name you are using. Believe it or not, this concept is connected to the Aaronic Blessing and the Ten Commandments.

> And the LORD spake unto Moses, saying,
>   Speak unto Aaron and unto his sons, saying, On this wise ye shall bless the children of Israel, saying unto them,
>   The LORD bless thee, and keep thee:
>   The LORD make his face shine upon thee, and be gracious unto thee: [26] The LORD lift up his countenance upon thee, and give thee peace.
>   And **they shall put my name upon the children of Israel**; and I will bless them. (Numbers 6:22–27, emphasis added)

God placed His Name upon Israel, and they became His representatives on the earth. They bore His Name, walked in His ways and commandments, and were a testimony in a world filled with the darkness that flowed from Babylon.

> Thou shalt not take the name of the LORD thy God in vain; for the LORD will not hold him guiltless that taketh his name in vain. (Exodus 10:7)

We have always interpreted the command in Exodus 20:7 to mean, "not to use God's name as a curse word." While this is extremely important, much more is being said here.

I remember an old story I heard years ago. There was a good man who lived in a little Midwestern town. It was in a time when men were taught that a man was only as good as his name. Names carried weight, whether good or bad. This man came from a line of good men who always sought to do the right thing. Now, he was facing a day that he had dreaded. His son was now of age and longed to leave the Midwest for the bright lights of Chicago. This man took his son by the shoulders, looked straight into his eyes, and said:

"Son, when you leave here, don't forget who you are. Don't forget the name that you are carrying. What you do can affect that name and all who bear it!"

That father knew that if his son forgot who he was and began running with the wrong crowd, it would affect the reputation of his family's name, which he had guarded his whole life.

God was warning Israel, "I am placing My Name upon you, and it will create a blessing; but don't leave here and conduct yourselves in such a manner that brings reproach on My Name. I will hold you responsible!"

There have been so many fleshly activities and false doctrines being perpetrated today in the Name of Jesus that it would make Heaven weep (if that is a possibility). We have taken the most precious Name in all of creation and used it to promote the very spirit and heart of Babylon and its founder, Nimrod. My friends, this must change!

I want Heaven not only to recognize the Name of Jesus upon my lips, **but His nature within my heart and in my prayers.** I want Hell to also recognize the Name of Jesus when I stand in my authority in Christ, **but I also want it to see His fire in my eyes and His righteousness upon my heart!** I must reverence, respect, and guard His Name and reputation on the earth!

4. **Obedience:** Jesus is our example of how to live our lives and to conduct spiritual warfare. He did it all from a life of matured obedience to the Father.

We need to realize that we cannot play with the devil all week and then expect to be able to effectively fight him on the weekends!

Never engage in spiritual warfare, if there are any areas of disobedience in your life. This is why we see prayer and fasting so much in the book of Acts. I have always been amazed at just how much members of the early Church prayed and fasted. It was almost as if they would pray and fast to get ready to pray and fast. However, these men were very conscious of the life-and-death situations that faced them around every corner. They knew obedience to God's Spirit and His Word was paramount in all things. The same holds true for us today, but most Christians are oblivious to that fact. The veneer of civility within Western culture has put us to sleep spiritually. We need to be fully awakened, before our society's ultra-thin veneer is pierced by those who thrive on iniquity and anarchy.

Spiritual Mapping and Storming the Heavens

I want to go back for a moment to my discussion on the reality of the multiverse and the three Heavens. Paul states:

> For we wrestle not against flesh and blood, but against principalities, against powers, against the rulers of the darkness of this world, against spiritual wickedness in high places. (Ephesians 6:12)

Third Heaven
Eternity
Second Heaven
Principalities and Powers
First Heaven
Our Universe
Sheol
Place of Torment/Abraham's Bosom
Outer Darkness
Tartarus

It has become quite popular for ministries to conduct spiritual mapping expeditions to discover what principalities and powers are over their geographic areas. I have personally read many of the books and articles on spiritual mapping, and I walked away somewhat disappointed.

I found these writings on spiritual mapping very informative about how to determine what principalities or powers were controlling an area, but severely lacking in biblical protocols for conducting successful spiritual warfare against them. You cannot engage in warfare against a principality or power the same way you would a demonic force. Demons are Nephilim spirits that seek out physical bodies to manifest through. Principalities are very ancient and powerful fallen angels that prefer to control regions like puppets on strings. It could be compared to using a little stick to chase off the neighbor's dog that strayed into your yard, and then using the same stick to poke a grizzly bear that is asleep on your back patio. Too many have poked the bear and ended up on today's menu for the bear!

Now, I am not saying that the Name of Jesus is a little stick. I am only using this comparison for the purpose of contrasting a small, two-pound dog to a ten-foot, 1,500-pound bear! The warfare is completely different.

I have counseled many pastors and believers who used the incorrect protocols for engaging principalities and powers. They had awakened ancient spiritual wickedness of untold power that previously took little notice of them. They discovered that their warfare had backfired, and were not prepared for the retaliation that followed. I have seen pastors die, congregations scatter, and churches close down. All of this could have been avoided if proper protocols had been followed. What seemed to be "good preaching" caused a whole lot of tragedy and broken lives.

When God gave authority to man in the garden, it was over His creation in the First Heaven. When Jesus won back that authority by His victory over death, Hell, and the grave, it was over the First Heaven. Nowhere in Holy Writ will we find the instructions on how to transverse into the Second Heaven and engage in spiritual warfare with the fallen angels residing there.

When the apostle Paul speaks of "wrestling" with principalities and powers, he is discussing the continual struggles we have because of their influence within in our reality. Paul never attempted to go into the Second Heaven and dethrone the principality over the Roman Empire. Paul knew, from the book of Daniel, that it takes angels to fight other angels; those warring angels can only be sent from the throne of God.

I would like to provide a proper protocol for Second Heaven warfare. Please note that this is only a brief outline. (An exhaustive study would be a book in itself.) This outline includes some common-sense biblical approaches to the warfare in the Second Heaven.

Basic Protocols for Second-Heaven Warfare

1. Conduct spiritual mapping. This is helpful in discovering the tactics of the particular principalities or powers over an area. This will reveal what schemes and devices are being used to control and to maintain spiritual darkness in an area.

2. Follow this brief list of safe steps:

- Pray that Heaven will move to break the strongholds that the ruling powers have in your area. Ask the Father to send warring angels to begin to combat these powers.
- Ask forgiveness for the sins that created their power base, including the shedding of innocent blood to defile the ground.
- Pray to bind up the influence of principalities. Although we are not instructed in Scripture to directly assault principalities, we have been given authority by Jesus to bind up their spiritual influence in our lives (Matthew 16:18–19, 18:18). When the influence of principalities, powers, rulers of darkness, or even Watchers begins to intrude upon our lives, we have both a right and the obligation to pray and bind up their influence through the power of Jesus' Name. The next step is to ensure that there is no spiritual void remaining; this can be accomplished by releasing the power of the kingdom of God to replace their influence. This should always be followed by intense study in the Word of God that will counter their incursion.
- Add fasting to your prayers. The story in Daniel seems to indicate that his fasting was crucial in the battle being waged in the Second Heaven. It would be appropriate to have a prolonged, declared fast—perhaps calling the saints of God to stand with you

and fast one or two days a week until the power is broken or you receive a clear release from Heaven to end the fast.

- Use your influence to direct people toward God. Principalities increase in power in an area because their influence gains a foothold and increases until it holds more sway over the citizens of the region. The preaching of the gospel and the turning of men's hearts from sin to righteousness will begin to reduce their influence and power. I believe when a substantial portion of the population is turned to God and begins to walk in righteousness, the evil principality can be displaced by a godly one. Although a detailed study in this area would be a volume within itself, we can easily see the reality of it in the life of Israel. When they drove out the ungodly inhabitants in the Promised Land and began living according to God's ways, the principalities that once ruled were displaced by God's agents within the Second Heaven. If Israel fell too deeply into sin, the displacement occurred again. This time, the kingdom of darkness was placed back into the seat of power. This is why revival and walking in godliness are so important. How we live our lives affects more than just ourselves. It can affect those around us, and **it can affect the government within the Second Heaven!**

- Teach and encourage fellow believers. Once we see men and women saved, we must make disciples of them. The Great Commission includes teaching them to walk in the ways of God. The stronger the body of Christ gets in an area, the weaker an evil principality becomes!

After we have done all of these things, God can move upon a seasoned man or woman of God to release a prophetic indictment against the local principality or power. Many in the body of Christ have confused such events with regular spiritual warfare. In actuality, the warfare had already been conducted successfully. Now Heaven was using a vessel of honor (1 Thessalonians 4:1–6) to speak into the First Heaven what God had accomplished in the Second Heaven.

We must seek to walk in a continual state of revival. I am not talking about having meetings five times a week in perpetuity. For the believer, revival is a state of spiritual alertness. **He or she is actively being a disciple of Jesus** by praying, fasting, getting into the Word, sharing the gospel, encouraging other believers, etc. The apostle Paul called for the saints to awake out of slumber in his day, and I pray that this book is a similar call for the saints in ours!

> And that, knowing the time, that now it is high time to awake out of sleep: for now is our salvation nearer than when we believed.
> The night is far spent, the day is at hand: let us therefore cast off the works of darkness, and let us put on the armour of light.
> Let us walk honestly, as in the day; not in rioting and drunkenness, not in chambering and wantonness, not in strife and envying.
> But put ye on the Lord Jesus Christ, and make not provision for the flesh, to fulfil the lusts thereof. (Romans 13:11–14)

> Awake, awake; put on thy strength, O Zion; put on thy beautiful garments, O Jerusalem, the holy city: for henceforth there shall no more come into thee the uncircumcised and the unclean.
> Shake thyself from the dust; arise, and sit down, O Jerusalem: loose thyself from the bands of thy neck, O captive daughter of Zion.
> For thus saith the LORD, Ye have sold yourselves for nought; and ye shall be redeemed without money. (Isaiah 52:1–3)

chapter twelve

Preparing the Remnant

Part 3: Covenant and Kingdom

Why do the heathen rage, and the people imagine a vain thing?

The kings of the earth set themselves, and the rulers take counsel together, against the Lord, and against his anointed, saying,

Let us break their bands asunder, and cast away their cords from us.

—Psalm 2:1–3

W e now begin our last chapter in *The Shinar Directive*. We have examined the reality of conspiratorial history. Truly, the kings of the earth, both at the United Nations and in the international banking cartel, have labored to complete the unfinished work of Nimrod that had its genesis in the ancient plains of Shinar.

God speaks through the psalmist with uncanny accuracy. Today, these heathen of the earth are raging. The Hebrew word used for "rage" is *ragash* (raw-gash'), which means not only "to be in a tumult or commotion," but to "to conspire, plot."[247] These ungodly conspirators have set themselves against the God of Heaven and His Anointed One. They seek to break asunder and cast out God's ways, His commandments, His Covenant, and His plan for the redemption of mankind and creation. They passionately hate the gospel and the Word of God.

The only way we can counter their rage-infused directive against God is to love God with a matured (or perfected) love. Moses instructed Israel long ago:

> Hear, O Israel: The LORD our God is one LORD:
> And thou shalt love the LORD thy God with all thine heart, and with all thy soul, and with all thy might.
> And these words, which I command thee this day, shall be in thine heart:
> And thou shalt teach them diligently unto thy children, and shalt talk of them when thou sittest in thine house, and when thou walkest by the way, and when thou liest down, and when thou risest up.
> And thou shalt bind them for a sign upon thine hand, and they shall be as frontlets between thine eyes.
> And thou shalt write them upon the posts of thy house, and on thy gates. (Deuteronomy 6:4–9)

These verses are a part of a prayer called "the Shema." These words have been prayed twice a day by the Jewish people for millennia. The concepts embedded in the prayer are so powerful that Jesus considered it the greatest commandment of all:

> But when the Pharisees had heard that he had put the Sadducees to silence, they were gathered together.
> Then one of them, which was a lawyer, asked him a question, tempting him, and saying,
> Master, which is the great commandment in the law?
> Jesus said unto him, Thou shalt love the Lord thy God with all thy heart, and with all thy soul, and with all thy mind.
> This is the first and great commandment.

And the second is like unto it, Thou shalt love thy neighbour as thyself.

On these two commandments hang all the law and the prophets. (Matthew 22:34–40)

Notice the powerful statement by Jesus regarding these commandments: "On these two commandments hang all the law and the prophets." For everything else to work properly in the kingdom of God, these two commandments must be in place. Isn't that what John was expressing in his first epistle?

Whosoever believeth that Jesus is the Christ is born of God: and every one that loveth him that begat loveth him also that is begotten of him.

By this we know that we love the children of God, when we love God, and keep his commandments.

For this is the love of God, that we keep his commandments: and his commandments are not grievous.

For whatsoever is born of God overcometh the world: and this is the victory that overcometh the world, even our faith.

Who is he that overcometh the world, but he that believeth that Jesus is the Son of God? (1 John 5:1–5, emphasis added)

The Elite have taken advantage of the error that the Pharisees from the School of Shammai made in teaching Gentiles salvation through circumcision. These workers of absolute darkness have convinced us that if we look at the commandments of God as part of our Christian lifestyle, we are trying to "earn our salvation." They have embedded a jaundice within our theologies and collective consciousness to avoid God's loving instruction known as the Torah.

At this point, we might ask ourselves, "Then what is the purpose of the Torah in the life of the believer?" It is the same as it was for those that God redeemed thousands of years ago from Egypt.

Therefore shall ye lay up these my words in your heart and in your soul, and bind them for a sign upon your hand, that they may be as frontlets between your eyes.

And ye shall teach them your children, speaking of them when thou sittest in thine house, and when thou walkest by the way, when thou liest down, and when thou risest up.

And thou shalt write them upon the door posts of thine house, and upon thy gates:

That your days may be multiplied, and the days of your children, in the land which the LORD sware unto your fathers to give them, as the days of heaven upon the earth.

For if ye shall diligently keep all these commandments which I command you, to do them, to love the LORD your God, to walk in all his ways, and to cleave unto him;

Then will the LORD drive out all these nations from before you, and ye shall possess greater nations and mightier than yourselves.

Every place whereon the soles of your feet shall tread shall be yours: from the wilderness and Lebanon, from the river, the river Euphrates, even unto the uttermost sea shall your coast be.

There shall no man be able to stand before you: for the LORD your God shall lay the fear of you and the dread of you upon all the land that ye shall tread upon, as he hath said unto you. (Deuteronomy 11:18–25, emphasis added)

The commandments are not a matter of "gaining" salvation; they are a part of spiritual warfare for those who have been redeemed! The law of God reveals what belongs to Babylon and what belongs to His kingdom (that which is clean and unclean or separating that which is righteous from unrighteousness). As a believer begins to observe the command-ments the way Jesus did, the spiritual force of the kingdom that is released from his heart will begin driving back Babylon and establishing divine order and blessing.

Family, Covenant, and Training

When we examined the goals of the Illuminati, two were:

- Abolition of private property and inheritances
- Abolition of family life and the institution of marriage, and the establishment of communal education of children[248]

These goals are direct attacks on what was established in the Torah for the people of God.

- Each family was given land and was taught about inheritance.
- The concepts of marriage and family were established in the Torah, as well as the need for parents to teach their children the realities of the covenant and how to walk with God.

Our traditions have reduced the Old Testament to a group of children's stories of miracles that God no longer performs today. Then, we expect our children to believe in the story of Jesus presented in the New Testament. It is all one book authored by one God. As the book of Revelation unfolds before our very eyes, this wonderful, amazing God will show His wonders on the earth again.

We need to go back to the Word of God and allow it to become the ultimate reference book in our lives—allow it to define sin, righteousness, conduct, and truth. We need to begin a fresh dialogue about that old, old story of the power of the cross, the cleansing blood of Jesus, the need for personal faith in Him, and how we are to walk with Him daily as a people. We need our elders to be filled with God's wisdom and to teach us the ways of God. We need to eliminate biblical illiteracy from our midst, and we need to rediscover an ancient Hebraic truth: the highest form of worship is the study of the Word!

I have a dear friend and colleague, Dr. Karl Coke. Karl has spent a great portion of his life developing the Timothy Program. A vital part of this program is teaching Christians how to study the Word of God and how to read (or at least have a working understanding) biblical Hebrew. He has also reintroduced the body of Christ to the concept of Yeshiva (the Hebrew form of group study). I have witnessed a large group of Christians gather with Bibles and reference books in hand for a full day of study. Shortly after breakfast, a topic was chosen, and the study began. The research and discussion were only brought to a halt for lunch and dinner. That evening, the need to end the study was brought up by one of the elders. Complaining immediately erupted from some of the teenagers. They were disappointed that the Yeshiva had to end! Multiple hours of Bible study and research were not enough; they wanted more. Now, compare that to the average teenager today in a traditional church setting, complaining that the pastor's forty-five-minute sermon is too long. When we stop explaining away the Word of God and start teaching believers how to study and live it, the dynamic completely changes—the work of the Elite will begin to unravel, families will be strengthened, and the next generation will become stronger in God than the previous one.

It is time to untangle ourselves from Nimrod's web of deceit and iniquity! It is time to walk in the kingdom the way Jesus did—the same way that He taught His disciples. You cannot separate Jesus and His teachings from the Old Testament, for truly, He is the God of the Old Testament come in the flesh to redeem His creation!

Moving beyond the Elite's Label Game

Something seems to be encoded within the psyche of man that compels him to place labels on everything. We tend to resemble someone suffering from an out-of-control version of obsessive-compulsive disorder, in which we are driven to place labels on everything within our world. Although such a scene can be humorous in a television sitcom, such behavior places us at a great disadvantage regarding the **Shinar Directive**. The Elite will use this natural tendency against us.

The use of labels functions well when we are identifying cans of food within our pantries or seeking to specify which variety of cricket we have found in our backyard. (It is always aggravating to find a can of food in our kitchen that has lost its label.) Yet, when we attempt to place labels on something more complicated than a can of soup, labels completely fail in their general function and can become tools of deception and control.

For well over a century, the Elite have endeavored to use this unconscious need for labeling everything within mankind to their advantage. They have sought to expand the use of labeling to absolutely everything, from people groups to concepts. In doing so, they have reduced the conversation about most topics to a controllable sound bite. Then, they are the ones who can alter the meaning of a label for their purposes and slowly transform society.

There are no detailed, truthful discussions about anything within our Western culture anymore. If an honest discussion was allowed, facts and logic could then be addressed within the framework of whatever the debate was about. This would unravel their Orwellian control of society. They have created their labels within our culture as carefully orchestrated sound bites wrapped in preprogrammed emotional responses to control all of us.

We are witnessing a relabeling of "sin" as "acceptable lifestyles" within our culture. This shift in our society will soon move far beyond the biblical definition of family to include same-sex unions, multiple-partner unions (bisexual polygamy), marriage to a consenting minor (pedophilia), and even union with animals (bestiality). The primary mechanism used to facilitate this dynamic change is the use of labels, and the secondary mechanism is the creation of an environment in which the definitions can be in flux.

Another example of a label in flux is "evangelical." Not long ago, "conservative evangelicals" were held in high esteem; in fact, evangelicals were considered the backbone of our nation. Yet today, that label is being used to represent just the opposite. On October 23, 2013, a revealing article was posted to the Fox News site entitled, "Does Army Consider Christians and the Tea Party a Terror Threat?" In this article, reporter Todd Sterns reveals:

Soldiers attending a pre-deployment briefing at Fort Hood say they were told that evangelical Christians and members of the Tea Party were a threat to the nation and that any soldier donating to those groups would be subjected to punishment under the Uniform Code of Military Justice.[249]

It is amazing to me that, at a base where a Muslim officer committed a horrendous act of terrorism, evangelical Christians are being "labeled" as the problem and not Muslims! However, to control the use of labels and their ever-changing definitions, the Elite must also control all sides of the conversation.

The only way to overcome this linguistic/psychological strategy of the enemy is to follow the example of Abraham, who stepped outside of Babylon's control. To do that, we must reevaluate our use of labels and the definitions they carry. We must ask:

- "Who created the definition I am using for that label?"
- "Has the definition been changed and by whom?"
- "How is that label really being used by society?"

The apostle Paul admonishes us to "prove all things; hold fast that which is good" (1 Thessalonians 5:21). Although I have already shared this verse, I cannot stress it enough. We cannot continue to allow the agents of the mystery religions to create the definitions of the labels (or terms) we use in the body of Christ. It is time to remove their uninvited influence and begin returning to God's definitions of literally everything.

Before I continue, I want to address this issue of labels and definitions from a spiritual warfare perspective. This short discussion will help those who are seeking to regain true biblical spirituality in many areas of their lives. A label is nothing more than a few words strung together to describe an object, person, belief, practice, event, etc. **The origin of anything determines its spiritual power.** For instance, we can trace the origin of the family all the way back to the Garden of Eden. Marriage was God's idea. The Almighty created Eve to be the life partner of Adam. God did not create Bob, or Bob and Eve, or Eve and Betty to serve as Adam's help-mates. Within the concept of true marriage, the very act can tap into the spiritual force of the kingdom of God to bring blessing. Even if someone who does not know God enters this union with a good heart, blessings can flow.

Now, there are those in our world that want to redefine marriage. They are not using the Word of God as the source for their definition. They are drawing from another kingdom and another spirit, that of Babylon. Babylon was founded through the Watcher/Nephilim seeds carried in the family line of Ham. Within Babylon, marriage can include all of the contradictions to God's Word I have already listed in its redefinition being presented today. So far, the only Babylonian concept of marriage I have not included is incest (Nimrod married his mother). Although, there have been recent discussions among the legal community that mild forms of incest should no longer be considered taboo.[250] Whenever someone enters these unbiblical types of "marriage," another spiritual force is released into his or her life and into society as a whole.

For the more tech savvy, I will express this truth by using the icons on your computer's desktop as an analogy. Anyone who has used a computer is familiar with the program icon. Let's say that you want to use Microsoft Word. You have the icon on your desktop and when you click on that icon, it causes a chain reaction of preprogrammed code to begin. Soon Microsoft Word is ready for you to use. You can change that icon and program name to read something else. What would happen if you changed it to the name of your favorite video game and even exchanged the Word icon for the one matching the game? Every time you click on the new icon, expecting your favorite video game to begin, you would always end up in Microsoft Word. This is the reason Lucifer is known as the "god of a thousand names." He doesn't care which name you call him, as long as you access him instead of Jesus. He also doesn't care how you relabel his practices, as long as you do them. You can give them Christian-sounding names, but it doesn't matter; Lucifer's power is released every time they are enacted.

This is why we must PROVE all things. We cannot allow the world to relabel and redefine everything, nor can we accept previous labels and definitions because they were used prior to our involvement historically. Everything must go back to what God's Word clearly says. We must move beyond sound bites and relabeled concepts and study the original meanings. Then, we can separate God's kingdom from Babylon.

Sound Bites Are Not Answers

We need to move beyond labels and on to real discussions. Years ago, I conducted Wednesday evening Yeshivas for some of our local men. We all enjoyed those evenings of researching the Word of God with reference books and computers at our disposal. Most evenings, we went well past our designated study times for the sheer joy of discovery, regarding some aspect of biblical truth.

Occasionally, we would have one of the men invite another Christian in the area to visit and participate. The background of our visitors would be either Baptist or Pentecostal (which is typical for this part of Missouri). As the study would begin, our visitors would respond to questions by giving a label (a short, one- to four-word answer). Within their minds, this short sound bite was the end of the discussion. To their amazement, the group would begin dissecting their sound bite by thoroughly examining what the Word of God actually said. Many times, the examination of the Word would cause their carefully crafted sound bite to fall completely apart. We all witnessed emotions from our visitors that ranged from discomfort to downright dismay. One evening, as we examined one of those sound bites, our visitor commented, "I feel the conviction of the Holy Spirit. I cannot remember the last time I have felt that in church." Unfortunately, that was the last time he ever attended our Yeshiva.

This situation illustrates a truth: Our faith and the situations in life require more than sound bites to address them. As we proclaim our sound bites, which pacify our flesh, Nimrod's workers are advancing their agenda of neutralizing the church and then marginalizing it within our society. We must move beyond sound bites to conduct deep and honest discussions about our faith and what it means to walk in the covenant established through the shed blood of Jesus.

Truth loves examination, while lies resist it at every turn. Careful examination brings each subject into the light of day. The enemy's lies are like the mythological vampires that burst into flames when exposed to pure daylight.

This Generation Longs for More

The current generation is waking up to realize the complete failure of materialism, which had its conception at the Tower of Babel. In an interview Glenn Beck conducted with Rabbi Daniel Lapin, the two men discussed how the mortar used in building the tower was equivalent to materialism. Rabbi Lapin said:

Yes now, in Hebrew, mortar is very related—same word really as the word materialism. And you can actually even hear the similarity transfer into the English language. Mortar —M, T, R are the key consonants. Material—matter—same word essentially.

And it's very important because the lesson from ancient Jewish wisdom here is that you can bond people and unify people with a sense of common spiritual purpose, but if you're going to eliminate the spiritual—if you're going to take God entirely out of the picture—then you can unify people through materialism.[251]

He then added:

What any tyrant knows is that you cannot enslave a people that believe in the boss. And so, therefore, any tyranny will always begin to develop a hostility to traditional biblical faith, a hostility to the God of Abraham, Isaac and Jacob, a hostility to biblical commitment of any kind at all.

You always find that, whether it's Cuba or the Soviet Union or anywhere else, secularism becomes the religion of the day. In fact, I gave it a name—secular fundamentalism, I think, is the religion of the day.[252]

The good rabbi reveals a powerful truth here: Materialism is not about seeking happiness through ownership of things, it is the religion of secular fundamentalism. This religion of materialism declares:

- Man is just an animal.
- There is no creator.
- There is no god, except for yourself.
- There are no absolutes.
- There are no consequences for what we do.

Those who are part of this current generation are beginning to wake up with a sour taste in their mouths and havoc in their lives from this false religion. Here is the crux of the matter: We can either move past sound bites to real and lasting answers from God's Word, or we will allow Islam to fill the void materialism has left! We must move beyond sound bites to a faith that is practical, powerful, and transformative!

If we do not answer this call to a living and vibrant faith, based on true covenant with the God of Abraham, Isaac, and Jacob and established through the shed blood of Jesus, our legacy in Western society will be that our materialism gave the world over to the return of the Son of Perdition! Let us answer the call given in the book of Joel now and not wait for the transgenic army of the Antichrist. There is no more time for games, only for revival surrounding those who will know their God and do great exploits!

Notes

1. Alexander Hislop, *The Two Babylons* or *The Papal Worship Proved to Be the Worship of Nimrod and His Wife* (2010-05-14), (Kindle Edition) 20.
2. Singularity: The technological singularity, or simply the singularity, is a hypothetical moment when artificial intelligence will have progressed to the point of a greater-than-human intelligence, radically changing civilization, and perhaps human nature.
3. MPD (Multiple Personality Disorder): Dissociative identity disorder (DID), previously known as multiple personality disorder, is a mental disorder on the dissociative spectrum characterized by at least two distinct and relatively enduring identities or dissociated personality states that alternately control a person's behavior, and is accompanied by memory impairment for important information not explained by ordinary forgetfulness.
4. Terrance Moore, "Hating the Constitution 101: The Common Core on the Nation's Founding," http://townhall.com/columnists/terrencemoore/2014/01/06/hating-the-constitution-101-the-common-core-on-the-nations-founding-n1771633/page/full.
5. Dave Bohon, "West Point Terrorism Study Targets 'Far Right' Conservatives," http://www.thenewamerican.com/usnews/item/14301-west-point-terrorism-study-targets-%E2%80%9Cfar-right%E2%80%9D-conservatives.
6. http://dailycaller.com/2014/04/01/george-washington-voted-for-obamacare-pelosi-says/.
7. Ralph Epperson, *The Unseen Hand: An Introduction to the Conspiratorial View of History* (Tucson, AX: Publius Press, 1985) 6.
8. http://en.wikipedia.org/wiki/William_E._Jenner.
9. Barry Goldwater, *With No Apologies* (New York: William Morrow, 1979) 293.

10. Curtis Dall, *My Exploited Father-in-Law.* (New York: Action Associates, 1970).

11. http://millercenter.org/president/speeches/detail/3429.

12. Source: Letter to George Washington, Snyder, October 24, 1798, Mount Vernon, in *The Writings of George Washington*, vol. 20, p. 518.

13. Definition for the Hebrew word "Torah." R. L. Harris, G. L. Archer, and B. K. Watke, *Theological Wordbook of the Old Testament.*(Chicago: Moody Press, 1980) 404.

14. Ed. F. Vallowe, *Biblical Mathematics: Keys to Scripture Numerics* (Columbia, SC: Olive Press, copyright date not available) 66–73.

15. T. Robertson, *Word Pictures in the New Testament* (Nashville, TN: Broadman Press, 1933), Romans 10:4.

16. There were two schools of thought for the Pharisees. The School of Shammai believed in the letter of the Law. The School of Hillel believed in the spirit of the Law. Paul belonged to the School of Hillel.

17. Rabbi Edward Lavi Nydle-B'nai Avraham, *PaRDeS: The Four Levels of Torah Interpretation for Beginners,* PDF File accessed here: http://www.bnaiavraham.net/teaching_articles/english_teachings/RabbiEd/PaRDeS.pdf.

18. "#H1961," *Strong's Enhanced Lexicon,* BibleWorks for Windows 7.0 (Norfolk, VA: BibleWorks, 2006).

19. Ibid., "#H8414."

20. Robert Jamieson, A. R. Fausset, and David Brown, *Commentary Critical and Explanatory on the Whole Bible* (Oak Harbor, WA: Logos Research Systems, 1997) Genesis 1:2.

21. *Strong's*, "#G225."

22. *Dake's Study Notes,* WORDSearch Bible Software Version 7 (Notes and charts copyright 1961, 1963, 1989, 1991 by Finis Jennings Dake).

23. *Strong's*, "# H8508."

24. Ibid., "# H2451."

25. Albert Pike, *Morals and Dogma,* 321.

26. Abraham Cohen, *Everyman's Talmud: The Major Teachings of the Rabbinic Sages* (New York: Schocken Books, 1949) 17.

27. Apotheosis—(from Greek ἀποθέωσις from ἀποθεοῦν, *apotheoun* "to deify"; in Latin *deificatio* "making divine"; also called "divinization" and "deification") is the glorification of a subject to divine level.

28. Hermeneutical or hermeneutics: the study of the methodological principles of interpretation (as of the Bible).

29. Idiom: a form of a language that is spoken in a particular area and that uses some of its own words, grammar, and pronunciations.

30. Exegetical or exegesis: an explanation or critical interpretation of a text.
31. John D. Garr, *Family Worship: Making Your Home a House of God* (Atlanta: Golden Key Press, 2013) 12–13.
32. Transhumanist (abbreviated as H+ or h+): an international cultural and intellectual movement with an eventual goal of fundamentally transforming the human condition by developing and making widely available technologies to greatly enhance human intellectual, physical, and psychological capacities.
33. *Strong's*, "# H07227."
34. Chuck Missler, "Mischievous Angels or Sethites?" http://www.khouse.org/articles/1997/110/.
35. George H. Pember, *Earth's Earliest Ages* (Crane, MO: Defender, 2012) 175–176.
36. D. E. Thomas, *The Omega Conspiracy* (Oklahoma City, OK: Hearthstone, 1986) 107.
37. Graphic of the Masonic hierarchy was used with permission from Dr. Bill Schnoebelen and was taken from his book, *Masonry: Beyond the Light*.
38. William Schnoebelen, *Exposing the Illuminati from Within*, DVD (Topeka, KS: Prophecy Club). Note: Information included in both the 1998 and 2005 editions of the video.
39. http://en.wikipedia.org/wiki/Book_of_Enoch.
40. *Strong's*, "#H05799."
41. Stephen Quayle, *Aliens and Fallen Angels: The Sexual Corruption of the Human Race* (1997) 36.
42. Ibid., 86.
43. Ibid., 172.
44. Ibid., 173.
45. Ibid., 174.
46. This video interview with Russ Dizdar is available on YouTube: https://www.youtube.com/watch?v=ijzG5AHRslA.
47. http://en.wikipedia.org/wiki/Foo_fighter.
48. I believe that males were also abducted so research could be conducted to overcome the physiological changes that occurred in both men and women after the Flood. It appears that not only was our life span shortened, but the changes greatly hindered the creation of hybrid offspring. This may also be part of the agenda of transhumanist research.
49. *Strong's*, "# H05303."
50. K. A. Mathews, "Genesis 1–11:26," *The New American Commentary*, vol. 1A, (Nashville: Broadman & Holman, 1996) 336.
51. John Peter Lange et al., *A Commentary on the Holy Scriptures: Genesis* (Bellingham, WA: Logos Bible Software, 2008) 286.

52. Wilhelm Gesenius and Samuel Prideaux Tregelles, *Gesenius' Hebrew and Chaldee Lexicon to the Old Testament Scriptures* (Bellingham, WA: Logos Bible Software, 2003) 556.

53. D. E. Thomas, *The Omega Conspiracy*, with endorsement by Francis A. Schaeffer on the back cover (Oklahoma City, OK:Hearthstone1986).

54. http://beforeitsnews.com/alternative/2014/03/russian-archaeologists-uncover-skeletons-of-satyr-and-giant-horse-video-2921836.html.

55. Finis Jennings Dake, *Dake's Annotated Reference Bible: Containing the Old and New Testaments of the Authorized or King James Version Text* (Lawrenceville, GA: Dake Bible Sales, 1997) WORDsearch CROSS e-book, "Chapter 26."

56. Ken Johnson, "Ancient Post-Flood History," 2012-06-12 (Biblefacts.org, Kindle Edition) Kindle location 1114–1126.

57. Mathews, "Genesis 1–11:26," *New American Commentary*, 418–420.

58. Dake, *Dake's Annotated Reference Bible*, WORDsearch CROSS e-book, "Chapter 10."

59. Mystery religion: Refers to the many initiatic pagan religions and secret societies that sprang forth from ancient Babylon. These religious systems have many occult symbols and teachings that have levels of interpretation in which only those considered "adepts" are privy to. Until you reach the highest levels within their systems, the meanings of their symbols and teachings are either lied about or obscured. In the Bible, it is referred to as "Mystery Babylon."

60. Hislop, *The Two Babylons*, 18.

61. Ibid., 19.

62. In the KJV, *"the author"* is in italics. This means the phrase did not occur in the original Greek, but was added for clarity by the translators. It could have read, "For God is not of confusion," which would have completely separated the God of Abraham from Cush or Janus "the god of gods" in Babylon within the minds of his readers.

63. *Complete Jewish Bible* (Clarksville, MA: Jewish New Testament Publications, 1998).

64. *Strong's*, "# H03569."

65. Francis I. Andersen and A. Dean Forbes, *The Hebrew Bible: Andersen-Forbes Phrase Marker Analysis (V 0.90, Aug 09)* (Bellingham, WA: Logos Bible Software, 2009).

66. Kenneth L. Baker, *Micah, Nahum, Habakkuk, Zephaniah*, vol. 20, *The New American Commentary* (Nashville: Broadman & Holman Publishers, 1999), 464.

67. Robert Jamieson, A.R. Fausset, David Brown, *A Commentary: Critical,*

Experimental, and Practical on the Old and New Testaments, (Toledo, OH: Jerome B. Names & Co., 1884), WORD*search* CROSS e-book, "Chapter 10."

68. Walter A. Elwell and Barry J. Beitzel, *Baker Encyclopedia of the Bible* (Grand Rapids, MI: Baker Book House, 1988) 1805.

69. M. G. Easton, *Easton's Bible Dictionary* (New York: Harper & Brothers, 1893).

70. David Noel Freedman, Allen C. Myers, and Astrid B. Beck, "Canaan," ed. David Noel Freedman, Allen C. Myers, and Astrid B. Beck, *Eerdmans Dictionary of the Bible* (Grand Rapids, MI: W.B. Eerdmans, 2000) 212–213.

71. Ronald F. Youngblood, F. F. Bruce, and R. K. Harrison, Thomas Nelson Publishers, eds., *Nelson's New Illustrated Bible Dictionary* (Nashville, TN: Thomas Nelson, 1995).

72. K. A. Kitchen, "C. Religion," ed. D. R. W. Wood, et al., *New Bible Dictionary* (Leicester, England; Downers Grove, IL: InterVarsity Press, 1996) 164.

73. Practices: Concerning with action or practice, as opposed to one concerned with theory.

74. James E. Smith, *The Pentateuch*, 2nd ed., Old Testament Survey Series (Joplin, MO: College Press, 1993) Genesis 10:8–12.

75. Thomas Horn, "Forbidden Gates," Part 19, http://www.newswithviews.com/Horn/thomas155.htm.

76. Adam Clarke, *Adam Clarke's Commentary*, (New York: Abingdon-Cokesbury Press, 1826) WORD*search* CROSS e-book, "Genesis."

77. Ibid.

78. http://www.apollyonrising2012.com/.

79. Thomas Horn, *Zenith 2016: Did Something Begin in the Year 2012 That Will Reach Its Apex in 2016?* Kindle Edition (Crane, MO: Defender, 2013), Kindle Locations 5056–5075.

80. Dake, *Dake's Annotated Reference Bible*, "Chapter 10."

81. Arthur W. Pink, *The Antichrist* (Swengel, PA: Bible Truth Depot, 1923) WORD*search* CROSS e-book, 96–99.

82. Alfred Edersheim, *Bible History Old Testament* (London: Religious Tract Society, 1890) WORD*search* CROSS e-book, "Chapter 8."

83. Arno C. Gaebelein, "Fulfilled Prophecy a Potent Argument for the Bible," *The Fundamentals: A Testimony to the Truth*, ed. R. A. Torrey and A. C. Dixon (Los Angeles: Bible Institute of Los Angeles, 1917) WORD*search* CROSS e-book, "Chapter 6. Fulfilled Prophecy a Potent Argument for the Bible."

84. "The Apocrypha," *The Researchers Library of Ancient Texts*, Vol. 1 (Crane, MO: Defender) 295.

85. Flavius Josephus and William Whiston, *The Works of Josephus: Complete and Unabridged* (Peabody: Hendrickson, 1987).

86. E. W. Bullinger (1837–1913), *Commentary on Revelation* (Chicago: F. H. Revell, 1909; repr., Grand Rapids, MI: Christian Classics Ethereal Library, 2003) WORD*search* CROSS e-book, "The Sixth Vision on Earth."

87. http://www.bibliotecapleyades.net/cienciareal/cienciareal20.htm.

88. Anthony L. Podberscek and Andrea Beetz, *Bestiality and Zoophilia: Sexual Relations with Animals* (Google eBooks: Berg Publishing, 2005).

89. Ibid.

90. Elwell and Beitzel, *Baker Encyclopedia of the Bible,* 362–363.

91. Edward F. Murphy, *Handbook for Spiritual Warfare* (Nashville: Thomas Nelson, 1996) 231.

92. Frank Gaynor, ed., *Dictionary of Mysticism* (New York: Philosophical Library, 1953) 136.

93. Joseph Seiss, *The Apocalypse: A Series of Special Lectures on the Revelation of Jesus Christ* (New York: Charles C. Cook, 1901) WORDsearch CROSS e-book, 388.

94. http://www.biblebelievers.org.au/moongod.htm.

95. http://en.wikipedia.org/wiki/Europa_(mythology).

96. Robert James Utley, *How It All Began: Genesis 1–11*, vol. Vol. 1A, Study Guide Commentary Series (Marshall, Texas: Bible Lessons International, 2001) 127.

97. Alfred Edersheim, *The Life and Times of Jesus the Messiah* (WORD*search* CROSS e-book) 1411.

98. Joel Richardson, *The Islamic Antichrist: The Shocking Truth about the Real Nature of the Beast* (Los Angeles: WND Books, 2009) 62–63.

99. *Dune* was written in 1965. Herbert not only describes how the Elite think, but he foretells the fight for oil (spice is used as a metaphor) and the rise of an Islamic messiah who will oppose and gain the upper hand over the Elite by being transmuted into something else.

100. *Strong's* "# G3180."

101. Ceslas Spicq and James D. Ernest, *Theological Lexicon of the New Testament* (Peabody, MA: Hendrickson Publishers, 1994) 462.

102. Timothy Friberg, Barbara Friberg, and Neva F. Miller, *Analytical Lexicon of the Greek New Testament*, Baker's Greek New Testament Library (Grand Rapids, MI: Baker Books, 2000) 256.

103. Albert Pike, *Morals and Dogma of the Ancient and Accepted Scottish Rite of Fremasonry,* new and revised ed. (Richmond, VA: L. H. Jenkins, Inc., 1950) 104–5.

104. Hislop, *The Two Babylons,* 43.

105. Dake, *Dake's Annotated Reference Bible,* "Chapter 17."

106. *Strong's* "# H1980."

107. *Strong's* "# H8549."

108. Martin Gilens, Benjamin Page, *Testing Theories of American Politics: Elites, Interest Groups, and Average Citizens,* http://www.princeton.edu/~mgilens/Gilens%20homepage%20materials/Gilens%20and%20Page/Gilens%20and%20Page%202014-Testing%20Theories%203-7-14.pdf.

109. http://en.wikipedia.org/wiki/Oligarchy.

110. Title IV Funding, through the Guaranteed Student Loan Program, has the potential of destroying virtually every Christian institution of higher learning who participates in its system. There will eventually be a move to only allow student loans for politically correct degrees, subjects, and institutions—for the good of the economy, of course! This will bankrupt all Title IV Christian institutes overnight.

111. Flavius Josephus, *The Works of Flavius Josephus*, trans. William Whiston (Hartford, CN: S. S. Scranton, 1905) WORD*search* CROSS e-book, 46.

112. For more information, I would highly recommend the book *Yeshua: A Guide to the Real Jesus and the Original Church* by Dr. Ron Moseley.

113. Theodoret, *Ecclesiastical History*, Book 1, Chapter 9.

114. Hislop, *The Two Babylons*, 18.

115. Dake, *Dake's Study Notes*.

116. *Strongs* "#H2856."

117. *Strong's* "# H2451."

118. Pike, *Morals and Dogma*, 321.

119. William Schnoebelen and Sharon Schnoebelen, *Lucifer Dethroned* (Chick Publications, 2009-08-18) Kindle Edition, 158–160).

120. Manly Hall, *Lost Keys of Freemasonry*, 48.

121. A.W. Tozer, *KJV Study Bible* (Grand Rapids, MI: Hendrickson Publishers).

122. "Accuser" in Revelation 12:10 is the Greek word *kategoreo* (κατηγορέω; kat-ay-gor-eh'-o), which means "accuser before a judge: to make an accusation, of an extra-judicial accusation." *Strong's* "#G2723."

123. *Strong's* "#H05771."

124. R. Laird Harris, Gleason L. Archer, Bruce K. Waltke, eds., "1577:עָוַן" in *Theological Wordbook of the Old Testament*, (Chicago: Moody Press, 1980), WORD*search* CROSS e-book, 650.

125. *Strong's* "#G0458."

126. http://en.wikipedia.org/wiki/Thelema.

127. *Strong's* "#G2032."

128. Paradox Brown, *A Modern Guide to Demons and Fallen Angels*(2007–2013) chapter 3, http://paradoxbrown.com/powersprincipalitiesfallenangels.htm/.

129. Michael Heiser, "Should the Plural Elohim of Psalms 82 Be Understood as Men or Divine Beings?" http://www.thedivinecouncil.com/Heiser%20Elohim%20of%20Ps82%20Gods%20or%20Men%20ETS2010.pdf .

130. "The Apocrypha," *The Researchers Library*, 4.
131. Ibid., 7.
132. http://en.wikipedia.org/wiki/Gog_and_Magog.
133. Horn, *Zenith 2016*, Kindle Locations 1915–1929).
134. "History of the Illuminati," http://people.virginia.edu/~sfr/enam481/groupa/illumhist.html.
135. http://www.blogtalkradio.com/cfp-radio/2014/06/06/henry-gruver-steve-quayle-on-the-hagmann-hagmann-report.
136. "The Rothschilds and Rockefellers Join Forces in Multi-Billion Dollar Deal," http://vigilantcitizen.com/latestnews/the-rothschilds-and-rockefellers-join-forces-in-multi-billion-dollar-deal/.
137. John D. Rockefeller, *Memoirs of David Rockefeller*, 405.
138. http://www.prometheas.org/mythology.html.
139. "President Bush's Second Inaugural Address," http://www.npr.org/templates/story/story.php?storyId=4460172 (emphasis added).
140. http://www.blogtalkradio.com/revolutionaryradio/2013/01/10/canaanite-altars-and-the-federal-reserve.
141. Horn, *Zenith 2016*, Kindle Locations 2267–2285.
142. "New World Order and Utopian Globalism," http://www.illuminati-news.com/adam-weishaupt.htm.
143. Schnoebelen, *Exposing the Illuminati from Within*.
144. http://en.wikipedia.org/wiki/Adam_Weishaupt#Philosophical_works.
145. Willian Schnoebelen, *Blood on the Doorposts* (Chick Publications, 2010-06-18) Kindle Edition, 145.
146. Winston Churchill stated this to the London Press in 1922; see http://www.globalistagenda.org/quotes.htm.
147. http://hidhist.wordpress.com/churchill/the-greatest-story-never-told-winston-churchill-and-the-crash-of-1929/.
148. "World Religions and Spirituality: Discordianism," http://www.has.vcu.edu/wrs/profiles/Discordianism.htm.
149. Ibid.
150. http://www.politifact.com/texas/statements/2012/apr/27/ron-paul/ron-paul-says-40000-new-laws-were-put-books-first-/.
151. "The Hegelian Dialectic and Its Use in Controlling Modern Society," http://realnewsaustralia.com/2013/08/09/the-hegelian-dialectic-and-its-use-in-controlling-modern-society/.
152. http://online.wsj.com/news/articles/SB122721278056345271?mg=reno64-wsj&url=http%3A%2F%2Fonline.wsj.com%2Farticle%2FSB122721278056345271.html.
153. http://in.reuters.com/article/2009/03/06/us-eu-climate-clinton-idINTRE5251VN20090306 .

154. http://www.brainyquote.com/quotes/quotes/w/williamsha166828.
html#lgCSR5Qd1lg3oEbL.99.

155. http://www.sianews.com/modules.php?name=News&file=article&
sid=2253.

156. Walter J. Veith, *The Secret Behind Secret Societies* (Delta, Canada: Amazing
Discoveries Ministries, 2004).

157. Bill Schnoebelen, *Masonry: Fatal in the First Degree* (Dubuque, IA: With
One Accord Ministries).

158. http://www.henrymakow.com/251102.html.

159. Anthony C. Sutton, *America's Secret Establishment: An Introduction to the
Order of Skull and Bones* (Billings, MN: Liberty House Press, 1986) 5.

160. Ibid., 19.

161. Ibid., 5.

162. Ibid., iii.

163. Ibid., 25.

164. Ibid., 27.

165. Ibid., 27–28.

166. *The Protocols* is not a rabbinical Jewish document about taking over the
world. Both Freemasonry and the Luciferian Elite are trained in Kabbalah.
In addition, after a courier was struck by lightning and the Illuminati codes
were broken, it produced unwelcomed focus on dismantling their work.
By writing the documents in Hebrew, if *The Protocols* were discovered, the
Jewish people would be blamed rather than the Illuminati. Remember,
although the Rothschilds are Jewish, they make up just one-thirteenth of the
bloodlines.

167. Albert Pike and other Illuminati members planned all three world wars
around the time of the Civil War. Christian J. Pinto, *Megiddo: The March to
Armageddon,* DVD (Mount Juliet, TN: Adullam Films 2003).

168. http://quotes.liberty-tree.ca/quote_blog/Nikita.Khrushchev.Quote.7174.

169. http://washingtonexaminer.com/fec-chair-warns-of-
chilling-regulations-book-ban-on-conservative-publishers/
article/2551197.

170. http://en.wikipedia.org/wiki/Round_Table_movement.

171. Lindsay William, *The Elite Speak,* DVD (Topeka, KS: Prophecy Club).

172. https://www.youtube.com/watch?v=3sGs8eFld1U#t=60

173. "Who Owns the News?" http://www.whoownsthenews.com/.

174. With the *Diagnostic and Statistical Manual of Mental Disorders,* 4th Edition
(DSMIV), MPD was renamed "Dissociative Identity Disorder" or DID.

175. Mary Lou Lake, *What Witches Don't Want Christians to Know,* Expanded
Ed.(Marshfield, MO: Biblical Life Publishing, 65706, 2014) 12.

176. Ken Adachi, "Mind Control—The Ultimate Terror," http://educate-
yourself.org/mc/.

177. Jim Keith, *Mass Control:Engineering Human Consciousness* (Lilburn, GA: IllumiNet Press, 1999) 30–31.

178. Colin A. Ross, MD, *Bluebird: Deliberate Creation of Multiple Personality by Psychiatrists* (Richardson, TX: Manitou Communications 2000) 24–25.

179. "Project MKUltra," Wikipedia,http://en.wikipedia.org/wiki/Project_MKUltra.

180. Alexander Constantine, "The False Memory Hoax," http://educate-yourself.org/mc/falsememoryhoax1996.shtml#2.

181. Russ Dizdar, "Satanic Super Soldiers: The Sinister Reality of Trauma-based Mind Control," http://www.paranoiamagazine.com/2013/06/satanic-super-soldiers-the-sinister-reality-of-trauma-based-mind-control/.

182. http://www.scientificamerican.com/article/do-people-only-use-10-percent-of-their-brains/.

183. "The Effects of TV on Your Brain," Applied Neuro Technologies, http://appliedneurotec.com/neuroscience/effects-of-tv-on-your-brain/ .

184. Joseph Mercola, "How Television Affects Your Brain Chemistry— And That's Not All!" http://articles.mercola.com/sites/articles/archive/2007/10/20/how-television-affects-your-brain-chemistry-and-that-s-not-all.aspx .

185. *Strong's* "#G1381."

186. Merriam-Webster Dictionary, http://ww.merriam-webster.com.

187. Ibid.

188. Nick Begich, *Controlling the Human Mind: The Technologies of Political Control or Tools for Peak Performance* (Anchorage, AK: Earthpulse Press, 2006) 50.

189. Ibid., 29.

190. "The Mind Has No Firewalls," U.S. War College, *Parameters,* (Spring 1998), 84–92.

191. Begich, *Controlling the Human Mind*, 33.

192. Nick Begich, *Weapons of the New World Order*, video (Topeka, KS: The Prophecy Club, 2000).

193. CBC TV Canada, *Undercurrents* 1998/99 Season, Program #612-2160-8C19 (February 7, 1999). (Special thanks to Dr. Begich for providing the citation.)

194. "ADHD," Centers for Disease Control, http://www.cdc.gov/ncbddd/adhd/data.html.

195. "Attention Span Statistics," http://www.statisticbrain.com/attention-span-statistics/.

196. "People Choose Electric Shocks Over Sitting Quietly for 15 Minutes and Thinking," PsyBLOG, http://www.spring.org.uk/2014/07/people-choose-electric-shocks-over-sitting-quietly-for-15-minutes-and-thinking.php.

197. *Strong's,* "#H07503."
198. http://www.goodreads.com/author/quotes/30691.Adolf_Hitler.
199. http://www.worldviewweekend.com/worldview-times/article. php?articleid=6568#sthash.cX3L010G.dpuf.
200. http://www.great-quotes-powerful-minds.com/famous-conspiracy-theory-quotes.html#sthash.7vWw8Rxe.dpuf.
201. http://www.un.org/depts/dhl/dag/meditationroom.htm.
202. "The Apocrypha," *The Researchers Library,* Kindle Locations 3014–3015.
203. Ibid., Kindle Location 3029–3034.
204. http://freemasonry.bcy.ca/biography/wells_h/wells_h.html.
205. http://www.scientificamerican.com/article/ multiverse-controversy-inflation-gravitational-waves/.
206. http://en.wikipedia.org/wiki/Aleister_Crowley.
207. http://en.wikipedia.org/wiki/Babalon_Working.
208. Perry Stone, *Secrets from Beyond the Grave* (Lake Mary, FL: Charisma House, 2010) 19.
209. http://www.bibliotecapleyades.net/mapas_ocultotierra/esp_mapa_ ocultotierra_11.htm.
210. http://en.wikipedia.org/wiki/Ley_line.
211. Ibid.
212. http://discovermagazine.com/2011/ jun/03-our-universe-may-be-a-giant-hologram.
213. Dake, *Dake's Annotated Reference Bible,* WORDsearch CROSS e-book, "Chapter 13."
214. *The Preacher's Outline & Sermon Bible—Matthew I* (Chattanooga, TN: Leadership Ministries Worldwide, 1991) WORD*search* CROSS e-book, "B. Jesus Heals a Centurion's Servant: Receiving and Rejecting Men, 8:5–13."
215. *Strong's,* "#G5020."
216. http://www.thefreedictionary.com/Tartarus.
217. http://en.wikipedia.org/wiki/Interdimensional_hypothesis.
218. Thomas Horn, *Nephilim Stargates: The Year 2012 and the Return of the Watchers* (Crane, MO: Anomalos, 2013-11-13) Kindle Locations 2537–2540).
219. "Scientists Claim That Quantum Theory Proves Consciousness Moves to Another Universe at Death," http://www.spiritscienceandmetaphysics. com/scientists-claim-that-quantum-theory-proves-consciousness-moves-to-another-universe-at-death/#sthash.NVof0jKc.dpuf .
220. http://en.wikipedia.org/wiki/Interdimensional_hypothesis.
221. http://www.theregister.co.uk/2008/03/28/ lhc_cern_hawaiian_botanist_lawsuit/.
222. http://www.examiner.com/article/cern-logo-resembles-666.

223. http://en.wikipedia.org/wiki/Shiva.

224. http://www.sanatansociety.org/hindu_gods_and_goddesses/shiva.
htm#.U-fpuvldV8E.

225. http://en.wikipedia.org/wiki/Transhumanism.

226. Michael Anissimov, "Top Ten Transhumanists Technologies," http://lifeboat.
com/ex/transhumanist.technologies.

227. http://litthe.oxfordjournals.org/content/16/1/65.short.

228. R. T. Kendall, *Understanding Theology,* Vol. 1 (Ross-shire, Great Britain:
Christian Focus, 1996) 15.

229. *Strong's,* "# G4352."

230. Thomas Horn, *Blood on the Altar: The Coming War Between Christian vs.
Christian*(Crane, MO: Defender Publishing, 2014) 105–108.

231. http://en.wikipedia.org/wiki/Transhumanism.

232. Dake, *Dake's Annotated Reference Bible,* WORDsearch CROSS e-book,
"Chapter 32."

233. "The Apocrypha," *The Researchers Library,* Kindle Locations 2691–2695.

234. Stephen Quayle, *Xenogenesis: Changing Men into Monsters*(Bozeman, MT:
End Time Thunder Publishers, 2014) 229.

235. http://plato.stanford.edu/entries/chimeras/.

236. *Strong's,* "#H03045."

237. Ibid., "#H02388."

238. Ibid., "#G726."

239. Ibid., "#G04982."

240. Ibid., "#G0739."

241. Ibid., "#101."

242. Ibid., "#H05254."

243. David Bivin, Roy Blizzard Jr., *Understanding the Difficult Words of Jesus:
New Insights from a Hebraic Perspective* (Shippensburg, PA: Destiny Image
Publishers, 1983, 1984) 154–155.

244. http://www.biblicalresearch.info/page48.html.

245. *Strong's,* "# G5281."

246. Ibid., "# H01471."

247. Ibid., "#07283."

248. "New World Order and Utopian Globalism," http://www.illuminati-news.
com/adam-weishaupt.htm.

249. http://www.foxnews.com/opinion/2013/10/23/
does-army-consider-christians-tea-party-terror-threat/.

250. http://www.housepricecrash.co.uk/forum/index.php?/
topic/199678-incest-no-longer-a-taboo-says-australian-judge/.

251. http://www.foxnews.com/story/2010/11/17/
glenn-beck-lessons-from-tower-babel/.

252. Ibid.